how to start a home-based

Antiques Business

Fifth Edition

Bob Brooke

gpp®

Guilford, Connecticut

To buy books in quantity for corporate use
or incentives, call **(800) 962–0973**
or e-mail **premiums@GlobePequot.com**.

Editorial Director: Cynthia Hughes
Editor: Katie Benoit
Project Editor: Tracee Williams
Text Design: Sheryl P. Kober
Layout: Kevin Mak

Chart on page 54 courtesy of Oregon Small Business Development Center Network

ISSN 1552-728X
ISBN 978-0-7627-6361-0

Printed in the United States of America
10 9 8 7 6 5 4 3 2 1

This book's purpose is to provide accurate and authoritative information on the topics covered.
It is sold with the understanding that neither the author nor the publisher is engaged in render-
ing legal, financial, accounting, and other professional services. Neither Globe Pequot Press nor
the author assumes any liability resulting from action taken based on the information included
herein. Mention of a company name does not constitute endorsement.

Contents

Introduction

Have you been collecting antiques for some time and dream of operating an antiques shop from your home? Are you tired of the corporate rat race or the uncertainty of your job's future? If you answered yes to either question, then running an antiques shop from your home might be for you. Sure, you'll make a few mistakes, but, hopefully, they'll be small ones. After all, your responsibilities will be limited, and you won't be working with a big budget. And your contact with the public will be low-key and pleasant. If you think this is for you, then you'll find much of the information you'll need, plus additional resources, within the pages of this book.

Chapter 1 poses some questions about owning your own business. It discusses the advantages and disadvantages of owning a home-based antiques shop, as well as offering practical advice on researching to see if your town and neighborhood might be able to support an antiques shop. Plus, it will make you examine your home to see if it's suitable as a location for your shop. Lastly, it will make you think about whether you're suited for your new business venture.

In chapter 2 you'll learn about two government-sponsored sources where you can get practical, down-to-earth information on managing your business. The extensive information you'll gain from their counselors is actually free. It also shows you how and where to apply for any necessary permits and how to choose and record your shop's name, plus it offers guidelines on ways to adapt your home to accommodate your shop and will help you estimate the costs of remodeling. You'll also discover what you need to know if you choose to work with a partner.

Unless you've owned a business before, you may not understand the reason for creating a business plan. In chapter 3, you'll learn not only why you need one, but also what to include in it. To help you model your own business plan, you'll find a completed hypothetical sample plan to follow as you design your own.

Although you may not enjoy keeping detailed records, you'll have to learn to tolerate that if your business is going to be successful. Chapter 4 will help you understand which records you need to keep and how to go about the process. You'll even find suggestions on how to simplify record keeping.

Keeping your new shop stocked with salable antiques and collectibles can be a challenge. Chapter 5 shows you how to know, in advance, what your potential customers will buy. Here, you'll find descriptions of the places where most antiques dealers acquire their merchandise, plus other non-antique items you can sell to increase your profits.

Today, it's not enough to sell only from your shop. More and more antiques dealers have turned to the Internet to find what they need to fill out their inventory. Chapter 6 shows how you can reach a wider selection of buyers, as well as find some unique pieces to sell, on the Internet.

Knowing which antiques to buy is one thing. Pricing them to make a profit is quite another. In chapter 7 you'll discover the realities of overhead and how it can affect your pricing structure. You'll see how the services you offer have a direct bearing on your markup. You're bound to occasionally buy antiques and collectibles you can't sell at your usual markup. This chapter shows you how to move those items and recoup your investment.

Even though you've purchased salable antiques and have priced them to move, that doesn't guarantee they'll sell. How you display your inventory can make all the difference. Chapter 8 shows you how to display and light your antiques to the greatest advantage.

Once you've got your inventory in place and have hung out your sign, customers should beat a path to your door, right? Wrong. You've got to let everyone know you're there. Chapter 9 offers several creative ways to promote your business to the public, including traditional advertising methods and lesser-known but even more effective public relations techniques, including new Internet marketing ideas that cost little or nothing.

Finally, chapter 10 describes several additional ways you can use your knowledge of antiques to create extra income. You'll learn the nitty-gritty of selling at antiques shows, for example. You'll also discover how to expand your capabilities by holding estate sales, appraising antiques, and even teaching continuing education courses on antiques.

Be sure to read this book from cover to cover to get the big picture. Then go back and read each chapter closely and take notes. By this time, you should have gained enough insight to begin to visualize your new business. As you make your plans, refer to individual chapters for the detailed information you need on specific topics and other resources listed in the book. And don't put the book away, even after you've opened your shop. Use it as an everyday guide to make your dream of owning a successful antiques business come true.

01 | So You Want to Own an Antiques Shop

You have most likely come to consider opening your own antiques shop by chance rather than on purpose. The road to becoming your own boss begins at local yard or garage sales where you buy items you like for your own home. Eventually, you'll find yourself buying similar items and eventually beginning a collection. This collection leads to exposure to other items, which leads to another collection and, soon, another. By now your house is so full that in order to continue collecting, you resort to selling some of the pieces that perhaps aren't as good at your own yard or garage sale. While yard and garage sales are where many antiques and collectibles enter the market, prices can be limited here because buyers are looking for bargains. So you seek out flea markets where you can not only sell your items for higher prices, but also become available to collectors seeking those items. Thus begins your route to becoming an antiques dealer.

Unfortunately, that isn't the best route, and it's why most new dealers fail in their first year or two. While you may get a better feel for what to buy for your collections, you don't learn to buy salable items—ones that your customers won't be able to resist.

Many dealers start out selling antiques part-time. Some of them use this as a sideline business to supplement their regular job. Others see it as a profitable hobby, a way to have the fun of working with antiques and make a little money, too. A few dealers started out buying and selling antiques simply because their own collections became too large. That's exactly the way one dealer got into the business. He filled his small home with bowls, urns, and plates. Shelves held even more pottery. So, he began selling off the less desirable pieces. Of course, that just gave him money to buy *more* pottery. Since he had the knack of finding fine pottery everywhere he went, he never really solved the problem of his overcrowded house, but he did make a lot of money.

If you decide to sell antiques part-time, after a year or so you'll gain confidence in your ability to spot good buys you think may sell. You'll also learn what types of antiques people in your area are looking for. But while you may learn how to buy, you won't really learn how to sell—and selling is what the antiques business is all about.

After a while, when you are addicted to buying antiques, you may imagine yourself owning an antiques shop, but not feel confident enough to open one in a commercial building. The obvious solution is to open a small shop in your home.

You may have a fairly decent job now but are looking for one by which you can make a living without having to put up with a demanding boss. You may be retired—or close to it—and casting about for a working situation in which you can supplement your retirement income and keep active in the community. You may be a homemaker who needs to add to the family income but who doesn't want to be away from home for most of the day. And while all of these are legitimate reasons for considering a home-based antiques shop, none are a good enough reason. To run a successful antiques business, you have to not only be passionate about antiques, but also be a good businessperson, too. Should you decide to go ahead with such a shop, you'll be one of a growing number of people who are discovering the advantages of working from their home. Before you call the painter in to make a sign for your front yard, however, you need to sit down and do some honest soul-searching. The decision to run an antiques shop from your home is not one you make some morning before you've had your coffee. Not everyone is cut out for self-employment, in spite of how enticing it may sound.

Ideally, you'll be a high-energy person who takes personal responsibility for your own actions. You enjoy competition and have a fine sense of your own worth. You like people and people like you. You enjoy working and expect to be rewarded well for your efforts.

What are some of the pros and cons of the antiques business you ask? Read on to find out.

Disadvantages of Owning a Home-Based Antiques Shop

Like most of us, you've probably worked at a *regular* job at one time in your life. In spite of having to put up with all its problems, you did have a regular paycheck, maybe health benefits, paid vacations, and perhaps some job security.

You'll have none of that, except that you can't get laid off or fired, when you're self-employed as the owner of a home-based antiques shop. Here are some disadvantages:

- Your only paycheck will be the profit from your sales, and that will fluctuate with the seasons—boom and bust. You'll probably have months when sales are very high—spring until the winter holidays—and other months—usually January and February—when you'll wonder if anyone will ever come in the door again.

- You'll have to pay for your own health insurance, and because of your status as a self-employed person, your social security contributions to the government will be doubled.

- If you want to take a vacation, you'll have to either close the shop or hire someone to run it for you in your absence.

- You can also forget the forty-hour workweek. Even if you keep your shop open only eight hours a day five days a week, you'll spend many additional hours acquiring stock and doing book work.

- Since you'll operate out of your home, most people won't think you're really working. Friends will drop by, expecting you to sit and share a cup of coffee or tea with them. Some of them may call you on your business phone just to chat.

- Customers won't respect your posted hours, either. One owner of an in-home antiques shop had people banging on his shop door at 10:00 p.m. because they knew he was at home upstairs!

- Unless you have another source of income—or your spouse is bringing home a paycheck—opening a shop is highly risky for anyone with dependents. It may be many months before you show a profit.

- Since you'll work at home, you'll never be able to get away from work. Unless you have more willpower than most people, you'll manage to wander back into the shop area almost every night after closing, every Sunday, even on holidays, to take care of some little detail.

- Unless you hire an assistant, you'll be working alone, and the sense of isolation can become genuinely distressing. You won't have the companionship of fellow workers or the fun of office parties.

- If you decide, for whatever reason, to close your business, you may lose all your investment and have to remove any remodeling you did to your home.

It sounds depressing, doesn't it? But let's look at the upside.

Advantages of Owning a Home-Based Antiques Shop

There are many advantages to owning an antiques shop in your home. Perhaps you have become fed up working within the corporate bureaucracy or, even worse, the government. You realized that no matter how hard you work, you always seem to be a small frog in a big pond. Your strings always seem to be pulled by someone who has more clout than you could ever hope to have. Or maybe you're a person who wants to be in the business world, perhaps for the first time, but who likes a slower lifestyle than the one offered by the average job. Or maybe you're one of those people who's always dreamed of owning your own antiques shop, and you've decided now's the time to do it. You're willing to take a few risks to make it happen. If this sounds like you, read on.

- You'll feel a sense of pride and accomplishment when you see that sign go up outside with *your* shop's name on it.
  As the owner of your own shop, you'll be totally in control of your business. If you want to open your doors earlier and stay open later than your competition, you can do so. Open on Monday? Close on Monday? It's up to you. Should you decorate your windows with cheery checked curtains or elegant lace panels? Do whatever suits you best. You'll have the freedom to make all the decisions yourself about how you run your business.
- Your commuting time and expenses will drop to zero, since you won't have to go any farther than from the back of the house to the front. If your former workplace was thirty minutes from your home, you'll save a full five hours a week in commuting time, as well as many dollars each week for fuel or transit fares.
- You'll be able to dress in a more casual style than most offices allow, thus saving hundreds of dollars every year on clothing.
- As the owner of a business, you'll garner prestige among other business-people in your community, and your friends will admire your courage, independence, and self-reliance. You'll have the opportunity to join the

chamber of commerce and service clubs. Your network of friends will double, triple, or even quadruple, within months of opening your shop.

■ There are also numerous tax advantages to operating a home-based shop. You'll make one mortgage or rent payment, pay one utility bill, and you can take a large portion of those bills off your income tax as legitimate business deductions—your accountant will explain just what you can and cannot deduct.

■ Since you'll be running the shop from your home, your operating expenses will be less than those of a dealer who rents commercial space, yet your markup ratio can be the same as that dealer's, meaning that you'll make more profit per sale than he or she will. If you wish, you can sell your antiques at prices lower than those of the "downtown" dealers, thereby developing a reputation among regular customers for offering quality at lower prices. Yet you'll *still* make a profit.

■ Although your profits may be slim at first—at least until you've recouped your start-up costs—you have the potential for a good income. Everything depends on your initiative and how hard you're willing to work.

Doing Preliminary Research

Hopefully after reading the preceding pages, you're still excited about opening your own antiques shop. Your first step will be to research the demographics of your town and then take an informal survey of the existing antiques shops to determine whether they're successful or not.

Visit your local chamber of commerce, which can provide you with all the demographic data you'll need. Be sure to check on the following:

■ *What is your town's median income level?* People buy antiques for their homes with discretionary income, after they've paid their mortgage and bought their groceries. These customers must have some extra cash to spend on luxuries. It's important, therefore, that there be a solid base of people in town with comfortable incomes.

■ *What is the growth potential of the area?* Are companies moving to town, bringing with them jobs and additional discretionary income? Can young people find employment? Since opening a shop is a long-term proposition, it's important that the prognosis for a town's economic future be one of health and growth.

■ *What is the turnover rate of shops in town?* Do most businesspeople stay in business for many years, or is there a constant opening and closing of different enterprises?

■ *What is the traffic count on your street in front of your home and on nearby arteries?* A large part of your business will come from people who see your home/shop as they commute to work or drive by on their way to somewhere else. If your chamber of commerce doesn't have these figures, go to the highway department in your city or county.

Once you're satisfied that your town has a bright future for business in general, you need to check out the future for the antiques business itself. Almost every town of any size in this country has at least one antiques shop, whether in a commercial space or in a home. It's a given in this business that any well-run antiques shop will succeed if others in the general area are successful, too. Most people don't patronize only one antiques shop. Whether they're shopping for a specific antique or just browsing, they'll cruise through every shop in town.

If there are no existing antiques shops, you should ask yourself why not. Maybe the population base is too small to support a shop, or perhaps sports and recreation interest most people rather than collecting or investing in antiques.

Hopefully, you live in a town where many of the residents enjoy antiques. One way you can determine the success of existing shops is simply to observe the number of customers going in and out of them. Watch especially to see how many come out with bags in their hands. This is pretty good evidence that they bought something.

Most owners of antiques shops are friendly people who don't mind at all helping those new to the business, so don't hesitate to simply ask a shop owner how his business is going. If the shop has been there, under the same owner, for at least a year, you can be sure that person is making money. No one continues pouring funds into a losing business for more than a year. But do ask about the average number of customers the shop gets in a day and if the owner is making a reasonable profit.

Now ask yourself two important questions: (1) Is my home *suitable* for a home-based shop? and (2) Am *I* cut out to manage one? To help answer these questions, take a few minutes to complete the following self-surveys. After each question you'll find space to check off an answer.

Each question relates to subjects that are covered in later chapters of this book and therefore these are useful to consider.

If you don't want to write in this book, make a copy of the surveys. And while you're at it, purchase a package of manila folders and label one "Background Research for My Antiques Business." File surveys, notes, charts, and any other information that may be pertinent to starting your antiques business in it. Use the remaining ones for filing invoices, tax forms, etc.

Now stop and take the two surveys found on pages 8-9 and pages 10-13.

There are no right or wrong answers to any of the questions in the "Is Your Home Suitable for a Home-based Antiques Shop" and "Are You the Right Person to Run a Home-based Business?" surveys. But your *overall* answers will show whether owning a home-based shop is practical for you. Go back and look at your check marks. One or two *nos* aren't critical, so if you can answer *yes* to most of the questions, then you, too, should be able to open an antiques shop in your home with confidence.

Like any other business, the antiques business thrives when the economy is good. Despite the recent "Great Recession," the general profile of the antiques business is generally good. However, what people are buying has changed considerably. Those who collect fine antiques, dating from before 1830, are still buying them, but the market has shifted in the past few years. New collectors are shying away from the favorites of their parents and grandparents. Instead, they're collecting items from the thirties, forties, and fifties—items that fit better into their techno lifestyle.

Knowledgeable people have always invested in quality antiques for their homes. Those who can afford them have at least a few. These people realize that antiques, like real estate and fine art, can be good investments.

The beauty of this business and for you as the owner of a home-based shop, however, is that today people don't have to be wealthy to buy antiques and collectibles for their homes. Thousands of shop owners across the country cater to middle-income Americans. They fill their shops with useful and often beautiful furniture, prints, tableware, stained glass, and an infinite variety of memorabilia, all at affordable prices.

Real estate salespeople have a formula they use to help determine the selling value of a piece of property. It's *location, location, location.* Location is vitally important to the success of a home-based antiques shop, too.

Look at your home objectively, both from a customer's point of view and as a commercial establishment, and complete the following site evaluation. A quick glance at your answers will tell you whether you should go ahead with your plans to use your home for your shop.

1. Many local zoning laws do not allow commercial businesses in private homes. And, even if they do, the bylaws of many upscale housing development homeowners' associations don't.

   Question: Do your town or township's zoning laws permit commercial businesses in private homes?

   Yes _____   No _____

2. Since customers will come to your home instead of to a commercial building, it should be easily accessible to them. You don't have to be right in the center of town, certainly, but you should have good access by automobile. To be successful, you should be located on or near major traffic arteries. Customers will drive a few blocks out of their way to reach a shop, but most won't travel much farther than that.

   Question: Is your home located in a neighborhood where customers can find you easily? Is it situated near a major artery where there is reasonable traffic flow to create drive-by interest in your shop?

   Yes _____   No _____

3. Most of your customers will drive to your home, but parking is forbidden or restricted in some neighborhoods.

   Question: Will your customers be able to park at the curb in front of your home/shop or at least nearby?

   Yes _____   No _____

4. For many weeks in winter, your shop will be open after dark. Some people are hesitant to park their car on a street that isn't well lighted.

   Question: Does your street have adequate overhead lighting that illuminates it and the entrance to your shop on late afternoons in winter?
   Yes _____   No _____

5. There's nothing wrong with starting out in a small front room. But as your business grows, you'll need more display space.

   Question: Is the layout of your home such that you can either remodel it to include more display space in the future or add another wing or room?
   Yes _____   No _____

6. Unless you live alone, you must consider the needs and feelings of other family members. In most cases the space used for a home-based antiques shop usurps a living room, dining room, or some other area that was once used by the family. Understandably, they may feel displaced if you fill that room or others with antiques and customers and the family has to move to the back of the house.

   You shouldn't consider turning part of a home into a shop if it's going to cause tension within your loved ones. It's just not worth it.

   Question: Does your home have a family room or some other space where everyone can still gather for games, television, conversation, and entertaining friends even after you've allocated space in your home for your business?
   Yes _____   No _____

Many of us have a blind spot or two regarding our own faults and qualities, so you might copy down these questions and ask a close friend or your spouse to evaluate you based on his or her own judgment of your entrepreneurial abilities.

1. A home-based antiques shop is still an antiques shop, not a hobby. It's not so different from one in a commercial space as far as its day-to-day operation is concerned. Barring genuine emergencies, the doors must be open for regular hours on specific days. In most cases this means that you, as the owner/manager, must be there to greet customers during those hours and on those days. Certainly, you can hire part-time help (more about that later), but the main burden of running your shop will be on you.

   One home-based antiques shop owner had hung a rather crudely painted sign out front. It informed potential customers: "Open whenever I'm home. Call first—555-3485." Guess how many customers took the time to call first and set an appointment to browse through her antiques? Not many.

   So even though maintaining your shop in your home can be far more pleasant than working eight to five for someone else, it's still a full-time job.

   Question: Are you looking at managing a home-based antiques shop as a full-time job (instead of a profitable hobby)?

   Yes _____   No _____

2. Loving antiques isn't enough to ensure a profit in your shop. You must be a good businessperson, too. This means understanding how to keep good records, what the relationship of profit to expense is, ways to control inventory, how much to allocate to advertising, how to establish good public relations in the community, and much more.

   Question: Have you ever worked in a business in which you were responsible for or had exposure to the behind-the-scenes side to retail selling?

   Yes _____   No _____

   Question: If the answer to the above question is no, would you be willing to get practical experience or training before you open your shop?

   Yes _____   No _____

3. Most financial advisers suggest that anyone planning a home-based antiques business have enough cash on hand or readily available to pay for the necessary remodeling and to buy the initial stock without having to obtain a bank loan. The reason is simple: It often takes months for a new business to begin showing a profit, yet lenders expect loan payments to come in on time every month, whether or not the shop is making money.

   Question: Do you have enough cash on hand or readily available to take care of the inevitable remodeling and opening expenses of your antiques shop?
   Yes _____   No _____

4. Most people consider self-employment because they want to be free of the corporate bureaucracy, want to have the opportunity to make as much money as their intelligence allows, and want to make their own decisions. They are independent thinkers. These people often come up with creative ideas and solutions to problems. They're self-starters who can get out of bed in the morning and begin work even though there's no time clock to punch or supervisor to please. They stick with a project until it's finished. They're reasonably well organized and get a sense of accomplishment from a job well done. These people have usually served as officers or on committees at their churches or synagogues, in clubs, or at their children's schools.

   Question: Do you consider yourself a self-starter, creative, and independent?
   Yes _____   No _____

5. Only someone who genuinely loves antiques will be able to sell them with enthusiasm. That means all antiques, too, even those whose style may not be exactly to your liking. You may not be overly fond of Mission Oak, for example, yet Mission Oak is very popular right now and brings in high prices.

   A middle-aged man recently moved from Philadelphia to a small town west of St. Louis, bringing with him pieces of top-quality Chippendale and Queen Anne furniture, the type he preferred. Looking ahead to opening an antiques shop in his new home, he scouted the antiques shops and malls in the area, checking out their stock, prices, and so on. Since he had moved into an area of small towns where most people wanted late-nineteenth-century oak and primitives, that's what he noticed in the shops. He hadn't realized that his Eastern tastes may not be the same as those of the Midwest. If he did open a shop, he'd have to sell oak and primitives, among other things, or his business would fail.

Question: Do you love and appreciate antiques enough to be able to sell any and all of them with enthusiasm?

Yes _____   No _____

6. As with many other aspects of life—skirt lengths, architecture, music, even pets—trends in antiques change from time to time. Savvy dealers keep up with these trends.

    Remember when everyone was collecting insulators? Dealers scoured the countryside, buying all they could find for their shops. Prices went through the roof, and these dealers sold the insulators for top dollar, but that trend passed and others took its place.

    Signed aluminum ware, for example, has become a legitimate collectible. Dealers and collectors now search for aluminum trays, bowls, and novelty items of the thirties, forties, and fifties—things they would have previously ignored.

    To be successful as a dealer in antiques, you must keep up with such trends, on both a national and a local level. If there appears to be a surge in interest in some period or item, then you know to begin stocking it. You can keep up with trends by reading several of the excellent trade journals and books published for dealers in antiques, such as *AntiqueWeek, Antique Trader,* and *Southeastern Antiques and Collectibles Magazine.* Some newspapers print syndicated columns devoted to antiques. A few national magazines, such as *Forbes,* have regular departments for antiques and collectibles. By reading these publications regularly, you can keep up with what people are buying, as well as current selling prices. This information is available to you no matter where you live.

    Keep up with what the decorating and home service magazines are featuring, too. New homeowners often follow the trends they see in home decorating magazines such as *Country Living, Better Homes and Gardens,* and *Southern Living,* or perhaps they've gotten home decorating ideas from one of the many home shows on cable television. They'll either bring in a magazine and point to an illustration of a piece of furniture or decorative item and ask, "Do you have one of these?" or tell you about one they saw on a cable show. If you have it, you've made an immediate sale.

You can tell when a trend is fading by reading the "For Sale" and auction ads in the major antiques trade papers. If many dealers and private collectors start selling off their stock in a certain category, you can be pretty sure the trend has peaked and prices will fall substantially.

Question: Will you be willing to devote several hours a week to studying antiques, their trends, and current prices?

Yes _____   No _____

7. Of course, you'll have the companionship of your customers. You'll become good friends with many of them, and their visits will be bright spots in your workday. Inevitably, however, you'll spend many hours alone in your shop. Can you handle this without becoming depressed?

Question: Can you work alone without being lonely?

Yes _____   No _____

8. Good health and energy are prime attributes of the successful entrepreneur. Some people seem to be blessed with this health and energy. Others have to work at it. Regardless, it's impossible to run a business successfully if you're listless and tired all the time.

You don't have to follow the regimen of an Olympic athlete to maintain good health. All it usually takes is a sensible lifestyle. Most doctors and physical therapists today recommend no smoking, moderate or no alcohol consumption, normal weight, a low-fat, high-fiber diet, and a half hour or so every day of some kind of exercise—an early-morning brisk walk or late-afternoon workout at a gym will do wonders for your energy level.

Question: Will you make an effort to maintain a healthy lifestyle so that you'll have the energy necessary to run your business?

Yes _____   No _____

Getting Experience Before You Hang Up Your Sign

Simply loving antiques or dealing in them part-time is fun, but making the transition to full-time dealing requires a good deal of thought and preparation. Almost every profession requires some kind of education or training. The antiques business is no different. You certainly don't need a degree in business management, but you do need to know the basics of retail merchandising and record keeping.

What's the best way to learn the ropes? Reading this book is a good start. It contains just about everything you need to know *that can be put in a book*. Unless you have some hands-on experience in selling antiques on a day-to-day basis, however, you might be letting yourself in for some problems.

We'll assume that you really do love antiques but have never owned a shop of your own with the full responsibility of management. You can get that training in several ways:

- *Get a job in a good local antiques shop,* then use your eyes and ears to absorb every bit of knowledge you can from the owner or manager. This way, you'll see how he or she manages inventory, works with customers, handles difficult situations, and so forth.
- *Work in an antiques mall.* Large antiques malls sometimes hire several people to assist in selling and bookkeeping, to help customers find specific items, to watch for shoplifters, and so forth. While this is often only part-time—three or four days a week—you'll get firsthand training in the antiques business.
- *Rent space in an antiques mall.* Doing so will teach you how to manage your own booth and stock. You'll also learn the best ways to display your antiques, how to shift them around to create interest, how to decorate, and how to price them realistically. In addition, you'll learn about profit margins and what people in your area are buying. At the same time, you'll build up inventory that you can move to your own shop when you open it. This is an excellent way to get started in the antiques business. And even after you open your own shop, you may want to keep your booth to sell extra items.
- *Join an antiques co-op.* If an antiques co-op is already in operation near your home, you could approach the owners and ask about joining it. In a co-op several dealers actually own the business jointly and usually have equal floor space in the shop. They share the responsibility of keeping the shop

open, cleaning it, and so forth. They also share all expenses: rent, utilities, advertising, and so forth. This is about the only way you can actually own an antiques shop without having the entire responsibility of management.

Business Courses Can Help, Too

To further your business knowledge, you might want to enroll in a basic business management course in the community education division of a local college or university. Seriously, look at your business skills and find courses that will help you improve them. A course in how to start or run a small business will be excellent, for starters. As you get into your new business, you may also want to enroll in basic record keeping, accounting, and tax courses.

And to broaden your knowledge of antiques, search for and enroll in antiques courses, either general ones or those dealing with specific topics, at community school nights held in local high schools and community centers. It's important to constantly be learning. The more you know about antiques, the better salesperson you'll become.

All right, so you've decided to take the plunge. You're going to become the proud owner of the best antiques shop in town. Before you put out the welcome mat for that first customer, however, you need to get some advice.

Receiving Free Advice from Professionals

Free services are invaluable for anyone who's never managed a business before. What can you expect from a meeting with volunteers? Hours and hours of one-on-one consultation! The helpful people at your local or regional Small Business Development Center (SBDC) will even meet with you regularly *after* you open your shop to help guide you toward success. These centers also offer short courses on running a business, such as Understanding Financial Statements, Changing Careers, Basic Bookkeeping, Advanced Bookkeeping, and Beginning Business Workshop—each for a modest fee.

Counselors from SCORE and SBDC

You can make an appointment to speak with someone from the Service Corps of Retired Executives (SCORE), as well as a counselor from your nearest SBDC. Both organizations, sponsored by the Small Business Administration (SBA), offer professional advice for entrepreneurs just starting out in business.

Why spend your time talking to two different counselors? Because they may have totally different perspectives to give you, and all of it is worth your while. The people at SCORE, for example, are retired executives who've spent many years managing successful businesses. Some of these men and women will have owned their own businesses, while others will have been high-level employees of major corporations. On the other hand, the counselors at the

Small Business Development Centers will have been involved in smaller businesses, perhaps not too different from the one you're planning to operate.

Although it's highly unlikely that you'll be assigned to anyone who has ever managed a home-based antiques business, the consultants who work with you will have had hands-on experience in *some* type of business. They can give you excellent information on how to set up and operate your shop. They'll walk you through many of the topics you'll read about in this book. They'll play devil's advocate to help you think through any problems you perhaps haven't considered in your enthusiasm to open your shop, and they'll give you an understanding of some basic management procedures, including writing the business plan that we'll cover in chapter 3.

You'll almost certainly be advised to estimate the amount of cash you'll need to take care of your personal living expenses for at least six months. While you may begin making a profit before that, don't count on it. They'll tell you to look back at what you spent last year for rent or mortgage payments, utilities, food, car payments, clothing, medical expenses, entertainment, taxes, and so forth. Then, in addition to what you will need for start-up expenses, plan to have that much cash in the bank—or readily available—so that you can draw on it immediately.

These counselors can also give you some government publications to study at home. You'll leave the meetings with a much better understanding of the practical side of running a business, the part that can make or break you as a dealer.

To make an appointment with a SCORE representative or someone from the SBDC, call the SBA office number listed in the U.S. Government section of your local telephone directory. In case there's no SBA office near you, call (800) 827-5722, the SBA Hotline Desk, and ask to have the *Small Business Resource Guide* for your state sent to you. This free guide lists dozens of helpful publications you can order for nominal fees. You can also check with a nearby college. Many have affiliations with an SBDC.

Check Your Local Library

Your counselors might suggest you pay a visit to your local library for some in-depth research about antiques shops in particular. The reference librarian will be happy to give you a hand in locating some up-to-date information sources.

One place to start is the *Reader's Guide to Business Periodicals*. This directory catalogs hundreds of current articles about every business topic under the sun. You might even find a few well-written articles that give statistics about the status of the antiques business as a whole while others might discuss trends, turnover rates, problems the industry is having, and other highly relevant topics.

In almost every case these articles will include quotations from experts in the field of antiques. Jot down the names of the authors of the articles and the experts quoted. You can nearly always get these people's address, telephone numbers, or e-mail addresses by writing to the editors of the magazines. Contact these experts and ask if they could help you with more information. You'll be surprised how accommodating they can be. However, remember that they're busy people, so be as efficient as possible and send a list of questions by regular mail or e-mail.

Some of the questions you might ask: *What's a reasonable turnover rate for a shop of XX square feet? What are the best advertising media for a home-based antiques shop? How do I build a strong and loyal customer base? If I start with and maintain an inventory of $XXXXX, what can I reasonably expect in revenue?* Make the questions specific to *your* shop. If these experts don't know the answers, they'll refer you to someone who does.

Obtaining Licenses and Permits

Virtually every city and town in this country requires business owners to apply for and receive a business license or permit before actually opening their doors. This permit will give you formal permission to operate your antiques business in your home.

The process for getting this permit isn't involved, but having one is absolutely necessary to carry on a business legally. In most cases all you'll have to do to start the process is fill out a form that asks for the type of business you plan to operate, your name, and the business address.

In your case the only hurdle you might have to jump after that surrounds running a business out of your *home,* not from a commercial location. Some communities have strict laws about what businesses can and can't be operated in a residential neighborhood. You might run up against a zoning law that prohibits or restricts home-based retail shops. Whether or not you're in the clear depends to a large extent on your town's attitude toward home-based businesses and the zoning of your neighborhood. Some neighborhoods are zoned for single-family homes only. Others allow multiple residential units. And still others allow many types of small businesses right along with residential homes. And even though your town may allow commercial businesses in homes, your homeowner's association—should you live in a housing development—may not.

So before you go any further, visit your city hall or local township building and explain your plans to someone in the business licenses or planning department. That person can walk you through the zoning regulations that spell out activities permitted in your neighborhood.

Some regulations that apply to you as a home-based dealer in antiques may include the size and placement of signs on the building itself or near the street, the number of parking places available to customers, how much alteration of the home itself will be necessary to accommodate the business, the approximate number of customers who will visit the shop per day, the number of employees you can hire, and so forth. In some towns the planning department schedules a meeting with or a survey of neighbors to approve a home-based business. Almost certainly, there'll be an on-site inspection of your home by a fire marshal.

Suppose you're turned down for your business permit. This isn't likely to happen unless you live in a neighborhood zoned for single-family homes *and* in an exceptionally restrictive town. But if it is turned down, are you out of luck? Not necessarily. Ask any builder or contractor. They routinely appeal turndowns, and the rate of reversal on applications is often good.

If you're not well versed in the vagaries of municipal regulations, your first step in getting that refusal reversed would be to find a local attorney who specializes in obtaining licenses and permits. Your legal counsel will probably tell you that you have two options: (1) You can apply to the appeals board for a review of your application, or (2) you can ask for a variance or exception to whatever rule tripped you up.

Be prepared to state your case politely, clearly, and firmly before a group of people from some municipal department. Emphasize that your antiques shop will be a nonpolluting, low-traffic impact, quiet business that will be a genuine asset to the community. Show your plans for landscaping and any remodeling of the building. Explain that your shop will be open only during regular business hours. Tell them you plan to be an active, contributing member of the local business community by joining the chamber of commerce, a service club, or other professional organizations. All this will show you to be a responsible person who will operate an attractive, desirable business.

Although there's a trend toward home-based businesses, you should be aware of the difference between a commercial business in your home and working out of your home. With the advancements in technology and the ease of access to files from any computer, many people are able to work out of their homes in a variety of businesses. None of these require direct access by the public. An antiques business is a commercial retail business, regardless of whether it's in a shop downtown or a shop in your home. So be prepared to argue your case. Your chances of winning are good. Once you're approved for the permit, you'll be required to register your business name. But if you strike out completely with zoning, consult chapter 6, for an alternative.

Choosing Your Business Name

Probably one of the first things you'll decided on when you get the idea for a home-based antiques shop is the name of your shop. After all, that's the most personal part of this business. The name you choose reflects you and how you plan to operate your shop. It shows whether you'll be a cozy little "Grandma's Attic" type of shop or one that blends into the general commercial fabric of the town. Whatever type of shop you choose, be flexible about the name and be willing to change your mind about your first choice. A company's name is a very important part of its image, and once you make the decision, the name will be with you for a long time.

One good idea is to make a list of all the names you might even conceivably call your shop. Brainstorm with your family and friends to come up with fifteen or twenty names. Go over the list and immediately eliminate any that don't appeal to you. Put the list away for a day or so and go back to it. You'll probably be able to eliminate most of the remaining names. Make your choice from the few that are left. Play around with them until you come up with a business name that's really suitable for your shop.

You'll save yourself some paperwork if you use your own full name, for example, "Laura Colter Antiques," or your initials and your last name, "R. E. Thompson Antiques."

You can, of course, choose what's termed an "assumed business name," such as "Colter and Sons Antiques," "Main Street Antiques," or "Antiques Unlimited," the regulations for which are on the following page. If you decide on an assumed name—and there's absolutely no reason not to—be sure it's one that describes your shop.

If you decide to choose a name other than your own, you'll have to register it with the state as an *assumed business name*. The regulations about business names in most states are pretty standard across the country. They define the terms *assumed business name* and *real and true name* as follows:

- An assumed business name is a name other than the real and true name of each person operating a business. A real and true name becomes an assumed business name with the addition of any words that imply the existence of additional owners. Examples include "Company," "Associates," "Sons," and "Daughters."
- A real and true name is the surname of an individual with the individual's given names(s) or initial(s), or a corporate name or limited partnership name already filed with the state's business registry.

You do not have to register a business name that's a "real and true" name. What's the purpose of registering an assumed business name? It's just to let the public know who is transacting business under that business name.

An assumed business name must be registered in every county in which a business is located, but this probably won't affect you as a home-based retailer. Failure to register an assumed name can be punished by a fine, so don't overlook this requirement. The fee for registering an assumed business name runs about $50 on average in most states.

To register your business name (if you use an assumed one), write to the Secretary of State's office in your state capital and ask for the proper forms. A clerk in your local city hall, township building, or courthouse can give you the address. That person can also walk you through the process of registering the name.

Applying for Your Sales Tax Number

If you live in a state that charges sales tax on purchases, you'll have to get a sales tax number. This number allows you to buy antiques for resale without paying a sales tax, and it requires you to collect tax on your own sales. Apply for this number at your local municipal building or at www.businesslicenses.com.

Do You Need a Logo?

A logo is simply a graphic that you have printed on your business cards, your sign, and any other place where you want to give your business a special identity. Antiques shops use logos that look like rocking chairs, cut-glass goblets, and framed pictures. All are attractive and certainly do add interest to the company names.

You can hire an artist to design and draw a logo for you. A less expensive alternative is to use "clip art." Clip art is line drawings reproduced on CD-ROM or available

Guidelines for Choosing a Business Name

The following guidelines will help you choose a business name that will not only stand the test of time, but will also make your shop easily identifiable to your customers:

1. Your business name should immediately identify your company as one that sells *antiques*. For starters, plan on using the word "antiques" somewhere in the name. A name such as "Alexander's Place" could belong to a furniture store, a cafe, a bed-and-breakfast, or even a copy center! However, there's no mistaking the business of "Alexander's Antiques."

2. Does your town already have several antiques shops? Then choose a name that begins with the letter A. For instance, your name could be James Alexander or Alexander James. While many people search for businesses on the Internet, in which case, it doesn't matter what letter of the alphabet your name begins with, there are still some who look first in a business directory or the Yellow Pages when looking for a particular product or service. As they run down the list of companies under the category "Antiques Shops," they will naturally see names beginning with "A" first. So, "Alexander's Antiques" would most likely be first on that list.

3. You may want to use your own name as your company name. That's fine as long as your name is easy to spell and pronounce. Granted, the United States is a melting pot, and any telephone directory lists plenty of names that, for most people, are difficult to spell and pronounce. If you happen to be the proud possessor of such a name, consider using an assumed business name that won't trip up your customers, instead.

4. The name should also be one that will differentiate your shop from others in town. Our minds tend to remember the primary word or words in a name and gloss over the less important words. If owners of two shops choose similar names, customers are going to remember the primary word or words and forget the rest. Eventually, customers will refer to the shop as "Alexander's," meaning his antiques shop.

It's easy to see how customers who read an ad placed by a shop called "Country Cousin Antiques" might end up driving to another shop named "Everything Country Antiques," especially if they weren't familiar with either one of them. The primary words *country* and *antiques* in each could be very confusing to them.

5. Your company name should be an accurate indication of the type of merchandise you carry. Will you specialize in high-ticket antiques? Or will you carry moderately priced antiques and collectibles? A name such as "Heirloom Gallery Antiques" might be suitable for the first type of shop while "Aunt Tilly's Attic Antiques" would fit the second one.

on the Internet. While some designs aren't copyrighted, others are; so it's best to find out before you use the design. If you decide to use clip art, just be sure it's of excellent quality, will reproduce well in print advertising, and will portray the image you wish for your shop.

The chances are good that a print shop won't charge for reproducing clip art on your business cards and stationery. You can, of course, do it yourself using the proper computer software. A sign painter may charge a fee for including a logo on your signs.

Specializing in Arts & Crafts furniture and accessories

123 Chestnut Road
Fraser, PA 19335

Phone: 494-555-6938
E-mail: ealexander@webservices.com

What Legal Structure Do You Want for Your Business?

Another decision you must make early on in the process of getting started is to determine just what legal structure your business will take. A home-based business can be structured in several ways, depending on the following:

- the size of your business
- the number of people involved in the venture
- the need for capital to start the business
- tax advantages or disadvantages

Your accountant can help you decide which is best for your particular situation and prepare any documents that may be necessary. Here is a brief summary of four basic types of structures and their differences.

Sole Proprietorship

Sole proprietorship is the simplest and most economical form of ownership. You can open your business with the least amount of paperwork and bureaucratic hassle, and your attorney and accounting fees—(both up-front and ongoing—will usually be less than for other forms of business. You're the sole owner of the business. You make all the decisions, take all the risks, pay all the bills, and enjoy all the profits. Your record keeping for the IRS will be minimal, and as the owner of a small business, you'll enjoy certain income tax advantages.

The biggest disadvantage to a sole proprietorship is that you're *personally* liable for all debts of the company. Also, the growth of the business is pretty well limited to your own energy, ambition, and finances.

Many owners of small businesses also have problems keeping their personal lives separate from their business affairs, and serious illness can mean the end of the business and the loss of all investment.

Partnership

When two or more people own a business jointly, that's called a partnership. They usually share equally all responsibilities in running the business and share equally in the profits, assuming each has an equal financial investment in the company. Record keeping is fairly simple, with profits taxed as personal income.

While the sole owner of a shop must make all decisions alone, a partnership has the advantage of two or more heads working together to solve problems. If additional capital is needed for the business, it's sometimes easier to obtain it from two or more partners than one person.

One unique partnership advantage for owners of home-based antiques shops is that it allows one partner to manage the shop while another scouts for antiques at estate sales or auctions or works a booth at an antiques show. Having one partner available to keep the shop open also allows the other partner the freedom to take care of personal or family affairs. This is especially valuable for those people with small children.

As with any relationship, disadvantages do exist in a business partnership. The partners must share the profits, which may be pretty slim for the first few months. If one partner eventually moves away or simply decides she doesn't like running the shop, one must buy the other out. This can mean a substantial outlay of cash.

There's always the possibility of a personality conflict, too. Two people who've been lifelong friends, or even close relatives, can discover irritating personality quirks in each other once they're in business together.

Family-Owned Business

A family-owned business may seem to be the ideal partnership. After all, it provides income for two or more family members and keeps the money in the family. In a perfect world that's the way it should work, and sometimes it *does*. Many home-based antiques shops are jointly owned by husband and wife, two sisters, mother and daughter, or some other combination of family members.

Unfortunately, it doesn't always work so well. Emotions can run high in families, and this easily causes sparks when it comes time to make important business decisions. One person may be a strong advocate of the "Advertise, advertise, advertise!" school of business, whereas the other thinks advertising is a waste of good money. Even worse are the situations where family members are brought into the business not because they know anything about selling antiques but simply because they need something to keep them occupied. That's just a disaster waiting to happen! So, think long and hard about sharing your shop with another family member. No one wants to damage family relationships over business.

If, however, you and a relative do plan to operate your shop as partners, you need to establish some definite guidelines long before you open your doors:

- First, agree on the purpose of the shop. Is it to provide the sole income of the partners, or will it serve as an adjunct to other income? The answer to this question might determine the amount spent on remodeling the home, the number of days and hours the shop is open, the promotion and advertising budget, and a dozen other facets of the business.
- Will *all* partners share in all responsibilities of running the shop, or will there be a division of labor and responsibilities? Often one partner will be a great salesperson, for example, while another couldn't sell a Lalique perfume bottle for $5 but might have a real talent for locating and *buying* antiques that can be sold at a profit.
- Can you forgo traditional family relationships—mother-daughter or father-son, for example—and work together as *business* partners, not as parent and child? To do so requires a strong sense of independence and a great deal of respect between two people.
- Finally, can you separate your working lives from your personal lives? The problems of home should not encroach on the hours at work, and the problems that arise in the shop should be forgotten, at least temporarily, when you hang that CLOSED sign in your window at the end of the day.

With loyalty, affection, and effort, a family partnership certainly can work. If this is your plan, enjoy your business and work together for everyone's happiness and financial well-being.

Corporation

Few small-business owners incorporate their companies today, especially in the first years of operation. There was a time when laws gave the owners of corporations broad protections. Those owners couldn't be sued for debts incurred by the corporation or for liabilities that sometimes ran into millions of dollars. Owners of incorporated businesses also received highly favorable advantages when the tax man came around with his hand out. Those days are gone. The few advantages for the small-business person today are outweighed by some of Uncle Sam's stringent rules. Corporations must hold formal meetings, keep endless records, and wade through a morass of red tape. It's hardly ever worth the hassle for an antiques dealer.

Working with Professional Counselors

Your antiques shop may be just a converted garage or living room at first. You may have no employees and plan on a low-key operation for some time. Even so, you'll find it to your advantage to establish working relationships with several professional counselors.

Many people going into business for the first time are reluctant to hire professional counselors. They have had little need in the past for an accountant or an attorney, and their banking and insurance requirements have been minimal. They may not know how to choose good professionals or what to expect from their services. They may not see the *need* for these services, which can, admittedly, be expensive. In the long run, however, you'll actually save money by seeking help from these men and women. They can show you ways to cut your tax bill. They can help you establish a legal business structure that is right for your lifestyle and personal situation. They can set up a simple bookkeeping system for you that you can maintain yourself.

> Tip: To find some of these paid professionals, you may want to try Local Search, a new online service offered in conjunction with Google and Yahoo Maps. Many businesses and professionals are registering themselves with these services, making it easier to find them. One advantage to Local Search is that you can read reviews by satisfied or not-so-satisfied customers which will help you choose wisely.

The following sections discuss your banker, your insurance agent, your accountant, and your attorney. You might want to interview two or three counselors in each category before settling on one. Be honest with them about exactly what your business encompasses, and expect straight answers from them about fees and what you'll get for your money.

Your Bank and Banker

Plan to open a business checking account separate from your personal one. You'll find it infinitely easier to reconcile expenses and deposits that way.

You may already have a good working relationship with an officer at your current bank. If so, continue with that bank. If for any reason you need to shop for bank services, check out a small, locally owned, full-service bank. Many people have had unsatisfactory experiences when dealing with a branch of a large national bank. By dealing with a smaller bank, where you're known by sight and name, you'll get better, faster, more personal service than from an institution where you're just an account number.

Don't select a bank just because it's the closest one to your home/shop, either. Although that may be convenient as far as making deposits and so forth, you need a bank that has a healthy attitude toward small businesses. Not all of them do. Larger banks, used to dealing with larger businesses, often refuse to make loans of less than $50,000. As an antiques dealer, you may need to borrow $10,000 or less. Find out the bank's attitude about expansion loans for small businesses *before* you open an account.

Your Insurance Agent

You definitely need liability, theft, and fire coverage for your shop, plus coverage on any vehicle you use for your business. You may also want to consider business interruption insurance, health and life insurance, and disability coverage. If you're satisfied with the agent who writes your personal automobile and homeowner's insurance, go to him first. Agents, however, usually work with only one company, and not all companies provide all types of insurance.

If your own agent can't write policies for everything you need, shop around among the insurance brokers in your town. Brokers deal with many companies, not just one, and they'll research the entire industry until they can put together a package that gives you the coverage you need.

Ask each broker to give you a bid that covers the entire package. You'll probably get widely differing figures, so study each package carefully to determine which is the best deal for your particular needs.

Your Accountant

If you've always plowed through the IRS regulations necessary to file your own income tax forms, you may never have felt the need for an accountant. Being in business is a different matter. You can hardly conduct a commercial business efficiently today without the advice and guidance of a qualified accountant.

Don't confuse the services of a bookkeeper with those of an accountant. A bookkeeper simply records expenses and receipts in one or more ledgers. By using the information in chapter 4, you can easily handle that job yourself. An accountant, on the other hand, prepares your tax returns for you, sets up your schedule of estimated tax payments, and prepares information about deductible expenses and depreciation on capital assets. She can also double-check your bookkeeping system to make sure you're taking advantage of every legal break the government gives a small-business person like yourself.

One word of advice about selecting an accountant: Choose one who is qualified to handle all the intricate ins and outs of small-business accounting. Basically, you'll find three types of accountants available:

1. *Enrolled Agent (EA):* a person who has passed a two-day exam prepared by the IRS, covering several areas of taxation. This person will probably advertise as a tax specialist.
2. *Accredited Accountant:* a person who has passed an exam prepared by the Accreditation Council of Accountancy and Taxation. These accountants may specialize in small-business accounting.

3. *Certified Public Accountant (CPA):* a person who has passed the American Institute of Certified Public Accountants' rigorous national examination on accounting, auditing, law, and related areas. These professionals must also complete additional training every year to keep up with constantly changing rules regarding taxes and all the other financial matters that affect businesspeople.

Of these three, the best choice for a small business is a CPA. While a CPA's fees may seem high, you'll find the advice will more than pay for itself in tax savings and profits.

A friend in business might be able to recommend one. You'll find accountants listed in the Yellow Pages and online with the American Institute of Public Accounts at www.aicpa.org or by typing "accountants and the name of your town" into a search engine. One of the most important criteria in choosing an accountant, however, is that she have *extensive experience* working with small businesses. This is vital, because the needs of the person managing a small business are quite different from those of individuals or of people who own large corporations. Any accountant you interview should be able to give you references from other clients and should deal with you openly about fees. The accountant should also be willing to come to your shop occasionally if you feel you need on-site help.

Your Attorney

An attorney can advise you about the many small legal aspects of a shop in your home. Most of these details will be simple ones that relate to local regulations, but an attorney can also show you how to protect yourself in case of a lawsuit based on a customer's having an accident on your property. Although the chances of any such litigation are small, it's always wise to have established a personal relationship with an attorney *in advance*.

If your business is to be managed as a partnership, you should work out the details with an attorney. A simple covenant agreed upon *in advance* can save a lot of misunderstandings later on. This includes partnerships between two or more family members.

Your local bar association may have a referral service that can give you the names of several local attorneys, or you can go to the American Bar Association's online referral service at www.findlegalhelp.org, which also has links to county bar associations. You won't find all attorneys listed with the referral service, so a recommendation from an existing client may be the best way to choose and retain an attorney. Ask your banker, your CPA, or a friend who is in business for referrals. As with the CPA, the attorney you choose should specialize in working with small businesses. For information on legal topics, go to www.abalawinfo.org.

The fees accountants and attorneys charge vary widely, so don't hesitate to ask what their hourly rate is right up front. Those associated with large firms usually charge the highest rates. They must support large staffs and expensive locations and usually deal with people whose needs are quite complicated. As a person in a small business with simple requirements, you'll probably find an accountant or attorney in a one- or two-person office a more affordable choice.

The services of these professionals can be expensive since most charge by the hour. If you have a list of questions or concerns *written out* and ready to discuss at your first meetings with them, you'll probably be able to wrap up all your preliminary needs in an hour.

Building a Customer Base Before You Open

It's best to have sold antiques in some way before opening your own shop. This could have been working in someone else's shop as a salesperson, operating a booth in an antiques mall, owning part of a co-op, or selling at flea markets that specialize in antiques. If so, then you probably already know many of the people in your town who can become *your* customers. Buy a pad with lined pages and start now making a list of these people. Keep the pad handy and add to the list every time you remember a name or contact. As your list begins to grow, look up the names at www .anywho.com, an online directory of individuals and businesses. By the time you have your grand opening, you'll have a fine, easy-to-use list of potential customers to invite to this very special event.

Estimating Your Start-Up Costs

Chapter 1 recommended that you have enough cash—in the bank or readily available from non-loan sources—to get your business off the ground. You'll need that cash now for the necessary remodeling and other expenses you'll face before you actually open your doors.

Counselors with the Small Business Development Center strongly suggest that you avoid using credit cards for these start-up costs. They advise paying as you go in case you find it difficult to make even minimum payments during your first months in business.

Let's consider some start-up projects.

Walls and Partitions

You may be lucky enough to have a large living room/dining room area where you can display your antiques in style. If, however, your rooms appear to be a little crowded now with just the family furniture, they're going to be a lot worse when you fill them with antiques. Better plan on taking out a wall or partition to open up some walking-around space.

Instead of turning two rooms into one large room, though, you might consider leaving a foot or two on each side of one original wall intact to form an archway, which is an attractive architectural feature. Even though the two original rooms are now, for all intents and purposes, one room, the archway can serve to divide *types* of antiques. Chapter 8 further describes this strategy.

Carpeting

I suggest you take up any existing residential-type carpeting in your display rooms. You know how hard it is to keep carpeting clean with just the family running in and out. It will be a hundred times worse with *customers* bringing in dirt, mud, and slush on their shoes.

You may have a good wooden floor underneath the carpet. It doesn't have to be hardwood, just firm and solid. If so, all you have to do is sand it smooth and give it a few coats of tough floor varnish. The warm wooden tones will be a perfect complement to your antique furniture.

If you find a composition base under the carpet, you can cover it with a good-quality vinyl flooring. I've seen antiques shops floored with a charming non-gloss, deeply textured, brick pattern vinyl that is very effective. Lay a few attractive area rugs over this type of flooring, and you have a perfectly acceptable and easy-to-clean background for your antiques. But be sure any rugs you lay down have an antislip backing to prevent customers from slipping or tripping on them, falling, and eventually suing you.

If you really want carpeting in your shop, purchase the low-looped style used in churches, schools, and offices. This kind will take an incredible amount of punishment and is relatively easy to clean.

Window Coverings

Remove heavy draperies. You need all the light you can get in your shop. Customers always prefer shopping in a place that's light and airy. Replace the draperies with lace curtains, checkered cafe curtains, or anything else that will carry an ambience of nostalgia.

Electrical Wiring

Your permit may require you to install modern wiring if your house was built many decades ago. Don't resent this expense. It will actually add to the value of your house, should you decide to sell it someday.

Light Fixtures

Whether or not you have to replace old wiring with new, you'll probably need to arrange for additional overhead light. Without it, your shop will be gloomy and depressing on dark winter days. Track or recessed lighting around the perimeter of your rooms is one solution, and so are fluorescent tubes hidden behind a valance, as described in chapter 8. If you're planning a more high-end shop, you could install elegant chandeliers whose crystal prisms glitter and glow in the sunlight.

While you're at it, make sure you have enough outlets on the walls. You'll need these for the lamps you stock. Avoid using electrical extension cords and consider using power strips with an on/off switch into which you can plug multiple small lamps. These small lamps also add to the ambience by providing pools of inviting light which especially complement the warm woods of antique furniture.

New Drywall and Trim

You may need new drywall and trim to fill in spaces where old walls were removed—not an expensive or difficult job.

Paint or Paper

Once you've enlarged or remodeled your rooms, you can paint or paper them any color you like. The obvious choice might seem to be a neutral, such as white, ivory, or light gray. Many dealers, however, find that brighter walls—sky blue, Pepto-Bismol pink, sunflower yellow—add real pizzazz to their shops. I think the reason the brightly colored walls work is that most antique furniture is medium to dark brown—not especially lively tones. If you place such furniture against neutral walls, you get a pretty blah combination of noncolors, and brightly colored paint or paper costs no more than a neutral. The only caveat here is to have plenty of daylight and artificial light to compensate for the colored walls.

Shelving

You'll discover that you will make many more sales of small antiques—glassware, china, silver, and so forth—than you do of large pieces such as furniture. This means you'll need quite a bit of shelving to display these little beauties. The best choice is to order plate-glass shelves from your local glass company. The up-front cost for glass shelves is more than for wooden shelves, but in the long run you'll come out ahead. You don't have to paint or varnish glass, and it cleans easily with window cleaner and a quick swipe with a paper towel. Another advantage of glass is that light shines through it, so the antiques displayed on lower shelves sparkle just as well as the ones on the top shelf.

Consider installing glass shelves in windows in place of curtains. Sunlight pouring through colored glass displayed on transparent shelves gives a rainbow-like glow to a room. Also, casual passersby who see your windows can't help but be drawn to their beauty. They may come in just to inspect the pretty colored glass.

Exterior Sign

You may have to construct your exterior sign to conform to municipal regulations. Some towns will allow almost any type of sign, while others won't allow one that extends at right angles more than a certain number of feet from the building itself. A few towns regulate the lighting of signs. Some towns, for example, will allow lighted signs but not neon lighting. Be sure to check out any restrictions before you order your sign.

Do order your sign from a professional sign painter. Don't try to save a few dollars by painting it yourself, unless you're an artist. Few things degrade the appearance of a business more than an amateurish, poorly painted sign. Many sign companies today can design a potential sign on their computers and print the result on paper for you to examine. The designer can make changes right before your eyes on the computer until the end product is exactly what you want. The computer then creates self-adhesive vinyl letters the sign maker applies to a painted wooden base.

As for the actual design of your sign, choose a pattern and lettering that convey the image of an earlier era. Avoid thin, spidery-looking letters. While they may be attractive, they're hard to read from the street. Drive around town and simply observe other signs that appeal to you. Then go and do likewise.

If you have a choice, the best type of sign is one that extends at right angles from the building or from a post on the lawn and can be read from both directions. You'll also generate interest and direct customers to your shop if you can place additional signs at corners or intersections. Be sure to get permission to do this, however.

In addition, you'll need a small sign for the front door that announces the days and hours your shop is open. Many home-based dealers, especially if they don't have family obligations, will also work with serious customers during hours they are normally closed if the customers call first. Should you want to do that, your sign might read as follows:

OPEN TUESDAY–SATURDAY

10:00 A.M.–5:00 P.M.

OR BY APPOINTMENT

CALL 494-555-6938

(You could use your cell phone number here.)

To be honest, this sign may *not* stop people from knocking on your closed door on Sundays, evenings, holidays, and any other time that suits them. One of the hazards of operating a shop in your home is that a few people seem to rationalize that, since you already live at your place of business, you won't mind opening your shop for a few minutes.

You actually may not mind opening your doors if you're not otherwise engaged. One dealer who manages an in-home shop has a sign such as the one described above, but it's not attached permanently to the shop door. He has a hook on the door and places the sign there when the shop is closed and he doesn't want to be disturbed. But if, for example, on a Sunday afternoon he's not watching sports on television, taking a nap, or entertaining friends at a backyard barbecue, he simply removes the sign. He has a brass bell attached to the inside of the door, and it jangles whenever anyone enters. His living quarters are close enough to the shop area that he can hear the bell easily. That way, he doesn't have to personally monitor the shop area during his off-hours, but if anyone comes in, he's there in seconds to welcome them.

Many home-based dealers have such a bell on their door for other reasons. After all, you're going to have to leave the shop area and go into your living quarters occasionally, for lunch and bathroom breaks if for nothing else. You'll find bells, like the one described above, at your local hardware store or home center.

Exterior Painting

While you're driving around looking for examples of attractive signs, also watch for color combinations on homes or businesses that you think would attract attention and draw customers to your shop. The same philosophy applies here as with painting the interior walls of your shop: Avoid the neutrals and go for strong colors that make a statement.

If you're a little hesitant about combining bold colors, check out a book called *Painted Ladies*. Here you'll find dozens of pictures of fancifully painted Victorian homes. While you may not want to get as wild as the paint on some of these old beauties, you'll see how effective strong, contrasting colors can be. By painting your shop in similar tones, I guarantee you'll create some preopening interest that's bound to establish you as an innovative antiques dealer.

Landscaping

Any landscaping around and in front of a home-based shop should be low-key. You don't want to detract from the business side of your shop by having too many large residential-type shrubs and flowers in front of the building. Brick walkways bordered by low-growing flowers, a miniature lawn, and a small tree or two are usually enough. You can always move any cherished roses or other ornamentals to the backyard and enjoy them there. The more appealing your entrance, the more it will attract customers. Avoid high hedges and narrow walkways.

Customer Parking

You may live in a neighborhood where some customers can walk to your shop. Most of them, however, will drive, and they'll need a place to park their cars. You may have two or three parking places at the curb in front of the shop, but you don't own the street. Anyone can park there—neighbors, visitors, people going to nearby shops, workmen. These people can easily usurp the parking spaces in front of your shop, leaving no place for your customers to park.

Try to find a way to create even two or three parking places on your premises. Can you remove the turf from your front lawn and pour blacktop there? Is the side yard wide enough to block off a couple of places? Do you have alley access that would let customers park in the rear? Try to come up with something. Anything you do will add to the professional image of your shop, in addition to making it far easier for customers to visit you. This is one expense that can certainly be postponed, however, if you're short of funds.

Calculating Your Office Expenses
Basic Supplies

Is there a major office supply chain store near you? If so, you can save a great deal of money by patronizing it. For example, a string of one hundred small price tags at a traditional family-owned stationery store in one dealer's town might cost $1.99, or about 2 cents each. A chain store twelve miles away charges $15, or 1 1/2 cents each, for a box of 1,000 of the same tags—a savings of 25 percent. Multiply that savings by all the paper goods you have to buy, and you'll see the advantage of shopping at a chain store, even if you have to drive some distance every two or three months to replenish your supplies. But with the high cost of fuel these days, you might want to consider shopping for the same supplies online at any of the major office chain sites. In fact, by doing some diligent searching, you may save even more by finding other sites with better prices. Most offer free shipping for orders over a certain amount, usually $50.

You'll need the following basic supplies:

- stringed price tags
- stick-on price labels (be sure to buy the peel-off type)
- bags (large and small)
- tissue paper for wrapping fragile items
- sales-receipt books
- a rubber stamp to imprint your shop name on receipts, invoices, and so forth
- a ledger or bookkeeping software for keeping records
- assorted markers and pens

While commercially printed sales receipts, stationery, and so forth look good, you can save money initially by having a rubber stamp made that shows the name of your shop, your address, your telephone number, and your e-mail address. You can then buy blank receipt pads and a ream of paper at your office supply store and stamp them to create your own receipts and stationery. An alternative method is to use a computer word processing program to create your own stationery, envelopes, and even receipts, for the cost of the paper and a print cartridge. To save on print cartridges, consider getting them refilled. You can get brand-name cartridges filled at national retail stores like Walgreen's for one-third the cost of a new one. However, for consistent good quality printing, only fill them twice before buying a new one.

Business Cards

Business cards are a great and inexpensive way to advertise your shop and services. You'll put them on your checkout counter, in every bag a customer carries out of the shop, and in numerous other places. Copy centers can print business cards in a rainbow of colors and typeface styles. If your home/shop isn't on a well-known street, you might have a map highlighting it printed on the reverse side of the card. Another hint: If you plan to offer appraisals, estate sales, or any other non-shop service, place a line or two on the card to that effect. And again, don't forget your e-mail address and website, if you have one.

You can obtain 250 free business cards on the Internet from VistaPrint (www .vistaprint.com)—but you will pay a modest fee for shipping. Although you won't have a lot of choices in designs, the cards are attractive, and you can input whatever information you want on them. The company also offers low-cost premium cards with glossy finishes.

Telephone

The variety and types of phone services have grown greatly in the last decade. With the advent of digital lines and chips, phones have become smaller and increasingly mobile. In fact, mobile phones, also known as cell phones, are fast equaling landlines in both quality and ease of use.

You most likely have a standard phone line coming into your house. Previously, you may have had an extension installed to place a phone in another part of your house. Today, you can purchase modular phone systems for $50 to $70. These come with three 5-inch handsets, two base units to enable each of two handsets to recharge, and a master base containing a digital—that means no tapes—programmable answering machine and a place for one of the handsets. By plugging the master base and each phone base into regular electric outlets, you can have a phone anywhere you want it, including in your shop. Also, don't forget to inquire about monthly phone/TV/Internet packages from your phone or cable company. These will pay for themselves, especially if you sell online.

If you install a modular system or just have an extension that will be in your sales area, your phone will also ring on any other phone in the house. This is no problem if you live alone or if no one else is in the house during your operating hours. Since you'll be using the phone for business, however, your telephone company may require you to get a separate business line regardless of your personal family situation. You may want to list your business in the Yellow Pages, and this type of listing may also require a separate business line. Look in the front section of your telephone book for the number to call for information about this.

To avoid the extra cost of a separate line for your business, you may choose to use a cell phone dedicated to your business. This would allow you to take and make calls from anywhere within its calling range—for most cell phones that's now nationwide. You can either sign up for a standard pay-by-the-month cell service like Verizon, AT&T, or T-Mobile or a prepay service like Tracfone (www.tracfone.com) or AT&T (www.att.net). If you're not sure how much you'll use your business phone to accept calls, you may want to try a prepay phone for six months or a year. In the case of Tracfone, for example, you can get a phone for about $20, then purchase "minutes" on cards at discount, drug, and convenience stores or online. You must purchase minutes every three months to remain active or purchase a yearly/400-minute card for about $100 that keeps you active for 365 days. Unused minutes roll over if they're not used. Double-minutes-for-life plans that double your minutes each time you buy additional ones are also available for about $25. And while prepay phones used to have only basic features, today you can get the latest full-featured phones, often at no additional cost when purchasing a one-year/400-minute card.

Answering Machine

Granted, most people hate to listen to recorded messages, but the fact remains that an answering machine is a necessity today for anyone in business. You can record a message that lists your open hours, one that describes upcoming special promotions, or anything else you choose. You can change it from day to day if you like.

Of course, you'll pick up the phone if you're right there and available, but that won't always be the case. Some dealers record a message that says something like this: "Hello, this is John Alexander of Alexander's Antiques. I'm either with a customer or away from the shop right now. Please leave your name, phone number, and a brief message, and I'll get back to you as soon as I can. Please wait for the tone."

Before recording your message, practice saying it over and over until your voice sounds relaxed and happy. You can even record music at the beginning and end of your message if you like. Just place a CD player or iPod nearby and insert your favorite disk. Turn the volume to an average pitch and start the recording mode on the answering machine. After a second or two, lower the volume on the CD player and record your message. At the end of your message, raise the volume on the CD player again. This recording procedure will make your message sound professional. For best results, use instrumental music.

Computer

While a computer isn't absolutely necessary to run an antiques shop, you'll find that having one will make record keeping and correspondence easier. In fact, many dealers today buy and sell online, so, for them, a computer is a necessity.

Should you decide to purchase a computer, your local computer store offers two types of systems: IBM-compatible personal computers, known as PCs, which use Microsoft Windows as their operating system and Macintosh computers, known as MACs, which use a different operating system devised by Apple Computers. The majority of businesses use PCs since they are more cost-efficient. Whichever type you buy, you'll need to get some basic training. Many community colleges offer relatively inexpensive basic computer courses. You might also check with your local library, which may offer courses through a computer club.

Before you purchase a computer, new or used, ask your friends and other businesspeople which ones they use. Recommendations go a long way when buying a computer.

In order not to throw your budget completely off, you should consider purchasing a refurbished computer from such online companies as Computer-Show.com (www.computer-show.com). For the type of work you'll do on it—word processing, spreadsheets for records, accounting, online searches, even sign making—you'll find that a computer with a Pentium III or IV processor will work fine. Since many larger businesses lease their computers, these, like cars today, come on the market again when the company needs to upgrade. And that gives you the opportunity to buy a refurbished computer for just a few hundred dollars, including monitor and keyboard. And since so many people are involved with computers today, you should be able to find someone you know to help you set it up and install the software you need—although most of these computers come with a recent version of Windows and other basic software installed.

Computer repair can be very expensive and when purchasing a refurbished model, it pays to buy a third-party extended warranty plan from a company like SquareTrade .com (www.squaretrade.com), which offers excellent plans for about $30 per year. Purchasing one of these plans will give you the peace of mind that, should your system stop working for any reason, you won't be hit with a huge repair bill.

Even though a desktop computer costs less, many antiques dealers who do shows choose to use laptops so they can keep their records up to date while on the road. Today, laptops come in two varieties: basic and desktop alternative, both of which come with wireless capabilities. You'll most likely not be able to access the Internet on someone else's service since many users block outsiders. Therefore, you'll need to obtain a wireless Internet card from companies such as Clear Wireless Internet starting at $35 per month. While the first works fine as a mobile addition to your desktop, the second has the same power and capabilities as your desktop, plus a larger screen, should you decide to buy just one computer.

> Tip: You can purchase a high-quality Dell or Gateway laptop for $350 to $450 from online outlets such as TigerDirect.com (www.tigerdirect.com), and if you're on a really tight budget, try refurbished models from UsedLaptopComputers.com. A full list of websites appear in the appendix.

Printers

When purchasing a printer to go with your computer, you'll find many options. You don't need to pay a lot of money for a laser printer. They're fine for offices that require high-quality printing. An ink-jet printer, on the other hand, will work fine for your needs. Cartridges for these can be expensive, so it pays to shop the Internet for discount remanufactured cartridges—used cartridges that have not only been refilled but have had their printing heads cleaned or replaced.

> Tip: Ink-jet printers come with a variety of ink cartridge arrangements. Look for one with two larger cartridges which will save you money since you won't have to replace them as often. Also, printing in "draft" or "fast" mode will nearly double the number of pages printed with a cartridge.

Software

You don't need to buy a lot of software to run an antiques shop. Your PC should come with a recent version of Microsoft Windows installed. Windows contains a lot of programs that can be useful, such as WordPad for basic word processing, Windows Fax and Picture Editor for editing digital photographs, computer maintenance programs, and so forth. You'll also need to buy an office suite package like Microsoft Office, which contains Microsoft Word for word processing; Excel for creating spreadsheets for record keeping; and Access, a database to list your inventory, but it can be prohibitively expensive. Just as good is an open-source program, Open Office—virtually the same as Microsoft Office—that you can download free from the Internet.

You'll also need accounting software. The best choice here is QuickBooks from Intuit. It will help you keep your books, plus print invoices and reports. Instead of installing the software on your own computer, you can go online and work on it there, thus safeguarding your information should your computer crash. While it will set you back about $200, it's worth every penny. Do an online search, and you may find an older version selling for half the price. It will still contain everything you need. And while you're at it, look for a used copy of a QuickBooks instruction book on Amazon.com (www.amazon.com).

Website

Once you get your antiques business started, you may want to consider having a website—or, at least, participating in an online antiques mall. Creating a website from which to sell your antiques is not something you'll be able to do yourself, and it won't be cheap. To begin, you may want to create a simple site that acts as your online presence or home on the Internet. This can show photographs of some of your inventory, as well as note your specialty, address, shop hours, and so forth. You can easily set up this type of site on Google using free templates. But before you can do that, you'll need to register for a free Google Account.

Tripod (www.tripod.lycos.com) or FreeWebSites.com (www.freewebsites.com) offer similar services. However, all come with a small ad, which a visitor can remove, that the company places on your site. For a site without an ad, you'll have to pay a monthly fee. Unfortunately, you won't have your own web address since your site will be a subsite of the company. For example, http://alexandersantiques.tripod.com.

To set up a commercial site with your own address—one from which you sell your antiques and collectibles—you'll have to not only pay a web designer about $150 per page to create it, but you'll also have to purchase your domain name or web address and pay more for hosting your site since you'll need a secure site to prevent identity theft. An alternative to secure shopping cart capabilities on your site is to set up a free PayPal account through which your customers can pay for their purchases. But you may want to wait until your business takes off a bit to undertake this.

Rather than paying for a full commercial site, you may want to become a seller in an online antiques mall like TIAS (www.tias.com) or Ruby Lane (www.rubylane.com). Here, you'll pay a monthly fee for an online "shop," which TIAS networks with others on its site. The fee includes everything you need to get your online shop up and running, including customer checkout capability. This may work out better in the long run if your business is a small operation.

Business Checks

Most owners of small businesses find the three-checks-to-a-page system quite adequate. Beside each check is a section for recording the amount of the check, to whom it was written, for what it was written, and the date. This system makes record keeping simple and fast.

> Tip: While you can get your checks from your bank, you can save up to 50 percent by purchasing them from third-party companies such as Checks Unlimited (www.checksunlimited.com). Most check printing companies will allow you up to four lines of text printed on your checks, giving you room to put your business name, address, phone, and perhaps your driver's license number.

Credit Card Affiliation

There's no getting around the fact that being a credit card merchant is to your advantage as a retailer. One survey showed that you can actually increase your sales by 11 percent if you accept credit cards.

A few years ago many owners of new businesses encountered a great deal of trouble qualifying to become credit card merchants. Some owners had to wait up to a year before a bank would even consider their applications. Banks felt it took that long to establish an acceptable credit rating. In most cases that doesn't happen today. Almost any person with a good personal credit record can apply to become a credit card merchant now. However, credit card companies, such as American Express, charge a fee based on a percentage of the sale.

It will cost you something to use an electronic terminal for credit card purchases in your shop. You'll just have to decide if your budget can handle that expense at first. Finding a place for the terminal in your budget as soon as possible will definitely increase your sales.

Banks are highly competitive when it comes to merchant accounts. Some offer deals like a free terminal for two or three months. But you have to be careful and not be swayed before asking how long a transaction will take. Typically, it takes two to four days for your customer's payment to be posted to your account. Some credit card companies take a long as six.

> Tip: When it comes to a merchant account, shop for availability and service as well as price. The price will be different for rewards cards and mileage cards. While one bank may charge higher fees, it may replace a broken terminal immediately, rather than waiting several days.

To apply for an electronic terminal, you can either go to your local or regional bank or a third-party company, such as Merchant Services (www.merchantservices .com) where you'll need to fill out a form like the one on page 45. You'll be told that you can either lease or purchase a terminal. While higher-priced terminals can handle larger volumes of business, less expensive ones are ideal for merchants whose credit card purchases are smaller. Unless you're dealing in high-end antiques, you'll probably want the latter type.

Once your bank or third-party company approves your credit, your application will be sent to the processing center. A technician will then come to your shop to install the terminal.

Every time you run a customer's card through your terminal, the processing center records the dollar amount of the purchase in the customer's credit card

Please supply the following merchant information:

Date: _____

1. Business Structure: (circle one)

   Sole Proprietorship   Partnership   Corporation   Nonprofit

2. Merchant Name (DBA) _____

3. Contact Person _____

4. Business Phone _____ Business Fax

5. Physical Address _____

6. Mailing Address _____

7. E-mail Address _____

8. Federal Tax ID or SS# (if sole proprietorship) _____

9. Owner's Information/100% ownership

   Name _____

   Address _____

   % of ownership _____ Home Phone _____ SS# _____

   Name _____

   Address _____

   % of ownership _____ Home Phone _____ SS# _____

   Name _____

   Address _____

   % of ownership _____ Home Phone _____ SS# _____

10. Current Processor

    Please fax 2–3 months current business checking account statements if new business.

11. Referral Bank _____ Branch _____

    Contact _____

account. The credit card bank then automatically deposits that amount, minus your merchant fee into your business account.

Calculating Your General Business Expenses

Trade Journal Subscriptions

As a dealer, you need to stay ahead of your customers when it comes to trends. Trade journals, such as *AntiqueWeek* and *Antique Trader*, can help you do that. At least a dozen times a week you'll have to refer to price guides or check online for help in pricing an item. Trade journals also offer hints on shop management and display through the experiences of other dealers. (See the appendix for a list of these publications.)

Business Memberships

Chamber of Commerce: You'll probably find it to your advantage to belong to your local chamber of commerce. This organization holds meetings where knowledgeable consultants and professionals in many fields speak on business-related topics. The chamber of commerce also sponsors social events where you're encouraged to network and promote your business to other members. As a member, you'll receive a window sticker that identifies you to customers as a responsible member of the business community. Although membership fees differ from town to town and region to region around the country, the average is about $380 per year. The website www .chamberofcommerce.com offers lots of information to help you run your business.

Service Clubs: You might also want to consider membership in a service club such as the Rotary, Kiwanis, or Lions. These are clubs for businesspeople with the purpose of increasing skills, knowledge, and visibility in the community. Membership fees for these clubs vary greatly from town to town.

If you're at all hesitant about joining a business organization, just ask if you can attend a meeting or two as a guest. You'll learn very quickly what the responsibilities and advantages of membership may be.

Business License

In most communities the fees for the various permits and licenses you'll need to open your shop run between $25 and $75 each. Call the permit and license department at your town's municipal building to find out the exact figures for your area.

Attorney and CPA Fees

Spend at least an hour with an attorney and a CPA as part of your preopening process. These professionals price their time by the hour, and the rates vary widely from region to region. It pays to call several of each to get an idea of local rates. But don't choose either on their rates alone. Referrals from friends and other businesspeople will go a long way to making sure you start out on the right foot.

Insurance

You also need good insurance coverage. Call the agent who handles your existing homeowner's insurance or an insurance broker and find out what additional coverage for your shop will cost. Remember, being open to the public opens you up to liability issues, as well as the need to deal with stolen or damaged goods.

Advertising

You should do some advertising for your grand opening. Budget for a large display ad in your local newspaper for this important event. This ad is vital for letting potential customers know you're in business. The representative at the newspaper's advertising desk can tell you exactly what such an ad would cost.

Truck or Van

With any kind of luck, you already own some type of vehicle that you can use to haul antique furniture to your shop. You may decide to deliver some pieces for your customers, which will also require a truck or van. In any event, you have to have one. One word of advice: If you have to buy a vehicle, don't buy an expensive new one. The payments will cut too deeply into your profits. Instead, find a good previously

> **Tip:** Before calling to place your ad, prepare by first studying ads from other businesses. Draw up a rough idea of what you want your ad to look like and determine its size. Ads placed in the upper right quadrant of the right page and upper left quadrant of the left page cost more because readers seem them first. Ask the representative for suggestions but don't feel obligated to use them. And, by all means, have a plan for your ad *before* you call. If you don't, you could end up paying much more than you should.

owned truck or van at a lot, from an ad in the newspaper, or online from AutoTrader
.com (www.autotrader.com). Have it inspected at a diagnostic center before you
invest your cash. You'll be ahead of the game. No one is going to judge the quality
of your shop by how shiny your delivery vehicle is. But it needs to be dependable and
get decent mileage.

Projecting Your Start-Up Costs

It's important to project your start-up costs so that you'll know if the cash you have
available will be sufficient to cover them. Use the Start-up Costs chart on page 49
to help you do that. Do a little research and estimate what each expense will cost
you. Depending upon the layout of your home and the requirements of obtaining
your permit, you may have to do less or more actual remodeling. Try your best to
hold down expenses by doing as much of the remodeling work as you physically
and legally can.

When Is the Best Time to Open Your New Shop?

March and April are the best months to open a shop. Statistically, most antiques
dealers do the largest portion of their business between Memorial Day and the
December holidays, unless you live in Arizona or another area where summer is
the low season. By opening early in the year, you have a chance to develop a strong
customer base before the heavy buying season starts.

Four Steps to a Successful Beginning

Before you charge ahead with your plans, study carefully these four steps to a successful beginning:

1. *Write down your goals.* Write a few sentences that describe exactly what
   you plan to accomplish with your antiques shop. Will it provide you with
   an income to supplement an existing source of funds? Or will the shop,
   in time, be your sole source of income? If so, when? Will the selling space
   remain the same, or do you plan to expand as your customer base and
   income increase? If so, when and how much? How much money do you
   plan (not hope) to make within a specified length of time? When and
   how much?

(Ignore any that don't apply to you and add any you feel will be necessary for your business.)

Removing any walls or partitions to enlarge selling area	$_____
Removing carpeting and/or draperies	$_____
Refinishing or recovering floors	$_____
Upgrading existing electrical wiring to satisfy codes	$_____
New light fixtures	$_____
New drywall and trim	$_____
Repainting interior walls and trim	$_____
New window coverings	$_____
Shelving	$_____
Exterior sign	$_____
Exterior painting	$_____
Landscaping	$_____
Parking area	$_____
Office supplies	$_____
Computer, monitor, and printer	$_____
Business cards	$_____
Business telephone line	$_____
Answering machine	$_____
Business checks	$_____
Credit card membership (if any)	$_____
Subscriptions to trade journals	$_____
Business memberships	$_____
Business license	$_____
Initial attorney and CPA fees	$_____
Insurance	$_____
Initial advertising	$_____
Truck or van	$_____
Total Projected Start-up Costs	**$_____**

Add the total of your projected start-up costs to the amount you think you'll need to live for six months and you have the total you should have in the bank or readily available for immediate use.

Make your statements positive. "I will by September of 20___ own an antiques shop that is grossing $_____ per year in revenue. I will accomplish this goal by maintaining an inventory of no less than $_____ of quality antiques and collectibles and by spending a minimum of ten hours every week pursuing an aggressive marketing plan."

Print out these statements and tape them on your dresser or bathroom mirror, where you'll see them every day. They'll then become transformed from a dream into an attainable goal. You won't be sidetracked when you have this statement to guide you every day.

2. *Put fear aside*. Don't become a victim of the "What If" syndrome: What if there's a depression, and I lose all my money? What if I don't really know how to manage a shop? What if I can't keep the shop stocked? What if my family feels I'm neglecting it? What if . . . ?

You'll accomplish nothing great if you allow fear and doubt to stand in the way of your dreams. George Washington would never have made it across the Delaware River if he'd worried, "What if the boat leaks and we all drown?" Stanley would never have found Livingstone if he'd feared, "What if I get eaten by a lion?" Babe Ruth would never have hit 714 home runs if he'd panicked, "What if I strike out?" every time a ball came his way. Katharine Hepburn would never have won four Academy Awards if she'd quivered, "What if I forget my lines?" Great things can be accomplished by an ordinary person just like you if you only have faith in yourself.

3. *Plan ahead*. Take positive steps toward owning your own shop. Attend antiques shows and talk with the exhibitors. Ask them what's selling at what prices. Go to auctions and watch the patrons and other dealers bid. What are they buying and at what prices? Cruise the antiques shops in your area regularly and observe their display and merchandising methods. Watch the papers and see how other shops advertise.

Spend every dollar you can spare on inventory for your shop. Fill your closets, your garage, your attic, and your guest bedroom with boxes and accessories and furniture ready to sell.

Build up a substantial savings account to use for start-up expenses, or prepare to transfer funds from investment sources to a savings account.

4. *Finally, and most importantly, act as though you already own a successful antiques shop!* Say to yourself, and to anyone who asks, "I own an antiques shop." In your own mind, see yourself hanging out the open sign every morning. Visualize customers flocking to your shop. See them picking up antiques and bringing them to your checkout counter. Imagine your cash box full of money.

Believe you're *already* successful, and you will be successful!

03 Your Business Plan

Behind every successful business lies a well-thought-out business plan. Becoming a success in business doesn't just happen. It takes intense forethought and planning. Without a plan of action—a strategy—you'll most likely founder on the rocks of the economy, much like a ship without a rudder. A business plan helps you think out your business. What is your purpose? What are your goals? Do you have enough start-up capital? How will you maintain good cash flow? What buying methods do you plan to use? What selling methods? How do you plan to keep track of your customers? And, most importantly, what kind of competition do you have and how strong is it?

What Is a Business Plan?

A business plan is a detailed strategy describing who you are and what your reason is for operating your antiques shop, how you plan to manage it, how you will finance it, what its projections for success are, which professionals will assist you, and what overall direction you plan to take in the years to come. It should also include a detailed breakdown of operations.

Why Is a Business Plan Necessary?

At the outset, creating a business plan may seem like a lot of work because you'll have to do hours of research before you begin writing, but there are several good reasons for you to have one.

1. *First and most important, constructing a business plan will force you to look at every facet of operating your home-based antiques shop.* Before you complete the plan outline in this book, or any other business plan outline, you must work your way through dozens of details—some

minor, some major—that are essential to the successful operation of your antiques shop. You'll find much of the information you need for your plan in this book, so it's imperative to read and digest it before starting.

You know antiques—that's a given. You may already know how to sell them, as well. But to be successful as the owner of a shop, you also have to understand such things as demographics, bookkeeping, promotion, and a dozen other aspects of any successful business. As you complete, one by one, all the necessary steps, from getting that first permit to planning your grand opening, you'll be gathering the information you need to write your business plan.

2. *A business plan will help you determine whether enough people in your area might actually become your customers.* Though operating an antiques shop may seem simple enough, it often can be a minefield of problems, many of which won't be obvious to you in the beginning. Your enthusiasm for opening a home-based shop, however, won't be enough to guarantee its success. There must be a need for the shop in your area, otherwise no one will come.

3. *A business plan becomes a guide to help you manage your shop efficiently.* You'll make your day-to-day decisions proactively based on your previously organized strategy rather than on your reactions to unrelated events or spur-of-the-moment choices.

This plan won't be just a boring document that you'll write, then stick in a drawer somewhere. It will become a blueprint you'll use to guide your decision-making processes in years to come. Nothing you'll write in it will be set in concrete. As time passes and you see problems with your initial concepts, or opportunities you missed at first, you can go back and adapt your plan to your current needs. The plan will provide you with the tools for analyzing your business and for any changes that become necessary. Most business counselors recommend that you reevaluate your business and adapt your plan to accommodate changes every year.

The graphic on page 54 shows how a system works. As you can see, by following the arrows, you decide on a course of action—opening your shop—then put the plan into effect. Events begin to happen—customers come to the shop and buy your antiques. You record the results of those events—you make a profit or you don't. You study the figures on your monthly balance sheets to determine whether your original projections are

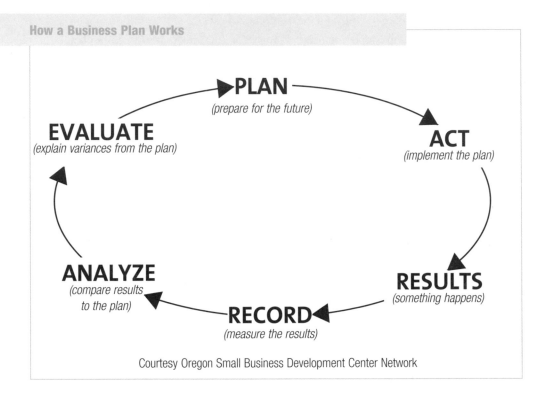

PLAN
(prepare for the future)

EVALUATE
(explain variances from the plan)

ACT
(implement the plan)

ANALYZE
(compare results to the plan)

RESULTS
(something happens)

RECORD
(measure the results)

Courtesy Oregon Small Business Development Center Network

working. If they aren't, you determine the reason—prices too low, markup ratio not high enough, incorrect inventory, too little advertising, and so on. You adjust your original plan to accommodate the results of this evaluation. You then have a new, revised plan to work with for the current year. Your revised plan will help you take advantage of practices that resulted in a profit and will eliminate or modify those that didn't.

Obviously, a great deal of thought must go into this evaluation, which is in reality a *plan for success*. As the old saying goes, "Nobody plans to fail, but you will fail if you fail to plan." That may sound corny but, unfortunately, it's true. Most businesses fail not due to a lack of a good product or expertise on the part of the owner but due to poor management. This plan will help you be a better manager of your shop. In other words, researching all the data needed for this plan will force you to think through many critical aspects of your business that you might otherwise overlook. It will help you anticipate the future, make well-informed decisions, and then act on those decisions.

4. *Your business plan will be a statement of your financial situation, your short- and long-range goals, and your prospects for success.* You may need such a statement as part of your application for a zoning variance to add parking spaces to your property or to use certain types of outdoor signs. Many municipalities have strict regulations about such things, but can often be persuaded to bend the rules if you can show you're a responsible businessperson and demonstrate that your plans won't detract from the ambience of the neighborhood.

You may someday need to apply for a bank loan to finance an expansion to your selling area or to buy a truck to haul your antiques. Most bankers won't be familiar with the antiques business, and they may be quite leery of lending money for an enterprise they consider marginal. To get any kind of loan, you're going to have to convince them you're in control of your business's future. A well-thought-out business plan can go a long way toward doing just that.

Your business plan should also include a *cash flow statement*. At one time or another, you probably kept a personal budget. You knew what your normal monthly expenses would be and what your normal monthly income would be. Without such a budget, you'd surely have too much month left when the money runs out. You'll keep a budget, too, for your business, so you'll have the money to pay your bills and buy stock based on past and projected income. Businesspeople refer to this as a "cash flow statement."

Your cash flow statement should have a section for each month of the year. In each monthly section you'll include your *monthly* expenses in running the shop—utilities, advertising, mortgage or rent, automobile expenses. You'll also factor in, for the appropriate months, expenses you have on a quarterly or an annual basis—insurance, taxes, and so forth.

The cash flow statement you include with your business plan will *project* your income for each month. These projections will be based on your research into what other, similar antiques shops are making. Granted, this may not be easy, but your counselors at SCORE and the Small Business Development Center can help you come up with approximate figures.

Once you actually have the shop in operation, you'll adjust these figures to reflect your actual income. The cash flow statement then becomes a tool to predict how much available cash you'll have at any given month. If you

Business Plan Questionnaire

To help you formulate your business plan, answer the following questions as best you can and research the information for the ones you can't:

1. Why do you want to open a home-based antiques shop?
2. What type of antiques will you be selling?
3. Where do you plan to get your inventory?
4. Will you specialize in any particular types of antiques and/or collectibles?
5. Will you carry other items that are antiques related?
6. What experience do you have that will enable you to successfully run an antiques business?
7. List the skills you have acquired that will enable you to operate your business.
8. When do you plan to open your shop? Why?
9. What are the demographics of your area?
10. What is the economic status or median income of its residents?
11. Are there other antiques shops close by? If so, what sort of antiques do they sell?
12. How will your shop differ from others in the area?
13. Do you foresee any problems operating your antiques business?
14. What are you business goals?
15. What type of business structure will your shop have?
16. Will you seek the advice of business professionals—lawyers, accountants, etc.?
17. How do you plan to promote your new business?
18. What are your planned pricing policies?
19. Where will you get the majority of the initial funding for your business?
20. How much debt do you currently have?
21. How much work needs to be done to convert a portion of your home into a shop?
22. Will you be doing the conversion yourself or hiring skilled workmen?
23. Will you be offering a delivery service?

know, for example, that your insurance comes due in March and that February is usually a slow month where income is concerned, you'll be careful about buying too much stock in January and February. Otherwise, you may not have the cash to pay for the insurance. The chart on pages 58 and 59 is a typical cash flow statement form for a home-based antiques shop. A copy of this form is in the appendix.

5. *Your business plan can also alert you to opportunities for profit that you didn't know existed.* Chapter 9 has some great ideas for promoting your business, and chapter 10 details some unique ways you can generate additional income from your knowledge of antiques. You might want to include some of these ideas in your business plan.

Formulating Your Business Plan

A business plan has a particular format. Most sample plans you'll find online are for larger small businesses, geared to companies that produce a product or provide a service. Unfortunately, the plan for an antiques business—much like any other retail shop—needs to be customized. What follows is a business plan outline especially adapted to the antiques business.

> Tip: To learn more about business plan basics, visit the Small Business Administration (SBA) website. (www.sba.gov) Once at the site, click on "Starting and Managing a Business," and from that menu, click on "Writing a Business Plan." The recommendations you'll find on this site will help you to formulate your own unique plan.

An Outline for a Home-Based Antiques Business Plan

It will be easier to relate this outline to your own plan if you can see a completed business plan. With this in mind, beginning on page 65 you'll find a hypothetical plan for Alexander's Antiques, based on this outline.

Cover Page: Center on one page your business name, address, and telephone number along with the date you completed the plan and your name as owner.

	Jan.	Feb.	Mar.	Apr.	May	
1. Beginning Cash Balance						
2. Cash Receipts						
a. Cash sales						
b. Estate sales						
c. Appraisals						
d. Consignments						
e. Other						
3. Total Cash Receipts						
4. Cash Disbursements						
a. Merchandise						
b. Accounting						
c. Advertising						
d. Auto expense						
e. Contributions						
f. Delivery expenses						
g. Electricity						
h. Heat						
i. Insurance						
j. Laundry						
k. Legal expenses						
l. Miscellaneous expenses						
m. Office expenses						
n. Postage						
o. Rent/mortgage						
p. Repairs						
q. Telephone						
r. Dues/subscriptions						
s. Travel expenses						
t. Estimated tax payments						
u. Owner withdrawalv						
5. Net Cash Flow						
6. Ending Cash Balance						

	June	July	Aug.	Sept.	Oct.	Nov.	Dec.

Table of Contents: List the major topics of your plan and their respective page numbers.

Purpose: This is a brief, positive statement of your philosophy about dealing in antiques. It should express the main reason you chose to open a home-based antiques shop rather than some other type of business—a child-care center, floral shop, bakery, watch-repair shop, etc.

Description of Your Antiques Business: Give an overview of the antiques business in general followed by a description of your antiques business in particular. Discuss the types of antiques you plan to sell. Will you carry a variety of antiques from all periods, or will you specialize in one or two eras? Will you carry some reproductions? Will you carry antiques-related items, such as collectors' reference books or furniture and metal polishes?

Do you plan to become a certified antiques appraiser ? Will you manage estate sales for local people? Will you take in consignments? What about your shop's location? Present information about your neighborhood, the traffic count on your street, and the advantages and disadvantages of your particular location.

Management: This section includes personal data about you as the owner of your shop. Include your background in antiques, your retailing experience, and any education you have in marketing, emphasizing your skills and experience.

Business Structure: Will your business be a sole proprietorship, or will you have a partner? If the latter, will your partner be a friend or family member and how will you share the duties of the business?

Long- and Short-term Goals: Your reasons for starting a home-based antiques business are empty without a set of goals to back them up. Your goals are your clearly defined business objectives. They become targets to shoot for and, when fulfilled, make your business a success. Writing down your goals and updating them regularly is extremely important.

Divide your goals into long-term and short-term benchmarks. In the former category, you should list things you'd like to achieve in two to five years. In the latter, you should concentrate on what you'd like to achieve in a month or two. But goals, themselves, are empty if you don't list ways to achieve them.

Under each goal, list three things you need to do it achieve that goal. Listing too many things will cause you to procrastinate. Keep it simple.

Avoid writing abstract goals, such as "I plan to make great progress in my first year in business." Your goals should be concrete ones that can be measured. Include such things as the following:

1. Find and keep customers.
2. Hold regular promotional events.
3. Increase profit margin.
4. Expand business.

Take your goal of "find and keep customers." Under that you can list these three steps to achieve this:

1. Run a weekly ad in my local paper.
2. Develop a mailing list.
3. Record contact information for each customer.

Once you've set your goals, you need to create business strategies to go with them. These will help you keep your business on track. For instance, how many hours will you be comfortable working? Where will you obtain your stock? Will you eventually expand beyond your shop onto the Internet or to doing shows?

Projection for Success: No one can predict exactly how your antiques business will do in its first year or two, but you can make an educated guess based on the business climate of your town and the success of similar shops.

Analysis of Potential Problems: Do you foresee any problems in managing your shop, and how will you overcome them?

Professional Counselors: List the specialty, name, and contact information of the professionals who will assist you in managing your shop efficiently. Examples include:

1. attorney
2. accountant
3. insurance agent
4. banker

Market for Your Products and Services: What is the potential market like for antiques in your area? What is the current population in your town, its median income level, and the interest in antiques among those with discretionary income?

Competition: If you've found your area to be a viable market for antiques, how many other antiques shops already exist there? What are their locations relative to yours? Do they appear to be successful? How will your shop differ from them? What are the special features about your shop that will fill a niche in the antiques market? What are their strengths and weaknesses?

Marketing Strategies: Your advertising and promotion plans, like your overall business plan, are guides you'll follow on a month-to-month basis. Be sure to include the following:

1. targeted advertising to specific customers
2. general advertising in newspapers and the like
3. where and when you'll buy radio and TV spots
4. promotion plans for your opening and for the first year
5. Internet promotions and possible advertising
6. a budget for advertising and promotion

Buying Strategies: Decide how and where you're going to buy your stock. The more you pay for items, the less you get to keep. Will you restrict your purchases to smaller collectibles or mix them with larger pieces of antique furniture? Will you buy at yard sales, flea markets, estate sales, shows, auctions, or on eBay?

Selling Strategies: Decide how you will sell the items you buy. Will you sell only from your shop or will you branch out to sell at flea markets, smaller shows, local auctions, or on eBay as well?

Pricing Strategies: Your shop will quickly develop its reputation based primarily on the quality of your antiques and the prices you charge for them. You'll make decisions on pricing based upon your own market research. For example, how much markup on items will your local market bear? How much should you mark up an item to sustain a profit? Generally, retail shop owners mark up their goods by as much as 100 percent. If you purchase an item for $150, will you be able to sell it for $300? Perhaps, in a more affluent market. What if you mark it up only by 50 percent, pricing it at $225? The item sells quickly, giving you an income of $75. Will that be enough to pay your bills?

According to marketing studies, it takes between 17 and 23 percent of the purchase price of an item to run an antiques business. So if you originally paid $150, then you get to keep $40 to $49. Out of that take 18 to 23 percent for income tax, plus another 6 to 8 percent for state income tax, and you'll realize that you'll make more working at a fast-food restaurant.

Service Strategies: Secondary in importance to pricing are the services you will offer your customers. Most people shop for price and quality first, but every good businessperson knows that good service can make a positive contribution to your success. Will you offer any special services, such as free delivery or gift wrapping? What about gift certificates?

Financial Data and Strategies: This is the most critical section of your business plan, and it may seem to be the most formidable to construct.

This section should have all relevant financial data about your business. The figures you use should be as accurate and verifiable as possible. Include the following:

1. sources of funds
    a. savings
    b. loans (if any)
2. use of funds
    a. start-up costs
    b. inventory
3. cash flow projections
4. personal income statement

    a. mortgage or rent payments
    b. equity in home
    c. vehicles owned
    d. personal debt
    e. other income

> **Tip:** It costs more to fund a business that sells valuable early American furniture than one that specializes in collectibles. If you're selling furniture, you can start out with just twenty pieces, plus decorative accessories. If you're selling collectibles, you'll need over 120 items.

A Sample Business Plan

On the following pages you'll find a detailed business plan for Alexander's Antiques, a hypothetical home-based antiques shop. This detailed plan, for the owner Eliel Alexander, is an example of one that will be primarily for your own use to help you foresee and work your way through all the details of opening your shop. Should you, in a year or two, find you need a bank loan, you'll want to write a different, greatly condensed business plan to present to your potential lender. As one Small Business Administration counselor says, "Most lenders, at first, are not interested in all the details of how you run your business. They just want the bare facts to determine if you're a good risk. If they decide to pursue your application further, they'll ask for balance sheets, IRS forms, and so forth." Adapt the format and information on the following pages to reflect the facts about your own business.

Alexander's Antiques

123 Chestnut Road

Fraser, PA 19335

(494) 555-6938

January 18, 2011

Owner: Eliel Alexander

Table of Contents

Purpose of My Business

Many consider antiques one of the best investments today because quality ones nearly always increase in value over time. In addition, antiques bring beauty and pleasure daily to those who use them in their homes. It's for these reasons I've chosen to open an antiques shop.

Description of My Antiques Business

Men and women have collected antiques for centuries. No matter what the state of the economy, collectors will not stop collecting. Today, nostalgia is a major contributor to the success of antiques shops. A dozen national decorating magazines focus on the charm of yesteryear, complete with photographs of homes decorated with antiques. For the last three decades, Americans at all income levels have been buying antiques and collectibles for their own homes. Many purchase them in small- to medium-size shops while others buy them from eBay and other sites on the Internet.

Since antiques are one of a kind, they aren't available to dealers from commercial vendors as other retail items are. Astute dealers, therefore, are aware of nontraditional sources for their merchandise where they can purchase antiques and collectibles for a fraction of their retail value. This means that markup in antiques shops is usually far higher, and, therefore, more profitable to the dealer, than is possible in the average retail shop.

My home-based antiques shop will be located at 123 Chestnut Road in Fraser, Pennsylvania, a suburban community of 56,000 people. My street is in a residential neighborhood, one block off of Main Street, the primary thoroughfare through town. Fraser's zoning laws allow small, in-home businesses in this neighborhood, zoned R2. Pennsylvania Department of Transportation figures state that approximately 1,500 cars per day pass along Chestnut Road. Traffic on Main Street often averages 1,000 cars per hour, affording excellent visibility for my shop, especially with a directional sign pointing in its direction off of Main Street.

Although some customers will be able to walk to my shop, most will drive. There's street parking along Chestnut Road, plus I plan to add off-street parking for three cars in front of my shop. An alley at the rear of my property allows me to unload antiques for sale in the shop and to load those scheduled for delivery to customers.

For my shop space, I'm remodeling the former living, dining, and breakfast rooms of the home owned by myself and my wife, comprising 600 square feet of space, to adapt them to a shop atmosphere. Our home is large, so there are ample living quarters still available at the rear of the first floor and on the second floor.

I also plan to enclose a side porch, which now opens into the shop area, to provide an additional 150 square feet of retail space. In addition, I've had a ramp constructed along the front steps of our home to make the building wheelchair accessible.

In Alexander's Antiques I'll carry a wide variety of antiques and collectibles, including but not limited to: pine and oak furniture, nineteenth-century glassware and china, old baskets, old rugs, paper goods, and early twentieth-century collectibles.

In addition to managing my shop, I'll also hold professionally managed public sales for individuals who wish to sell an entire estate of antiques.

Most dealers in antiques see a definite trend regarding months of high sales volume and months when sales are low. Statistically, dealers in antiques make their greatest profits during the months between Memorial Day and Christmas. Profits are usually lowest during January and February. I plan to open my shop the first week in March. This will give me time to become established and for the shop to become known in the community before the summer/fall selling season begins.

Management of Alexander's Antiques

I have taught art in the public schools of Pennsylvania for the last forty years. As part of my college studies, I learned about the decorative arts, especially antique furniture styles. I have always collected various things throughout my life, but it wasn't until a friend of mine introduced me to collecting antiques that I became hooked on them. As I grew older, I began buying antiques to use in my home, and my natural interest in art led me to learn about their origins.

Last year, I decided to take early retirement and began to study antiques in earnest, visiting museums, and frequenting antiques shows and shops wherever I've traveled. I wanted to learn as much about the decorative arts as I could. I even took a couple of continuing education classes in antiques to familiarize myself with a wide range of styles and makers.

To fully prepare myself as a retail salesperson, I've worked weekends at the antiques mall on the edge of town. By helping customers there, I've learned what customers in my area are looking for and how much they're willing to pay. To educate myself on the business side of things, I've taken several courses in basic business practices, public relations, and computer use.

I've always been active in my community, but with my shop, I see that increasing as I join the local Chamber of Commerce and the Rotary Club.

Business Structure

I will own and operate my shop as a sole proprietor. Although my wife will assist me in the shop from time to time, the shop will be in my name.

To help me become a success in this business, I've enlisted the services of several local professionals who deal in various legal and financial areas:

1. James Monroe, Attorney-at-Law
2. William Seward, Certified Public Accountant
3. Helen Danforth, Central Insurance Agency
4. Roland Prospect, Vice President, First National Bank of Fraser

Each of these professionals has set up a system for the business based on his or her own specialty.

Long- and Short-Term Goals

My overall goal in opening and operating Alexander's Antiques is to provide a modest income to supplement my school retirement pension.

My long-term goals—two to five years—for my business are to enlarge the selling area and to create off-street parking. I also plan to begin making annual buying trips to New England and the upper South to enhance the variety and quality of the antiques I carry.

The short-term goals for my shop (one year) are to reach the break-even point within six months, create a mailing list of 300 customers, and increase inventory by approximately 10 percent a month.

The Market for Antiques in Fraser

With a population of approximately 56,000 people, Fraser's economic future looks good. The fastest-growing segment of Fraser's population consists of couples between the ages of thirty and forty-five, most of whom have children. Many of these men and women work at high-tech jobs in several local business parks, with another presently under construction.

The median family income of these professional employees is $70,000, and 85 percent of them hold college degrees, enabling them to be in a financial position to buy antiques. I plan to tap this large and growing market by carrying primarily antiques in the middle to upper-middle price range.

Competition for Alexander's Antiques

Three antiques shops already exist in Fraser. One shop specializes in expensive fine antiques but doesn't appear to be especially successful. Another carries a variety of low-end antiques that mostly fall into the collectible category. Because this crowded shop resembles a flea market, most of its customers come looking for bargain-basement merchandise. The third shop carries a good selection of antiques and appears to be quite successful. In addition, a large antiques mall opened six months ago in a vacant warehouse at the edge of town. This mall draws customers from a wide area.

Statistically, Fraser can easily support several antiques shops. Since Alexander's Antiques has the advantage of being the only home-based shop in town, is centrally located, and appeals primarily to middle-income buyers, the prognosis for its success is good.

Marketing Strategies

I'm allotting 3 percent of my budget for advertising during the first year of operation to gain high visibility for my shop. This percentage will drop to 2 percent in the second year. I plan to spend most of this money on print advertising in the local newspaper, the *Register*. Two weeks prior to my shop's grand opening, I'll run large display ads, switching to small weekly classified ads after that, for which I've arranged a discounted rate. A 3-inch, one-column ad, spotlighting different antiques each time, will run each week. I also plan to run spot announcements of my grand opening on a local radio station, WXYZ, the week prior to it.

I plan to schedule regular promotional activities throughout the year, including two annual sales, on-site talks by a local historian, a costume contest, and a display of valuable antiques. I'll announce these promotions through press releases to all local media. To promote my two annual sales, I plan to do mailings to previous customers.

Projections for Success

According to my research, income in antiques shops has been consistent with small-business income in general except for the last two years during a national recession. Statistics show a dramatic slump in sales during the first part of that period but an increase in high-end sales toward the end due to more investment in antiques.

Articles and photographs on antiques in national decorating magazines encourage homeowners to use antiques in their homes. Antique collecting is no longer just for the wealthy. Today, baby boomers born in the 1950s and 1960s comprise the largest group of new collectors. The number of antiques shops, nationwide, has increased 75 percent from 1990 to 2005. And while the number of shops has decreased somewhat in recent years due to the Internet, the total still remains high.

I've also spoken with the owners of three antiques shops in Fraser and two shop owners in a nearby city. One of the shop owners planned to close his store within two months as he was not making a profit. His problem appeared to be one of poor management, based on little or no advertising and an unattractive and dingy shop interior. One shop owner said he was breaking even, but not showing much profit. Apparently, he had been in the antiques business in another part of the country prior to moving to Fraser and hadn't realized the difference in customer demand between the two areas. The other owners, all of whom had been in business a minimum of three years, claimed to be making a good living from their shops.

Analysis of Potential Problems

I've analyzed my personal lifestyle and the business practices of other antiques shops in Fraser and determined I have two main problems to overcome:

1. Keeping the shop open six days a week throughout the year would mean no time for a vacation or visits to children and grandchildren in other cities. I decided to contract with a local temporary employment agency and hire a salesperson to work in my shop for three weeks every winter during the slow season.

2. Since my shop is the newest in Fraser, I'll have to do extensive public relations work in the community to let people know about it and to establish a following. To help promote my shop, I plan to offer to speak at various clubs and service organizations, giving information about understanding and collecting antiques, as well as to approach the continuing education department of the local community college and propose a short course in the same topics. I'll have flyers printed advertising my shop and distribute them in local hotels, motels, and bed-and-breakfast inns, plus contact local interior decorators and invite them to a private wine-and-cheese party in my shop to acquaint them with my inventory.

Buying Strategies

Antique dealers make their money on the difference between the price they pay for an item and the price they sell it for. I plan to buy items for my shop as cheap as I can get them, but at the same time, I hope to find several fine items for which I can get top dollar. These items may stay in my shop longer, but should give me a higher return on my investment.

To make sure that I don't overspend on inventory, I plan to pay no more than 10 cents on the dollar for most of the smaller items in my shop. To keep within this limit, I plan to purchase box lots or multiples of items whenever I can, then sell them individually and make more profit than if I bought just one. For instance, I might buy a box of fine Haviland china, containing only odd pieces from a set. I'll then price each piece—plates, cups, and saucers, etc.—individually for those who collect china.

Selling Strategies

For the most part, I plan to sell antiques out of my home-based shop. As the business progresses, I plan to expand by selling first on the Internet and then at local antique shows. I can supplement these sales by participating at the better local flea markets and by sending certain items to local auctions. I also plan to hold a private, invitation-only show in my shop once a year at the end of November in time for the holiday gift-buying season.

Pricing Strategies

Because Alexander's Antiques is home-based, I have a lower overhead for my shop than my competitors do. My shop comprises approximately 25 percent of the total square footage of my home, so I'm able to deduct 25 percent of what I pay on my mortgage, on my taxes, and for utilities. This saving will allow me to sell comparable antiques at a slightly lower price than other shops in town do.

Service Strategies

I own a 2006 Ford van, which I'll use to haul antiques to the shop and to deliver purchased antiques to customers. I plan to deliver any antique with a purchase price of $200 or more free of charge within a 10-mile radius of my shop and will add a surcharge of $10 for delivery of any antique priced at less than $200. For customers who live at a greater distance, I'll arrange for delivery through a local moving company.

I plan to accept only MasterCard and Visa credit cards, as well as debit cards. In addition, I'll offer a layaway service with a nonrefundable 30 percent down payment, the balance to be paid off within three months.

Financial Data

I had approximately $25,000 in ready cash and savings when I began the process of adapting my home to become a shop. I used $13,225 of these funds to remodel my home and for start-up expenses.

Approximate Projected Start-up Costs

Remove one partition to enlarge selling area:	$750
Remove carpeting:	$200
Refinish hardwood floors:	$500
Upgrade existing electrical wiring:	$1,100
New light fixtures:	$300
New drywall and trim (installed):	$650
Repaint two interior walls and trim:	$500
New window coverings:	$325
Shelving:	$650
Exterior sign:	$450
Exterior painting:	$1,500
Landscaping:	$800
Office supplies:	$300
Computer:	$500
Software:	$200
Business cards:	$75
Business telephone line:	$125
Phone system with answering machine:	$60
Business checks:	$65
Subscriptions to trade journals, price guides:	$225

Business memberships:	$125
Business license:	$25
Initial attorney and CPA fees:	$600
Insurance (shop and truck annually):	$1,500
Advertising (grand opening):	$500
Labor (minimum wage):	$1,200
Total projected start-up costs:	$13,225

I should have approximately $11,775 in cash as a reserve after paying for these start-up costs. I've been buying and storing antiques for about three years prior to the opening of my shop. These antiques, with a market value of approximately $5,000, make up my initial inventory. I expect my shop to break even within six months. Prior to that time, I'm aware that my expenses, using a prorated percentage, for the shop space in my home, for utilities and mortgage payments, plus advertising, attorney and CPA fees, and insurance will undoubtedly exceed my cash income. Based on my research of other shops in the area, I expect to begin making a profit of approximately $500 the sixth month, with steadily increasing amounts in the following months. I expect to be clearing approximately $1,500 a month by the end of my first year in business.

Personal Income Statement

My wife and I own our own home in Fraser. The current value of our home is approximately $210,000. We have an equity of approximately $65,000 in it, and our mortgage payments, based on a fixed 6.25 percent loan, are $620 per month.

We own two vehicles, a 2002 Honda Civic and a 2006 Ford van. The Honda is free and clear of a loan, but payments on the van are $350 per month. We have no other outstanding debts.

We have a fixed income of $1,485 per month. I receive a Social Security payment of $1,000 per month and a school pension of $835 per month. This income is sufficient to cover our personal expenses. I also have $86,450 in an IRA account.

04 | Keeping Records

Most antiques dealers don't like to deal with numbers. They'd rather work with objects that brought beauty, employment, or service to men and women generations ago. They love the patina on an old table, where a few nicks chart the thousands of meals served to loving families. Morning sunlight blazing through cut glass is as bewitching to them as diamonds. An old hand-tied Persian rug, though faded and worn, is, to them, an object of rare beauty.

Most find scribbling numbers in little squares boring, frustrating, and time-consuming. Who needs bookkeeping? You do. But it isn't as frightening as it used to be, especially with today's accounting software.

Bookkeeping is, essentially, "the recording of financial data, income, and expenditures that relate to your business." This information will come from sales receipts of antiques you sell, from receipts of things you buy or services you pay for, and from your check register.

Good records help you to see where your money is going and whether you're spending it wisely. Have you done too much advertising or too little? Are your insurance premiums too high for your budget or is more insurance needed? Is money available now for that computer package you've been eyeing, or should you wait a couple more months? Did the Christmas sale bring in as much income as your spring sale?

With good records it's easy to see when you bought each antique, how much you paid for it, when you sold it, and how much gross profit you made on its sale. Just as important, when you keep accurate and complete records, your accountant will make sure you take every legal deduction allowed by the IRS. This can mean a substantial lowering of your yearly tax bill come April 15 each year.

Keeping the IRS Happy

Another consideration is that the IRS looks closely at the records of all home-based businesses. If you don't have good records of your expenditures and income, the IRS could say you're running your shop not as a business but as a hobby. Then all your deductions would be disallowed and you'd have to pay a big tax bill.

Sure, it's a whole lot more fun to be out scouting for antiques or showing them to customers than keeping books. But if you want to make a profit in this business, you need to spend a few minutes every day entering your daily receipts. With accounting software, such as QuickBooks from Intuit (www.intuit.com), you'll only need to spend up to thirty minutes a day or perhaps less to enter your information. The program does the rest—adds up our totals, creates reports, prints invoices, etc.

Another program that will make it easier to keep track of both your business and personal expenses is Expense Director for Windows from Iambic.com. Unlike Quick-Books, you install the program on your PDA (personal data assistant) or iPhone. You enter your expenses into it as you get them, then synchronize them to your computer at the end of each month. The program enables you to produce a spreadsheet, and by sorting your entries by category, you'll be able to quickly tally them and enter them into QuickBooks. Once you learn how to use these programs, you'll discover that they'll do much of the work for you.

Fortunately, you won't have to maintain complicated records. Your buying and selling practices are far simpler than those of most retailers, so bookkeeping is simpler too. Just set a certain time of day, perhaps early morning when you expect few customers, to update the program or ledger with numbers from the previous day.

It's a good idea to get some basic instruction in bookkeeping, as well as the accounting software program you intend to use. Continuing education programs are available in both. These skills will make keeping records, once you understand the system, an easy task. Afterwards, you should be able to manage your daily record keeping on your own.

You can also hire a professional bookkeeping service to handle this task if you like. In this case, you would need to file all receipts for purchases you make, sales receipts for sales in the shop, canceled checks you've written, and so forth, in separate folders, then let the bookkeeper record those figures in a computer program. The bookkeeper can come to your shop to pick up the data, or you can drop it off at her office. Either way, she'll input the information into her computer and format it properly and accurately for your accountant. This is a reasonable alternative for dealers who simply don't want to handle the bookkeeping end of their business.

The biggest disadvantage of hiring an outside bookkeeping service is that you lose control over your records. The bookkeeper knows where all your money is going or coming from, but unless you spend a great deal of time analyzing the printouts she hands you, you won't have the foggiest notion of what the totals mean. Remember that you will have the bookkeeper's monthly service fee to pay, even during those first months in business when income may be spotty. The bookkeeper, too, cannot figure your taxes or advise you about management of the business. This task remains with your accountant. Regardless of whether you do your own books or hire a bookkeeping service, though, your accountant should be in on the system right from the start.

A record-keeping system that's right for you will meet the following criteria:

- It should be easy to learn and understand.
- It should be easy to maintain.
- It should foster accuracy.
- It should encourage timely entries.
- It should be complete.

You'll find several prepackaged commercial bookkeeping systems that will fulfill these needs at any office supply or computer store or online. (See the appendix for information about computer accounting software.)

The following information is for those who prefer to keep their records in a ledger. You might begin with a ledger while at the same time learning how to use your accounting software.

Remembering the K.I.S.S. Principle (Keep It Simple, Stupid)

As you peruse the ledgers offered you, look first and foremost for *simplicity*. Their chart of accounts should have predesignated categories that can be easily adapted to your needs. As you study the various systems, ask yourself these questions: Will I find it simple to transfer my daily income to a balance at the end of the month? Can I tell at a glance how much my monthly income exceeds my expenses or vice versa?

Whichever system you choose, be sure it's based on *single-entry bookkeeping*. These are the easiest to use and are quite adequate for a small- to average-size home-based antiques shop. With a single-entry system, you record each transaction only once. You would, for example, record the payment of your gas bill once in a column headed "Heat." A payment for repairs to your truck would be recorded once under "Auto Expense." Even the IRS approves single-entry bookkeeping for small businesses, saying, "This system can be used to record income and expenses *adequately for tax purposes.*"

You will hear another term, *double-entry,* used by bookkeepers and accountants. Double-entry bookkeeping requires you to record each transaction in two separate categories. This system does have the advantage of catching errors, but it's more time-consuming than single-entry bookkeeping and is far more difficult to manage for anyone who didn't make straight As in Accounting 101!

A single-entry system that's exceptionally easy to use is the Dome Simplified Monthly Bookkeeping Record. This ledger is also recommended by some Small Business Development Center counselors. It's designed by a CPA and is published by Dome Publishing Company. The book usually sells for under $15 at office supply stores, or call the company at (800) 432-4352, or see www.domeproducts.com.

For the person relatively new to business, some of the most valuable pages in this ledger are the three that list some 400 legal deductions the IRS allows small businesses. Did you know, for instance, that you can deduct the cost of Christmas presents you give temporary employees or the value of a Haviland plate your cat knocked off a shelf as she settled in for her midmorning nap?

Preparing a Chart of Accounts

Your records will be based on what accountants term a *chart of accounts,* which is simply a general list of your income and expenses in running your shop.

In the Dome ledger your expenses will be listed on a sheet headed "Detail of Monthly Expenditures." Since you're in the retail business, you'll separate your purchases into two categories, the first for antiques you buy for resale, on the left side of the page; and the second for non-merchandise purchases or expenses, on the right side of the page. (See pages 88–89.)

Every category of expenses in the second group has a predesignated account number. That account number will correspond to an identical code number in your monthly tally of those expenses (see pages 90–91).

The chart on pages 86–87 illustrates a typical commercial chart of accounts, along with its account numbers. The preprinted categories on this sheet are standard ones, formatted to cover the expenses of almost any small business. There is another copy of the chart in the appendix.

Assuming you wanted to use this form, record your expenses as follows:

Deductible Expenses

1. *Merchandise and materials.* These are the antiques you buy for resale.
2. *Accounting.* Most businesspeople like to meet with their accountants regularly. It's one good way to make sure that you're on the right track with your own bookkeeping and that you're keeping expenses in line.
3. *Advertising.* Here you'd list expenses for newspaper and radio advertising, cards to customers announcing special promotions, and so forth. If you advertise in the Yellow Pages, that expense goes here, not under Telephone.
4. *Auto.* You will use your car or truck to cruise the yard sales and to visit auctions. Enter all costs in operating those vehicles here, including repairs, tires, and minor purchases such as windshield wipers, tune-ups, and oil changes, and don't forget parking and tolls. Keep a separate log of your mileage when operating your vehicle for business. If you use your personal vehicle for business, deduct the business mileage from the total for it. Don't include a major purchase, such as a truck, here (see number 6). This is a depreciable expense, which your accountant will record elsewhere.
5. *Books and publications.* All the books you'll use for reference in your business—price guides, antique books, general references—are all deductible.
6. *Capital expenses.* Equipment, such as a vehicle, computer, or any other large purchase that's depreciable, should be listed here.
7. *Shipping expenses.* You probably won't package and ship your customers' purchases unless you sell on eBay or through one of the online antiques malls. You may choose to provide this service if your shop is in an area where tourists, who can't take purchases with them, constitute a large part of your business.
8. *Contributions.* As a businessperson, you will inevitably be asked to contribute to community charities and events.
9. *Delivery expenses.* You may decide to deliver some antiques without charging your customers for the service. This is a deductible expense for you.

10. *Electricity.* You'll probably pay only one electric bill, covering your home and shop. You'll enter the prorated portion of that bill, based on the amount of square footage in your shop, here.

> Tip: To figure the percentage of space your shop takes up your home, roughly measure the length and width of every room in your house, including your shop area, being careful not to forget storage areas. Then multiply the shop square footage by 100 and then divide that number by the total square footage. The result will be your prorated percentage.

11. *Freight and express.* Will you go on buying trips and ship some of the antiques back home by a freight or express service? Many dealers do this.
12. *Heat.* If you heat your home/shop with any fuel other than electricity, use the prorated percentage you calculated in number 10.
13. *Insurance.* Your monthly or quarterly payments for liability, fire and theft, and any other insurance directly related to the business belong here. Remember to take the prorated percentage of your home owner's insurance. Do not include premiums for life insurance or other personal insurance.
14. *Interest.* You may someday take out a business loan for expansion or another business expense. The interest on that loan is deductible. Do not include here interest on any personal loans.
15. *Laundry.* No, you can't sell the old Maytag and start sending your sheets and towels to the local laundry and claim that as a business expense. You may, however, want to have your shop curtains laundered or the carpet cleaned by a commercial firm.
16. *Legal expenses.* You will have some attorney expenses when you set up the structure for your shop. You will probably want to pay a brief visit to your attorney every year, too, just for an annual checkup. Do not include here any legal expenses for nonbusiness purposes.
17. *Licenses.* You'll have to pay for licenses and permits when you open your shop. In addition, you will undoubtedly be assessed annual fees to renew your dealer's license and any others your state requires.

18. *Miscellaneous*. Put here any expense that doesn't seem to fall readily into another category.
19. *Office supplies*. This can be a catchall for bags, price tags, sales books, computer software, printing cartridges, paper, etc.
20. *Postage*. Any postage you must use for business purposes goes here.
21. *Rent (or mortgage)*. Determine how much of your rent or mortgage payments are deductible as a business expense, based on the prorated percentage in number 10.Delete this category if you own your home outright.
22. *Repairs*. This category would include whatever you have to spend to keep the building in good condition. Suppose some roof shingles blow off during a windstorm. Your expenses in having them replaced would be entered here.
23. *Sales tax*. If you live in a city, county, or state that charges sales tax, you'll have to charge your customers tax on all sales and send that money to the appropriate agency.
24. *Social Security and Medicare*. You're liable for these taxes only if you have employees.
25. *State Unemployment Insurance*. The same applies to state unemployment insurance.
26. *Tax—other*. Enter any other taxes for which you're liable.
27. *Selling expenses*. This is a vague category that includes any expense you incur in promoting sales in your shop. One example might be gift certificates given away during a special promotion. The only catch here is that the IRS limits these expenses to $25 per customer.
28. *Cleaning supplies*. You'll need brooms, mops, soaps, and so on, to keep the shop clean. You'll also need brass polishes, ammonia, paper towels, furniture polish, and other agents for getting and keeping your antiques in salable condition.
29. *Telephone*. If you have a separate telephone line for the shop, list its charges here. Do not include your household telephone bill. But do include the monthly fee for your connection to the Internet, whether it be a dial-up or broadband connection through your phone company or through a cable television service.
30. *Trade association dues and subscriptions*. You may join the chamber of commerce or a service club and have to pay dues. You'll want to subscribe

to some of the trade newspapers and magazines read by everyone in the antiques business.

31. *Travel.* You're allowed to deduct most expenses incurred attending out-of-town antiques shows or on buying trips. This includes meals, motels, taxis, and so forth. However, the IRS does impose some restrictions. For instance, you can only deduct half of the cost of meals while traveling.

32. *Wages and commissions.* Do you pay wages to an employee? Payments to a temporary employment agency would also be entered here.

33. *Water and sewer.* Most cities include water service along with the electric bill. If yours is separate, calculate the amount using your prorated percentage in number 10.

34. This number is left blank for any deductible expense not covered above.

Nondeductible Expenses

51. *Notes payable.* Did you pay off a personal note?

52. *Federal income tax.* Sorry, this isn't a deductible expense.

53. *Loans payable.* Enter here any payment on a bank or personal loan.

54. *Loans receivable.* Did you lend money to anyone? If the loan is partially or wholly repaid, enter the amount here.

55. *Personal.* This is for your owner's withdrawal (your salary).

56. This number is left blank for any nondeductible expense not covered above.

Don't add too many unusual categories to this list. You might hire a photographer to take a photograph of your shop for a grand opening advertisement, but why have a separate category for "Photography" when you may not hire him again for more than a year? Just enter his charges under "Advertising." You and your accountant can always insert extra categories in your chart of accounts as time goes on if you find you need them.

None of these categories is written in concrete, however. Every business is different and has different expenses. Should you decide to use this chart of accounts, feel free to adapt it in any way that will suit your shop. Use this same list of expenses when setting up any computer accounting program you may use.

Now take a look at the chart of accounts on pages 90–91. As you'll see, the entries reflect the expenses and income for Alexander's Antiques (see chapter 3).The chart on pages 88–89 is a register of monthly expenses. The left side of the register records antiques bought for resale. The right side records non-merchandise expenses, using the account numbers described beginning on page 80. These hypothetical entries are similar to those you might have in your own business. A blank form is in the appendix for you to photocopy.

You'll notice an entry for "cash purchases" on the merchandise register. Many times you'll have to pay cash for the antiques you buy at yard sales. You won't have any receipts for these sales, so keep a small notebook in your car or use your PDA or cell phone to record each purchase with a description of the item and the amount paid for it. This record will come in handy later on, when you price the item. At the end of the month, total all cash purchases for antiques and enter that figure on the register as "cash purchases." Then write a company check to yourself to cover the amount.

To put some of the entries on the non-merchandise side of the chart in perspective, let's suppose you plan to hold a sale in April to generate business after the winter slump. Your biggest expense will be postcards sent to everyone on your mailing list. You buy one hundred stamped postcards at the post office for $44, which you paid for with check #115, then have a copy center print your message on the cards. The copy center charges you $35, which you pay with check #117. You enter the postcards under Postage, number 20, and the printing under Advertising, number 3.

A few days later you take time to pay some bills. You write check #125 for $80 to the Fraser Electric Company and enter it in number 10, Electricity. You write check #126 for $133.50 to the Super Fine Oil Company for an oil delivery, which you enter under number 12, Heat. You also order a copy of one of the new antiques price guides and send your check #139 for $26.95 along with your order, then enter this amount in category 5. And don't forget to record the amount of sales tax you collected—in this case, a total of $570.18 for three months.

At the end of the month, you transfer these entries to a sheet (see pages 90–91) that records your total expenditures for the month. Register these totaled expenditures on the right side of the chart.

The left side of the chart on pages 90–91 is for registering your income. You list there, every day, your total receipts for that day—not each individual sale, just the total amount. At the end of the month, you add those figures and enter the total at the bottom of the sheet.

In the receipts section you'll enter only *actual cash or checks received*, not money that's still due you. If you sell an antique for $300 and the customer puts it on layaway with a $100 down payment, for instance, you include $100 on the day she gives you that check. When she makes a second payment of $100, you enter $100. When she makes the final payment of $100, you enter that figure.

After you complete each month's records on these sheets, you'll carry the totals forward to identical sheets on which you record your expenses and income for the following month. (The chart on pages 90–91 shows figures carried forward from previous months.) This pattern continues until the end of the year. Each month you'll have a record of expenses and income for that month, along with a total of expenses and income for the year to date.

At the end of the year, you'll transfer the final totals to a sheet that you'll give to your accountant (see pages 92–93). With this information, he can quickly and accurately prepare your profit and loss statement and your IRS forms.

Spend a few minutes studying these charts, and you'll see how simple good record keeping can be. But remember that this is only a hypothetical example of a chart of accounts. You and your accountant can adjust this example to suit your own situation.

As time goes on you'll see how practical and useful this information can be. The income record, for example, will show you at a glance which days, weeks, and months of the year are the most profitable for you. This information can be highly valuable as you plan your merchandising schedule.

Let's say you decided at first to stay open Monday through Saturday. But after studying your income register for several months, you notice that you have few sales on Mondays. You just might choose to close the doors on Mondays and save on the electric bill.

You may also discover that you make many more sales during the first two weeks of the month than during the last two. Some dealers attribute this to many people getting paid on the last Friday of the month. By the middle of the following month, they're running out of discretionary cash. If your record shows this to be true for your shop, you'd know to hold any special sales during the first week of the month, when your customers have more cash.

Are sales way down the first month or two of the year? Then perhaps that's the ideal time to take a vacation.

TOTAL RECEIPTS FROM BUSINESS			EXPENDITURES				
Date	Receipts	Amount	Acct. No.	Account	Total This Month	Total Up to This Month	Total to Date
				DEDUCTIBLE			
1			1	Mdse./Materials			
2			2	Accounting			
3			3	Advertising			
4			4	Auto Expenses			
5			5	Books & Publications			
6			6	Capital Expenses			
7			7	Shipping Expenses			
8			8	Contributions			
9			9	Delivery Expenses			
10			10	Electricity			
11			11	Freight and Express			
12			12	Heat			
13			13	Insurance			
14			14	Interest			
15			15	Laundry			
16			16	Legal Expenses			
17			17	Licenses			
18			18	Micellaneous			
19			19	Office Supplies			
20			20	Postage			
21			21	Rent/Mortgage			

#	Item
22	Repairs
23	Sales Taxes
24	Social Security/Medicare
25	State U.I. Insurance
26	Tax - Other
27	Selling Expenses
28	Cleaning Supplies
29	Telephone
30	Dues & Subscriptions
31	Travel Expenses
32	Wages/Commissions
33	Water/Sewer Fees
34	SUBTOTAL

TOTAL THIS MONTH

TOTAL UP TO THIS MONTH

TOTAL TO DATE

#	Item
	NONDEDUCTIBLE
51	Notes Payable
52	Federal Income Tax
53	Loans Payable
54	Loans Receivable
55	Personal
56	

TOTAL THIS MONTH

TOTAL UP TO THIS MONTH

TOTAL TO DATE

MDSE AND MATERIALS PAID BY CASH AND CHECKS

Date	Payee	Check No.	Amount
1			
2			
3	Cash purchases		$43.15
4	SLI Estate Sales	118	$18.00
5	eBay Auction		$23.50
6	Red Barn Auction	123	$78.00
7			
8			
9	eBay Auction		$19.10
10	Jim Monty (yard sale)		$13.05
11			
12	Cash purchases		$6.25
13	Red Barn Auction	128	$24.50

OTHER EXPENDITURES BY CHECKS AND CASH

Date	Payee	Check No.	Acct. No.	Amount
1	Post Office	115	20	44
2	Penn Mortgage Co.	116	21	550
3	Speedy Copy and Print	117	3	35
4	K-Mart		28	7.95
5	American Heart Assoc.	119	8	15
5	Office Depot	120	19	25
5	Lincoln City Landscaping	121	22	60
6	Williams Glass Co.	122	22	7
6	Fraser News	124	3	55
7	Fraser Electric Co.	125	10	80
7	Super Fine Oil Co.	126	12	133.50
7	Schroeder's Hardware	127	22	12.95
15	Sam's Auto Repair	130	4	29.51

Left ledger:

Day	Payee	No.	Amount
14	R.C. Carry (misc.)	129	$150.00
15			
16			
17	Indy Land (yard sale)		$12.75
18	Cash purchases		$7.25
19	Cash purchases		$23.00
20	Red Barn Auction	133	$13.50
21			
22			
23	Maria Dalhy (19th sofa)	136	$95.00
24			
25			
26	eBay Auction		$8.50
27	Tom Kendall (misc.)	137	$200.00
28			
29			
30			
Carried Forward			**$735.55**

Right ledger:

Day	Payee	No.		Amount
15	Verizon Communications	131	29	67.66
17	H. James Accounting	132	2	100
21	Target	134	19	15.95
21	Chamber of Commerce	135	30	50
28	Allstate Insurance	138	13	99
30	Sunoco Service Station		9	28.76
30	Warman's	139	5	26.95
30	Water Co.	140	33	47.58
Carried Forward				**1,490.81**

TOTAL RECEIPTS FROM BUSINESS			EXPENDITURES				
Date	Receipts	Amount	Acct. No.	Account	Total This Month	Total Up to This Month	Total to Date
APRIL	2011			DEDUCTIBLE			
1	(rain)	$24	1	Mdse./Materials	$735.55	$972.20	$1,707.75
2		$76	2	Accounting	$100.00	$200.00	$300.00
3		$71	3	Advertising	$90.00	$110.00	$200.00
4		$105	4	Auto Expenses	$29.51		$29.51
5		$152	5	Books & Publications	$26.95		$26.95
6	Closed		6	Capital Expenses			
7	Closed		7	Shipping Expenses			
8		$95	8	Contributions	$15.00		$15.00
9		$98	9	Delivery Expenses	$28.76	$52.30	$81.06
10		$259	10	Electricity	$80.00	$169.00	$249.00
11		$174	11	Freight and Express			
12		$185	12	Heat	$133.50	$267.00	$400.50
13	Closed		13	Insurance	$99.00	$198.00	$297.00
14	Closed		14	Interest			
15		$42	15	Laundry		$39.00	$39.00
16		$69	16	Legal Expenses			
17		$29	17	Licenses			
18	(rain)	$15	18	Micellaneous		$4.50	$4.50
19		$176	19	Office Supplies	$40.95	$19.00	$59.95
20	Closed		20	Postage	$44.00		$44.00

#	Item	This Month	Up to This Month	To Date
21	Rent/Mortgage	$550.00	$1,100.00	$1,650.00
22	Repairs	$79.95		$79.95
23	Sales Taxes	$151.68	$418.50	$570.18
24	Social Security/Medicare			
25	State U.I. Insurance			
26	Tax - Other			
27	Selling Expenses			
28	Cleaning Supplies	$7.95	$0.00	$7.95
29	Telephone	$67.66	$135.22	$202.88
30	Dues & Subscriptions	$50.00	$100.00	$150.00
31	Travel Expenses			
32	Wages/Commissions		$500.00	$500.00
33	Water/Sewer Fees	$47.58	$93.34	$140.92
34				
	SUBTOTAL	$2,378.04	$4,378.06	$6,756.10
	NONDEDUCTIBLE			
51	Notes Payable			
52	Federal Income Tax	$75.00	$150.00	$225.00
53	Loans Payable			
54	Loans Receivable			
55	Personal	$1,000.00	$2,000.00	$3,000.00
56				
	TOTAL THIS MONTH	$3,453.04		
	TOTAL UP TO THIS MONTH		$6,528.06	
	TOTAL TO DATE			$9,981.10

#		Amount
21	Closed	
22	(rain)	$29
23	(rain)	$10
24		$49
25		$88
26		$421
27	Closed	
28	Closed	
29		$32
30		$329
	TOTAL THIS MONTH	$2,528
	TOTAL UP TO THIS MONTH	$6,975
	TOTAL TO DATE	$9,503

Expense Summary For Your Tax Adviser

YEAR ENDED 20____

CASH RECEIPTS FOR THE YEAR .... $____

Accounts Receivable:	*Accounts Payable:*	*Inventory*
January 1, 20____ $____	January 1, 20____ $____	January 1, 20____ $____
December 31, 20____ $____	December 31, 20____ $____	December 31, 20____ $____

Equipment Record:

(Equipment Purchased)

Date Acquired M/D/Y	Description	New or Used	Cost or Basis	Life Years	%	Annual Depreciation

(Equipment Sold)

Date Sold M/D/Y	Description	Sales Price or Trade-In	Date Purch. M/D/Y	Accum. Depr.	Remain. Cost or Basis	Gain or Loss

Other Information:

Name of Proprietor _____ Soc. Sec. # _____

Main Business Activity _____ Product _____

Business Name _____ Bus. Address _____

Employer Identification Number _____

Accounting Method: (1) Cash (2) Accrual (3) Other _____

Method(s) used to value closing inventory: (1) Cost (2) Lower of cost or market

(3) Other _____

EXPENDITURES

ACCT. NO	ACCOUNT	TOTAL FOR YEAR
DEDUCTIBLE		
1	MDSE./MATERIALS	
2	ACCOUNTING	
3	ADVERTISING	
4	AUTO EXPENSE	
5	BOOKS & PUBLICATIONS	
6	CAPITAL EXPENSES	
7	SHIPPING EXPENSE	
8	CONTRIBUTIONS	
9	DELIVERY SYSTEM	
10	ELECTRICITY	
11	FREIGHT AND EXPR.	
12	HEAT	
13	INSURANCE	
14	INTEREST	
15	LAUNDRY	
16	LEGAL EXPENSES	
17	LICENSES	
18	MISCELLANEOUS	
19	OFFICE SUPPLIES	
20	POSTAGE	

21	RENT/MORTGAGE			
22	REPAIRS			
23	SALES TAX			
24	SOCIAL SECURITY/MEDICARE			
25	STATE U. I. INSURANCE			
26	TAX—OTHER			
27	SELLING EXPENSES			
28	CLEANING SUPPLIES			
29	TELEPHONE			
30	DUES AND SUBSCRIPTIONS			
31	TRAVELING EXPENSES			
32	WAGES AND COMM.			
33	WATER			
34				
	SUBTOTAL			
NONDEDUCTIBLE				
51	NOTES PAYABLE			
52	FEDERAL INC. TAX			
53	LOANS PAYABLE			
54	LOANS RECEIVABLE			
55	PERSONAL			
56				
	TOTAL FOR YEAR			

Was there any change in determining quantities, cost, or valuations between opening and closing inventory?   Yes_____ No_____

Did you deduct expenses for an office in your home?   Yes_____ No_____

Do you have evidence for all listed property (autos, etc.) to support your deduction?   Yes_____ No_____

Is the evidence written?   Yes_____ No_____

Record-Keeping Rules for Business and Entertainment Expenses in General

Adequate records (a log) are required to substantiate:

(1) the business use of "listed property" (i.e., passenger cars or other property used in transportation, property of the type generally used for entertainment, recreation or amusement, computers or peripheral equipment),

(2) traveling expenses, including meals and lodging away from home,

(3) entertainment expenses,

(4) business gifts.

Meals and entertainment must be directly related and have a clear business purpose.

Also deductibility is subject to limitation.

IMPORTANT

NO DEDUCTION FOR TRAVEL, ENTERTAINMENT, AUTOMOBILE EXPENSES, ETC., WILL BE ALLOWED UNLESS ADEQUATE RECORDS (A LOG) ARE KEPT.

NO PROOF—NO DEDUCTION

Keeping an Orderly Filing System

To be successful in your new business, you need to have some sort of order in your filing system to be able to record the entries in your chart of accounts quickly and efficiently. Use a few of the folders you bought back in chapter 3 to file your receipts. Label one "Accounts Payable" and drop all bills into it as they arrive. Label another "Accounts Paid" and drop the invoices there after you've paid them. If you're doing any outside work such as setting up estate sales, label one file folder "Accounts Receivable" and place copies of the invoices you've sent to your clients in it. Once you get the checks for those services, place the invoices in a file labeled "Invoices Paid."

Reconcile your accounts every month *without fail*. Create a folder for the printouts of your canceled checks and bank statements. Most banks today send only a printout and not the actual check. Then if you ever have to prove payment of a bill, you can easily cross-check the paid invoice for that service or merchandise with its corresponding canceled check.

Open a *business checking account* for your business and deposit all checks and cash you receive for sales in the shop or any other service you perform into it. Most dealers make these deposits every afternoon, leaving enough in the till to make change the next day. If business is slow, you may choose to make deposits every few days, instead.

Computerized Record Keeping

Can a computer make record keeping easier? Sometimes. It can all depend on a few things:

- How computer literate are you? If you understand computer language and how to use a spreadsheet and a word processing package, then certainly, this is perhaps the way to go.
- Do you already own a computer and printer? If not, you'll have to spend perhaps $800 to $1,000 for hardware and software to service your bookkeeping needs.
- Will the volume of business you do warrant setting up computer programs to keep track of your sales? In the beginning, you may not have many sales, so it might be better to wait a few months and gradually work the computer into your routine.

Is a Computer Necessary to Keep Good Records?

Granted, this is the age of technology, and although everyone from kindergarten-age kids to moms and dads is talking bytes and bits, RAM and ROM, not everyone needs a computer. Do you have to use a computer to keep your records? No. If you're managing a shop with minimal bookkeeping requirements, you'll do just fine with a few pencils and a ledger. But once your business begins to grow, a computer can save you hours of work each week and perform some amazing tasks.

Computer Accounting Programs

The most popular computer accounting software is QuickBooks (see chapter 2). It's user-friendly and efficient.

What Can a Good Accounting Program Do for You?

Once you've installed QuickBooks, you'll just type your information in and the program will take over from there. Data about expenses and income will almost automatically land in the right place. The program can even write checks for your expenses, making paying your bills easy with virtually no chance of errors. However, you'll need to purchase special check printing paper. The program will also add columns of figures for you and transfer totals to the proper category. You can give your accountant a printout that's so accurate and complete that he will spend far less time preparing your tax returns and year-end profit and loss statements. Since your accountant charges by the hour, you'll save perhaps hundreds of dollars every year on that bill alone.

Mailing and "Want" Lists. In chapter 9 you'll find recommendations to keep an e-mail list of customers to whom you can send announcements of special promotions. Your word processing package can churn out hundreds of individually addressed letters, cards, and labels that look as though you typed them specifically for that customer. You may wish to keep a "want list" of antiques for your regular customers. Make a database of those wants and you can almost immediately access any item and who's looking for it.

Let's say one of your customers comes in looking for a collectible Hummel plate as a gift for her sister. You don't have any such plates at that time, so you file her name, telephone number, and the words Hummel plate in your "want list" data file. Three weeks later you locate such a plate, but you can't remember the customer's name. You just go into your "want list" database, tell it to search for Hummel plate, and in seconds you'll see the customer's name and telephone number flashing on the monitor.

Inventory Lists. You'll want to keep an ongoing record of every antique you buy for resale and the price you paid for it. This is the only way you can be sure the price tag you place on the antique reflects a reasonable profit for you. Yes, you can keep such a record in a notebook, but in time, after you've bought thousands of antiques for the shop, that record gets pretty unwieldy. Make a database for your inventory, though, and the chore becomes simple.

To create a database, you must first create "fields" or categories, each representing one part or the item description. Typically, you'll begin with the item number, item name, category, date purchased, location of purchase, price paid, condition, and a brief description. Some databases even allow you to insert a digital photo of the item.

It helps to devise a coding system, such as "SS" for sterling silver, "J" for jewelry, "G" for glassware, "C" for china, "F" for furniture, "B" for books, "L" for linens, and so forth. Assign sequential numbers to the antiques. For instance, the first piece of jewelry was given the code number "J100," the second piece "J101," the third "J102," and so on. One advantage of using a database is that you can sort the list based on these codes. If you use separate sections of the database for each type of antique, this will make it easy to locate any one item, when you bought it, and how much you paid for it.

Say you buy that Hummel plate for $35 and price it at $140. You give it the code number C253 because it's china and happens to be the 253rd piece of china you've placed in the shop. The customer buys the plate on June 21 and asks for the standard 10 percent discount, which you agree to give her. You bring up your "China" database file in your computer, search for that plate, and record the date of the sale, the dollar amount of the sale, and the percentage of markup you achieved on the sale (more about figuring markup percentages in chapter 7). You now have a complete record of that purchase and sale.

Alternatively, you can create a word processing file for each category in which you list the items in the order that you purchased them. But eventually these files will grow too large and unwieldy. The main disadvantage to cataloging your inventory this way is that you can't sort the list to find the item you want. The chart on page 98 shows how a page of such entries in the "China" category might look. A blank copy of this inventory form is in the appendix.

Analyzing Your Records for Profit

About twice a year you should take a few hours to analyze all your monthly records. By then you'll be able to see patterns in your sales and expenses that you can use to increase your profit ratio.

Examine Your Expenses

As you study your records, ask yourself four questions about any regular expenses that seem out of line:

1. Why are these expenses so high?
2. Is there any way I can reduce them?
3. Should I incur these expenses at all?
4. Can I get rid of them altogether?

Do your fuel and electric bills skyrocket during midwinter months? Maybe you should consider cutting back on your shop hours then, opening an hour later in the morning and closing a half hour earlier in the afternoon. Many antiques shops do this to save money during the slow months. Can you do without some of the office supplies you usually buy? Are you shopping for these supplies at the lowest prices available? Is there any way you can lower expenses on your trips out of town to

Code	Item Description	Cost	Price	Sold At	Date	% Markup
C246	Clown cookie jar	$3	$39	$39	4/13/2010	92%
C247	Blue china bowl	$3	$19	$19	5/17/2010	87%
C248	Small cream pitcher	$1	$12	$10	3/23/2010	90%
C249	Delft dish, 7 inches	$4	$29	$29	6/30/2010	88%
C250	Azalea vase	$10	$49	$45	4/23/2010	80%
C251	Art Deco salt and pepper set	$5	$15	$15	5/18/2010	67%
C252	Staffordshire tea bowl and saucer	$19	$95	$85	7/28/2010	80%
C253	Niagara Falls souvenir plate	$35	$75	$65	6/21/2010	53%
C254	Child's tea set	$25	$125	$115	7/30/2010	80%
C255	Perfume bottle	$5	$19	$17	5/15/2010	74%
C256	Washbowl and pitcher, c.1900	$35	$110	$88	3/20/2010	62%
C257	White chamber pot	$8	$45	$45	4/14/2010	82%
C258	Art Nouveau jardiniere	$38	$125	$120	5/5/2010	70%

antiques shows? For example, instead of driving in the night before and staying in a motel, you could get up early and arrive just as the show opens.

Often you can't eliminate an expense, but you can look for ways to use it more creatively. Let's take your advertising as an example. Say your original advertising plan calls for a large classified ad in your local newspaper at a certain date each month. If you see from your daily sales record that your greatest sales volume every month is nearly always the few days following the insertion of that ad, you know the money you spend on advertising is paying off in extra income. That same data may also tell you to increase your advertising budget and schedule additional ads.

If you notice an obvious glitch in your expense records and some item is way too high, take action immediately to lower or eliminate it. You can always refine your method as time goes on. Reducing expenses gradually over time works best.

If you examine your records for the purchase price and selling price of each antique placed in your shop, you'll see clearly where you should be investing your inventory money. Most savvy dealers look at the *ratio* or *percentage* of markup on an item as being just as important as, if not more important than, the actual *dollar* profit.

For example, an auctioneer advertised an estate sale that seemed promising, so the antiques dealer arrived bright and early. As the morning wore on, she watched pieces of furniture being sold for fairly good prices. A fine golden oak square side table went for $125. She didn't bid on it because she knew that the most she could expect to sell it for would be $175, a dollar profit of only $50 on an investment of $125, or a markup of only 30 percent. Other dealers didn't bid on that table for the same reason.

But when the auctioneer got to lots of cups and saucers, the dealer, along with most of the others, began bidding. She was able to purchase fourteen different sets for a total of $45. She knew she could easily sell those cups and saucers for an average price of $20 per set, with a total sales price of $280. She would make a dollar profit of $235 on an investment of $45, or a markup of 84 percent. She based her decision to buy the cups and saucers on her inventory records, which showed a *sustained pattern* of making a higher percentage on china than on furniture.

Storing Your Records Carefully

Buy what's called a "banker's box" at your office supply store to keep your records and receipts for at least three years. The IRS requires you to keep them for a minimum of three years, but most accountants advise their clients to keep records for six years. It won't hurt, and you just might need them someday if you're ever called in for an audit.

## 05

Stocking Your Antiques

Before you can sell antiques, you have to buy them to create your stock inventory. You'll obtain your stock from a variety of sources, including everything from garage sales to flea markets all the way to antique shows and online auctions. But just purchasing items at random doesn't mean that they will sell. Likewise, only buying what you like doesn't guarantee that items will sell, either. In order to be successful at selling antiques, you have to learn what sort of items your customers want and buy accordingly.

Knowing What to Buy and Stock

You'll be investing your good hard cash in the antiques you place in your shop. Obviously, the only way you'll make a profit is if you can sell them, within a reasonable length of time, at a profit. Unless you've been working in another antiques shop recently, you may not know just what your potential customers will want to buy.

A good way to get that information is to select a number of successful antiques shops, both commercial and home-based, in your general area and make a survey of the stock in them. The owners of these shops will carry what their customers want to buy, or they wouldn't stay in business long.

It's easy to believe you know what other dealers are carrying, but you can be misled. When you go into an antiques shop, you drift toward the types of things you like or collect, and you pass right by items you don't. Perhaps you love beautiful marble, for example, so you make a beeline for every marble-topped piece of furniture in every shop you visit. Yet you pass right by most wicker furniture because you don't particularly care for it. It would be very easy for you to believe that shops carry more marble-topped dressers and tables than wicker furniture, because you see the marble and not the wicker. But you'll have to train your mind to know that this isn't the case, since wicker furniture outsells marble at least ten to one.

What this boils down to is that you must open your eyes, ignore your personal preferences, and stock what other people want to buy. There are collectors of virtually every item ever created on this planet, from ice picks to toothpicks. Today, in the back of antiques trade papers, you might find classified ads for old cereal boxes with the cereal still in them, typewriter ribbons in their boxes, or even old firecracker packs.

As you walk through the shops, also make an educated guess about the amount of furniture the owners display in comparison to the china, pottery, glassware, paper goods, and so forth. This will tell you whether they make their greatest profits on furniture or accessories, for they know from experience what sells. You'll know then how to allocate your precious floor and shelf space.

Look carefully at the furniture you do see. How much of it is formal and how much casual primitives? Which woods do you see used most often—walnut, mahogany, oak, pine? That's what their customers ask for and buy.

Do you see many framed prints, mirrors, old photographs? Is Fiesta ware still hot? Do the owners of the shop display much Shelley, Belleek, Limoges? What about fine crystal? Have people in your area jumped on the fifties bandwagon? Does Orientalia seem to be popular?

What about the prices? Do the owners seem to carry antiques in a wide range of prices, or do they specialize in high, low, or moderately priced items?

The chart on pages 106-107 illustrates a form you can use to record this information after you've visited each shop. Make photocopies of the blank version supplied in the appendix for your own records. Then study the results and keep them in mind as you buy the stock for your own shop.

Finding Your Stock

Unless you inherited a three-story house jammed with antiques, you'll have to begin acquiring the inventory for your shop many months before you actually open the doors. You'll need hundreds of items to fill your shelves, cabinets, and floor space. Obviously, you have to buy these antiques at prices that will allow you to cover your expenses and make a profit. Also, each piece you sell must be quickly replaced with another. So, how can you develop a system that will provide you with a continuous, reliable source of antiques at substantial discounts? Also, remember that you'll need to store the items you buy while you ready your shop.

The usual places where most other antiques dealers buy their stock are estate sales, auctions, yard sales, individuals (who wish to sell anything from one copper teapot to a truck full of antiques), and other dealers.

Many dealers also go on annual buying trips. Some dealers, especially those who manage their shops alone and don't have time for much scouting on their own, employ a small army of what are known in the business as "pickers." Many dealers take in antiques on consignment. A few create *instant inventory* by buying the entire stock of another dealer who's going out of business.

Estate Sales

An estate sale often occurs when an elderly person dies or goes into a nursing home. The family takes what it wants from the home and hires a *liquidator* to come in, price the rest, then sell it to the public. These liquidators price the goods higher than they would be at a yard sale but lower than what would be charged in an antiques shop. You'll often find excellent-quality antiques at such a sale. I've bought sterling silver, fine sets of china, old prints, quilts, and numerous other antiques at estate sales.

The sale is usually held inside the home on weekends. In some towns local liquidators have quite a following and their sales always draw big crowds. Often when the home where the sale is to be held is small, they'll use a "take a number" system to control the crowds. The first person in line gets number one, the second number two, and so on. If this is the case in your town and you know from advance advertising that a sale appears to be promising, you should plan to arrive long before the starting time to get a low number.

Most liquidators advertise that anything left on Sunday afternoon will be sold at half price. You'll seldom find much of real value left at the end of such sales, but you can usually pick up a few collectibles—linens, kitchenware, and so forth—so you should always go back for one last look.

Auctions

Auctions are a great way to buy antiques—if you bid wisely. They fall into two categories—consignment and estate.

Consignment Auctions. Consignment auctions are usually held regularly on the same day of the week or month in a large building owned by the auctioneer. Dozens of people may bring merchandise to be sold, and the quality can range from good to poor. Many auctions, especially those in rural areas which once offered mostly lower-end merchandise, are disappearing. In their place have appeared more middle-market auctions, usually found in more developed areas, offering better items which go for higher prices.

You should plan to attend these auctions regularly even though auctioneers rarely advertise in advance. You'll take your chances on finding quality antiques at this type of auction. You couldn't, for example, attend one with the express purpose of buying a Victorian bed. Maybe there'll be one there, maybe not.

Estate Auctions. Another type of auction is the estate auction, a one-time-only event usually held in the deceased person's home to dispose of its contents. Auctioneers of these events usually place large display ads in newspapers advertising the sale, and they nearly always include a long list of items to be auctioned. You just might find that Victorian bed on the list, along with hundreds of other antiques.

Buying Procedures at Auctions. Regardless of the location of an auction, the procedure for buying is the same. You approach a table or counter where one or two people sit and ask for a *bidding card*. The person there will ask for some identification, then issue you a large cardboard card that has a number written on it. The card costs nothing, but you can't bid without it.

Always arrive at an auction at least a half hour before its advertised starting time. The first reason is to stake out a place up front close to the auctioneer, where it's easy to see the merchandise being auctioned. Most auctioneers will let you reserve such a seat in some way. One method is to tape a piece of paper with your name on it to the seat.

The second reason for arriving early is to look over the merchandise. Many auctioneers won't allow you to browse through the items once the auction starts, and if you haven't scrutinized everything carefully beforehand, you can make some big mistakes once the bidding begins. Few auctioneers are really dishonest, and most will point out a flaw if they know of it, but all merchandise at an auction is sold as is. No returns.

You should walk through the merchandise to be auctioned, taking note of anything you might want to bid on. Examine those pieces carefully for cracks, chips, missing pieces, or any other flaws. Every item will have a lot number, which auctioneers call out when the piece comes up before them. Write the lot number of antiques on which you plan to bid on the back of your bidding card. Beside the number, write the amount you're willing to bid for it, based on what you think you could sell the antique for. Dealers always write the highest bid they're willing to go on every item on the back of the card. This is good insurance against getting caught up in what's called "auction fever."

You bid by holding up your card. If a Wedgwood vase, for example, comes up, the auctioneer will start the bidding by saying, "Who'll give me $500 for this vase?" Who'll start the bidding at $500?" *Never bid at that first price.* That's just the auctioneer's way of getting the bidding started. No one bids. Then he'll say something like, "All right, who'll give me $100?"

If you're new to buying at auctions, I suggest you attend several of them before placing a bid. You can learn a lot about buying at auctions by watching the other dealers.

How do you know who's a dealer? They're the ones constantly checking the back of their bidding card as they bid. They're the ones who look so serious that you'd think they were in the middle of a business conference. They enjoy the auctions, but they don't get emotional about them, as do most bidders who aren't dealers.

Today, a lot of bidders are people who have just purchased large new homes, and they need to fill them. They're there because they perceive antiques as a good value and they want to impress their friends with the pieces they buy, not because they're collectors or have any knowledge of what pieces are worth. They'll stop at nothing to win a bid. This drives prices up even on mediocre items, which is bad for you. Remember, you have to mark up anything you buy in order to make a profit.

Any antiques auction offers the potential for finding good buys, but for real bargains you can't beat the ones held in the country. The farther the auction is from a large town, the better your chances will be to come home with your car full of treasures at rock-bottom prices.

A Virginia dealer was out for a drive on a beautiful fall day, but not out scouting. She stopped at a country store to buy a cold drink and noticed a flyer on the window announcing an auction. Being an auction addict, she asked the store owner how to get there. He told her to go 8 miles down the road and then 5 miles down another road before turning onto a gravel road. So she started out and drove and drove and drove. Pretty soon, she was heading farther and farther into the hills. She finally found the place and parked her car. There were quite a few people milling around looking at the merchandise spread out in front of the beautiful country home, but not many dealers, so she was able to make some excellent buys. One of the best was a large cardboard box that held a beautiful silver water pitcher, eight silver dinner plates, three silver trays, and several small silver bowls. They were all salable antiques, for which she paid $5 for the box.

Many auctions go on for hours and hours. Plan to stay until the end, because that's often when you'll get your best buys, maybe even some real bargains for 50 cents to a dollar or two.

Sometimes, you might find a treasure if you're patient and just a bit aggressive. Many auction houses hold weekly consignment auctions on a particular day of the week. Items in these auctions may be assorted or grouped on a theme, such as American folk art. Start attending these on a regular basis. Get to know the auctioneer. After you've attended a few of his or her auctions, you can boldly go up after the sale is over—usually the auctioneer will stop at a certain time and hold over any items not sold until the following week—and ask if you can buy one of the items that you had your eye on. More often than not, the auctioneer will say yes to your offer, and you may walk away with a real find to turn around and sell in your shop.

Individual Sellers

Once your shop is open, people will come to you with antiques they want to sell. Until then, however, while you're trying to build up stock, you might run an ad in the classified section of your local newspaper, actively soliciting sellers. You can continue this practice after you open the shop if you find it pays off. Such an ad could read like this:

BUYING ANTIQUES
I buy all kinds of antiques.
Must be in good condition.
Call (494) 555-6938

The only real problem you'll run into with buying from individuals is that most of them seem to think they should get, from you, just about the retail value of antiques. They don't understand the realities of markup.

At times someone will respond to your ad and say, "I'm moving and getting rid of everything, including some antiques. Take all or nothing." That's when you go to the seller's house to assess the value of the antiques in the lot. If you feel they're really salable in your shop, you make an offer for everything, based on what you think you can get for the *antiques*. Don't factor into your offering price anything for the rest of the lot.

Shop	Furniture	Glassware	China	Other	Prices	Remarks
Annie's Antiques	Diamond dye cabinet				$650	Somewhat high
			Blue & white pitcher		$300	Overpriced
			Watt pottery bowl 10"		$125	About right
	Country Victorian cupboard				$770	Underpriced
		Cranberry glass perfume bottle			$225	Too high
	Hitchcock side chair				$1,150	Somewhat high
	Victorian mirror				$748	Overpriced
Rustic Antiques	Primitive shelves				$235	About right
	Oak upright icebox				$450	Good price
	Paint decorated				$855	A little high
	19thc jelly cupboard					
			Stoneware crock 10"		$150	About right
	Pine blanket chest				$460	Good price
				19thc roller organ	$450	About right
		Handpainted glass lamp shade			$25	Excellent price
	Hoosier cabinet c.1900				$825	Good price

Shop	Furniture	Glassware	China	Other	Prices	Remarks
All-American Antiques		Carnival glass bowl 10"			$175	A bit high
	Wooten secretary				$12,800	Much too high
	Child's wicker rocker				$110	About right
		Mary Gregory decorated decanter			$195	About right
				Handel reverse painted lamp	$20,000	Way overpriced
				Mira floor-model music box	$6,000	Overpriced
R&J Antiques	Oak pressed back chairs c.1901 (6)				$560	A little high
			McCoy jardiniere with pedestal		$350	Good price
	Rococo Revival lady's chair				$525	A little high
	Tall chest of drawers				$2,760	Overpriced
		Vaseline glass compote			$125	About right
	Late Classical mahogany sofa c.1840–1850				$385	Underpriced
	Mission Oak desk				$805	Good price
				Fishing derby flask c.1925	$1,045	Overpriced

January–March 2011

Location	Date	Furniture	Glassware	China	Other	Cost	Price	Condition
Rustic Antiques	15-Jan				Small iron stove	$50	$125	A little rust
Rustic Antiques	15-Jan	Oak upright icebox				$350	$525	Very good
R.C. Carry (individ)	16-Jan	Glass-door Mission Oak bookcase				$135	$950	Needs cleaning
Rustic Antiques	22-Jan	Pine blanket chest				$375	$475	Nice patina
Rustic Antiques	22-Jan		Handpainted glass lamp shade			$20	$30	Excellent
Annie's Antiques	25-Jan	Country Victorian kitchen cupboard				$650	$1,275	Nice patina
Schoolhouse Show	13-Feb				Milk glass lamp	$15	$85	Excellent
Schoolhouse Show	13-Feb		6 ruby glass water tumblers			$30	$95	Excellent
Estate sale	13-Feb		Art glass vase			$16	$85	Excellent
Lincoln Antique Mall	14-Feb	Mission Oak clock shelf					$25	$125
Lincoln Antique Mall	14-Feb	Mission Oak library table				$50	$375	Very good
Tom Kendall (individ)	18-Feb	Morris recliner c.1910				$85	$450	Good upholstery
Tom Kendall (individ)	18-Feb	Mission Oak revolving bookstand				$75	$385	Excellent
Red Barn Auction	23-Feb		Milk glass compote			$22	$60	Excellent
Lincoln Antique Mall	28-Feb			Washstand bowl and pitcher		$35	$110	Very good

Location	Date	Furniture	Glassware	China	Other	Cost	Price	Condition
Estate sale	6-Mar			Souvenir plate Niagara Falls		$15	$75	Excellent
Estate sale	6-Mar		Rainbow Chrome Art Deco cordial set			$10	$95	Needs polishing
Estate sale	6-Mar				Papier-mâché lap desk	$25	$175	One corner chipped
Estate sale	6-Mar			Art Nouveau jardiniere		$38	$125	Very good
Lincoln Antique Mall	7-Mar		Cut glass decanter			$25	$98	Excellent
Red Barn Auction	9-Mar			White stoneware chamber pot		$8	$45	Excellent
Upcountry Auction	10-Mar	Oak captain's chair				$55	$125	Some repair
Jackson's Flea Mkt.	20-Mar	Mission Oak doll bed				$35	$145	Very good
Jackson's Flea Mkt.	20-Mar				Rocking blotter	$8	$25	Very good
Jackson's Flea Mkt.	20-Mar		Green Depression glass luncheon set			$12	$65	Excellent
Jackson's Flea Mkt.	20-Mar			Delft dish		$4	$29	Very good
Jackson's Flea Mkt.	20-Mar			Azalea vase		$10	$49	Excellent
Red Barn Auction	23-Mar				Tiffany-style lamp	$85	$470	Needs rewiring
Church sale	27-Mar			Clown cookie jar		$3	$39	Shows some wear
Church sale	27-Mar			Tea bowl/saucer		$19	$95	Hairline crack
Yard sale	27-Mar	Wicker fern stand				$4	$72	Very good
Yard sale	27-Mar			Child's tea set		$25	$125	Complete in box

You haul everything away, place the antiques in your shop, and store the rest. All right, you're thinking, what do I do with all that other stuff—the pots and pans, sheets and towels, romance novels, Tupperware, and ancient typewriters? One option is to hold your own special yard sale once a year and get rid of it then. You might also rent a space at a local Sunday flea market during the summer. Many dealers do just that and make several hundred dollars or so from all that miscellaneous junk. But you could also give it to the Salvation Army and get a tax credit. The Salvation Army uses any clothing and household goods to help people in need, then sells the rest at its thrift shops. Everyone benefits that way.

Once your shop is open, you can place an attractive sign near your checkout counter that informs customers you buy antiques.

Most dealers also put text such as "I buy antiques—one piece or a houseful" on their business cards, then keep a supply of these cards at their checkout counter. They make sure each customer leaves with a card, either in his hand or in the bag containing his purchases. Handing out these cards does pay off. Often people will be planning to hold a yard sale but will not want to sell valuable antiques at it. They'll bring them to you.

Yard Sales

The ubiquitous yard sale is an American institution, and what would a weekend be without them? Dealers find it hard to pass up yard sales.

Most people who cruise the yard sales every weekend are casual shoppers, driving from one to another. The serious dealer, however, knows that to find the salable antiques and collectibles hidden among the plastic kitchenware and cheap florist vases, you must have a plan. Here are some pointers:

- When you read the yard-sale ads on Thursday and Friday evening, mark those that mention antiques or collectibles. Don't waste your time noting those that don't advertise antiques. After all, you must complete your rounds in time to get back home and open your shop.
- As you read the addresses, map a route starting with the sales closest to your home (or those with the earliest starting times) and move on to more distant ones. The purpose is to get to the good sales before someone else snaps up the antiques.

- Every town is different when it comes to finding antiques at good prices at yard sales. You'll have to make your own judgment in this respect. You'll usually find more antiques at the lowest prices in older, middle-class neighborhoods. In many cases owners of these homes have lived there for years and years and have stored a mass of castoffs in their attics and basements. These people are usually not trying to get top dollar for their things. They just want to get rid of them.
- By contrast, the owners of homes in upper-class neighborhoods are usually quite knowledgeable about antiques values. At their sales they set close to retail prices on any antique or collectible, so you'll seldom find much to buy at such sales.
- At yard sales possession is nine-tenths of the law, so to speak. The unwritten code of the yard sale is that whoever has his hands on an item first has dibs on it. You need to be able to pick things up quickly and hold on to them. Take along a large sturdy plastic tote bag, into which you can drop anything that interests you. This way, you can pick up and carry much more than you could in your arms alone. Then examine your finds carefully, put anything that isn't promising back on the tables, pay for the antiques you do want, and move quickly to the next sale.

Since the inception of the *Antiques Roadshow* in the United States, many people perceive that anything old must have value, so they price their items higher whether they know what that value is or not.

To be honest, you probably won't find an antique or collectible of outstanding value at a yard sale. You'll find china, glassware, pottery, and kitchen collectibles, all of modest value. Every once in a while, you'll come upon a piece of furniture—a bed, small table, brass bridge lamp, framed mirror, or whatever. Inevitably, these finds must be refinished, polished, or rewired to make them salable.

Every dealer has at least one story of a spectacular discovery, a real treasure bought for a pittance. A dealer in Ohio discovered four sterling silver steak knives at a not-too-promising yard sale. On one table sat a worn pink satin jewelry box displaying a medley of cheap jewelry in its upper tray. She was about to move on when her instincts told her to pull out the lower drawer in the case. There, dropped in among more cheap jewelry, lay four antique sterling silver steak knives. Hurriedly, she picked them up and dashed to the seller. "How much for these knives?" she asked. "Oh, four dollars," the seller replied. After she had paid for them, she asked the seller why he sold the knives for four dollars. The seller's reply? "We have a new set of stainless steel and those didn't match." The knives were worth a minimum of $250.

> Tip: When you go to estate sales, auctions, and yard sales, take at least one of the current antiques and collectibles price guides along with you. Otherwise, unless you have a phenomenal memory, you'll have a hard time remembering the thousands of ever-changing retail values of items you'll run across. You might find an item you think is priced well, but you don't know for sure. With a price guide along, you'll be able to decide if the price is too high or not to enable you to resell the item.

Other Dealers

Dealers also buy from one another, receiving the customary dealer's 10 percent discount. Many owners of antiques shops make a regular practice of cruising the shops of other dealers. We're usually looking for antiques that are underpriced. Perhaps the dealer got an exceptionally good deal on the antique and priced it low, hoping for a quick sale, or maybe the dealer simply didn't know the value of the antique.

Sometimes you'll have a customer who wants a specific item and will pay you a premium for locating it. At other times you'll be looking for "orphan" pieces to fill out a set. For whatever reason, you'll be searching for antiques you can buy at prices low enough to sell and still make a profit.

The obvious and natural reaction you'll have when you sell an antique to a dealer is, "I didn't price it high enough!" Don't be upset. You'll make some profit, and the other dealer will make some profit. Next week you may buy an underpriced antique from him.

Buying Trips

Once you're established and have a strong feel for what your customers will buy, you may want to go on extensive annual buying trips. Many longtime dealers do just this, taking off for Iowa or Maine or some other area and buying dozens of small tables, dressers, hall trees, and other pieces of furniture. They fill box upon box with china, silver, glassware, jewelry, prints, and other antiques. Most of these dealers drive large trucks capable of holding all their purchases.

This is a fine idea as long as a few things fall into place. You can't be off for several weeks in another part of the country buying antiques and in your shop selling them at the same time. If you don't have a partner to keep the shop open, you'll have to either close the shop or hire someone to keep it open for you. To a large extent your decision would be based on your record of sales. If, for example, after one year in business you find your sales are low during January and February, as they are in many antiques shops, you might plan to close the shop for two or three weeks and do your buying then. If sales are consistent year-round, however, you could hire a salesperson to manage the shop while you're gone.

Buying trips can be difficult if you're on your own. If you aren't accustomed to it, you may not feel comfortable driving a large truck for long distances. Many people don't have the shoulder muscles necessary to lift heavy furniture into these trucks by themselves.

An alternative to this is to drive a van, fill it as you go with small items packed in sturdy boxes, and ship larger pieces home by freight. While shipping adds to the cost of the items, you won't have the expense or hassle of driving a large truck.

Pickers

Hidden among the hundreds of people who frequent yard sales and flea markets every weekend are an intrepid group of stealthy buyers. These buyers, called "pickers," aren't there to buy antiques for themselves but for the owners of antiques shops like yourself.

Here's how the picker system works. You create a network of pickers from among people who want the fun and potential profit of buying and selling antiques but who don't want the responsibility of managing a shop. You can recruit these people from among your friends, from people who come to your shop offering their services as pickers, or by simply putting the word out to other dealers and antiques collectors that you're in the market for pickers.

You tell these people the types of antiques you want to buy and what you're willing to pay for them. The prices you can pay pickers for the antiques they bring you depend to a large extent on the condition of the antiques, whether you have to repair or refinish them, and their salability. You don't guarantee to buy everything they bring to you. It's up to them to know what you can readily sell in your shop and to buy at prices low enough to make a profit when they subsequently sell the antiques to you.

For example, there might be a good market in your area for small antique pitchers that retail between $15 and $29. If you, as owner of the shop, have to go out and search for these pitchers yourself, you probably would be willing to pay the sellers between $4 and $7 for them, but the time you'd have to invest in locating these pitchers is worth something. So, your pickers know you'll pay them between $5 and $8 for salable pitchers. They scout secondhand stores, yard sales, consignment auctions, thrift shops, and so forth, looking for pitchers they can pick up for small sums. You pay the pickers $5 to $8 for the pitchers they bring in, and they make a profit on each one they sell to you. Your profit margin when you sell the pitchers is lower than if you had found the pitchers yourself, but you haven't invested any of your time in locating them.

Some pickers in large cities or in areas where there are many antiques dealers make substantial incomes from their business. Most pickers in less populated areas, however, don't expect to make a living from picking. They just want the fun of searching for the antiques as you did at one time. Those who work diligently, though, and come up with good buys can often create nice little side incomes for themselves. Some pickers will call dealers on their cell phones when they come upon an outstanding but pricey item. This way, they know in advance if the dealer is interested.

Inventory of Another Shop

You can create instant inventory for your shop by simply buying out the stock of a dealer who's going out of business. This isn't at all unusual. It's fine as long as you have the finances for the purchase, but the outlay can be considerable.

A real estate agent advertised the sale of an established antiques shop in a commercial location. The offer was for either the property and inventory or the inventory alone. This particular shop had been in business for years, and the owner had acquired a fine stock of excellent antiques. Buying the inventory alone would have been a great way for anyone opening a home-based antiques shop to stock it in a matter of days. Any offer such as this, however, should be examined carefully. Should you be tempted to consider such an offer, you need to check out a few particulars:

If you have limited funds after remodeling and opening your shop, but you still need more quality antiques to stock it, then you can do so by taking in antiques on consignment. This can provide you with three important benefits:

1.   You don't have to buy the antiques out of your own funds, which may be limited at first.

2.   By selecting good-quality consignment items, you increase the look of substance in your shop.

3.   When those antiques sell, you receive a nice commission.

Commission rates vary from area to area, shop to shop. Some dealers charge as little as 20 percent while others charge rates as high as 50 percent. The average seems to be about 30 percent. Check around and find out what other dealers in your area are charging, then do the same.

You'll probably want to modify your commission policy a bit on very expensive items. For instance, if you normally charge 30 percent commission on consignment items but someone brings in an expensive item that needs to sell for $5,000 and over, you could lower your commission to 15 percent and still make a tidy sum.

As an example of how consignment selling works, let's call the person owning the antique Mike and the person owning the shop Kitty. Mike has a walnut side table he wants to sell. He goes to Kitty and asks if she'll take it in and sell it in her shop on consignment. She examines the piece, decides it's good quality and should sell, and agrees to place it in her shop. She explains that her commission is 30 percent on consignment sales. When the table sells for $300, she retains $90 as her commission and Mike gets the remaining $210.

One bit of advice about the antiques you take on consignment: Whether they happen to be Oriental vases or mahogany beds, beveled mirrors or sets of china, you'd be wise to take only high-quality items that will sell for above-average prices. The reason is simply economics. Your commission on high-priced antiques is more than on low-priced items.

Let's say you're offered two library tables to sell on consignment. They're about the same size, and both are equally desirable in your area. The first table is a turn-of-the-century oak table, which has a selling price of $275. The second table is a fine mahogany piece, which can bring $600. You take in both tables and place them in the shop. Each one takes up approximately 9 square feet of the selling floor. Four months later both tables sell on the same day. Your 30 percent commission on the first table is only $82.50, but on the second table it's $180. You're making almost $100 more on the higher-priced table, yet it has required no more display space than the lower-priced one and you probably spent no more time showing and selling it.

If you have plenty of stock yourself, however, you'd be foolish to give up 9 square feet to a consignment antique. Suppose you have a nice library table of the same size as the ones in the above example. You paid $200 for it and price it at $600 (a reasonable markup). When the table sells, your profit is $400, far more than for either of the consignment tables.

Accepting antiques to sell on consignment, therefore, is usually a good policy only if you have plenty of space and not enough of your own antiques to fill that space.

Many dealers seldom take items on consignment unless they know the person who owns them. Why? Because too many people place too high a value on their antiques, especially since *Antiques Roadshow* has aired on PBS. The antiques may also be family pieces and, thus, have sentimental value. Or perhaps the owners bought them in an area with higher prices. Whatever the reason, the owners aren't too logical about setting reasonable selling prices on their antiques. They simply want too much for them, and they expect them to sell quickly, not realizing that a valuable antique can take months to sell. As a result, most dealers do business only with people who understand the realities of selling antiques.

You're probably wondering about the legal ramifications of this system. After all, you're taking someone else's valuable property into your shop. Almost all dealers have some kind of written agreement between them and consignors. It can be as simple as a typed sheet or as formal as one generated and printed using your computer.

You can make up your own consignment agreement, but the form on page 118 is typically used by many dealers. You'll notice on this form that you, as owner of the shop, don't accept responsibility for the consignor's antiques. Your own insurance covers your property and stock in the case of fire or theft, but it probably won't cover consignment antiques. Can the consignor be protected? Maybe. Some homeowner's policies will cover loss or damage of a consigned antique. Many won't. This is the reason you have a written agreement—to forestall any unpleasantness with your consignor in case of a problem.

One dealer learned the value of such an agreement too late. He took in a lovely Vaseline bowl on consignment, without any written agreement, and agreed verbally to price it at $75. He placed the bowl on the floor while rearranging some stock on an upper shelf. A heavy bookend fell off the shelf and landed squarely on it. Horrified, he watched it shatter into a dozen pieces. Since he didn't have an understanding with the owner of the bowl about loss or damage, he felt morally obligated to reimburse her with $75 out of his shop funds.

- *Why is the business being sold?* If the seller is ill or retiring, that's a legitimate reason to put the shop on the market. Be a bit suspicious, however, of any other reason. Perhaps he had invested in too much stock that won't sell in the area. You wouldn't want to buy someone else's mistakes. Examine the inventory carefully to make sure it's the same type that's selling in other antiques shops.
- *Is there a detailed inventory of the antiques being offered?* Without an inventory, you can't make a reasonable estimate of the value of the antiques.
- *Will the seller finance part of the purchase price?* Owner-financing is common in sales of this type. That might be the only way that you, as someone just starting in business, could buy the inventory, since many banks won't lend to owners of new businesses.

Occasionally, entire contents of an antiques shop come up at auction. Such might be the case if the owner has died and his estate needs to be liquidated. All things considered, this can be a good way to stock your shop, but be extremely careful of developing auction fever at the sale. You could easily pay more than the stock is worth if several other dealers are bidding against you. Just as important, you'd almost surely be expected to pay cash for the antiques. There'd be no owner-financing in such a sale.

Date _____

Received from _____

Address _____

Phone number _____

Description of antique _____

_____

Price to be set on antique _____

Commission rate _____

The antique will remain in the shop and on display until _____ ,
on which date the consignor is responsible for picking it up unless other arrangements are made
between consignor and consignee.

It is understood that the consignee is not responsible for damage or theft of the antique while it
is in his shop.

Signed,

_____

Consignor

_____

Consignee

Making Sure an Item Is an Authentic Antique or Collectible

To anyone who browses antiques shops these days, the question, "What is an antique?" seems to have many answers. Side by side with ancient-looking furniture and old-fashioned china, browsers may find ruffled pink glass and souvenir spoons, no older than themselves. The problem bewilders not only buyers but dealers, too.

In 1930, the U.S. government ruled that objects had to be *at least one hundred years old* to be classified as antiques and be admitted duty-free into the United States. But that was a legislative tax decision. Since then, antiques have often been defined as objects made before 1830.

In Europe, items as recent as that seem quite young. In contrast with a classic Roman head, an eighteenth-century chair is modern. Antiques shops in European cities are often called "antiquities" shops. Except for Native American relics and a few Spanish buildings in the Southwest, the oldest American antiques are about 350 years old.

Yet American dealers experience the same contrast in their shops. To a New England dealer who might sell pine furniture from Pilgrim times, a Victorian sofa doesn't seem antique. But in Iowa or Washington it does because it represents the earliest furnishings in the region. The age of antiques seems to vary in relation to their environment. And so the perception of an antique tends to change from region to region.

Americans often count among their antiques items made by machine as well as those wrought by hand. Most handmade items date prior to 1830, which serves as the dividing line between the handcrafted age and the machine age.

The salability of an antique can also depend on the story behind it. As a piece gets handed down from generation to generation, its history takes on added flourishes. A spinning wheel made in 1820 becomes the spinning wheel brought over on the *Mayflower*. A bed from 1790 becomes a bed George Washington slept in.

But while the personal associations of an heirloom add to its interest, they can't be relied upon to place its date and source. Not all old pieces have a pedigree or a maker's mark or label, but each has characteristics that identify it and make it valuable to someone else. The secret of where and when and by whom it was made is in its material, its design, and its workmanship. So an antique is what dealers and collectors perceive it to be.

If you stock what people in your area want to buy, whether it's a genuine Chippendale or Fiesta ware, you'll make money.

How can you be sure the pieces you buy to resell are genuine antiques and not fakes or reproductions? First, there's a world of difference between *fake antique furniture* and *reproduction furniture.* You'll hardly ever be offered fake antique furniture. A fake is a deliberate attempt to deceive by using old construction techniques on wood that's been deliberately distressed to simulate age. The piece is then passed off as an antique. Yes, this does happen, but because the process is so time-consuming, it's usually practiced only by charlatans trying to emulate extremely valuable furniture.

You'll occasionally read about a table or cabinet, supposedly a fine seventeenth-century French piece perhaps, that sold for many thousands of dollars in some prestigious antiques auction house. It later turns out to be a fake. The chances of any of us being offered such a piece are about as good as winning one of those mega-million-dollar sweepstakes prizes.

Reproduction furniture, on the other hand, is furniture constructed with modern methods in the styles of earlier eras. Some of this furniture is of excellent quality, but no manufacturer ever advertises or sells it as antique. A good example is Shaker chairs. Craftsmen construct reproductions of these finely made pieces using original methods, so most sell for almost as much or the same as the genuine article.

The problem occurs when a reproduction passes from hand to hand, garnering wear along the way until it really looks old. All knowledge of its origin is eventually lost, and the present owner might honestly believe it to be an antique. A well-worn reproduction can fool anyone who doesn't have some information on how furniture looked and was made generations ago.

Should you carry reproductions in your shop? Only you can make that decision. Some antiques shops do carry a few reproductions, although many dealers frown on the practice, saying it diminishes the value of genuine antiques. You should probably follow the lead of other shops in your area.

Limit reproductions to small items such as black iron match holders, rhinestone jewelry, and the giftware being reissued today by manufacturers, such as Fenton for example, that distributed the same patterns years ago. Just be sure to label each piece "Reproduction" on the price tag.

Considering Other Items to Sell

You can add substantially to your profits by carrying a few antiques-related items. Here are some of the best sellers.

Reference Books

Collectors are always looking for books to help them learn more about their hobbies or to help them identify pieces they own. These books are easy sales in your shop.

Hundreds of such books have been written by experts on every subject: dolls, toys, chalkware, carnival prizes, marbles, majolica, gambling devices, Oriental pottery, Victorian jewelry—you name it, it's in print. Each book is a valuable source of information for beginning or experienced collectors.

> **Tip:** Keep a small, battery-operated black light in your car when you go shopping for stock. It'll help you detect any hidden crack or repair in china. A black light will also illuminate genuine Vaseline glass with that traditional fluorescent glow, helping you differentiate it from ordinary glass.

Some publishers wholesale their books to antiques shops, and all have catalogs and websites from which you can order. (See listings for some of them in the appendix.) In most cases you have to stock only one book of each title you select, and you buy at a discount of usually 40 percent off the cover price, which allows you to make a decent profit when you sell the books to your customers at the cover prices.

> **Tip:** Consider selling a series of small paperback books, each covering a particular topic about antiques or collectibles, published by Shire Publications, Ltd. of Oxford, England (www.shirebooks.co.uk). These low-priced books, filled with information and good photographs on not only antiques and collectibles but related history, sell for $12 to $20. Place them on your checkout counter and don't forget to recommend an appropriate book when someone buys an antique in your shop.

Determining the Age of Antiques

To determine the age of an item in your shop, you can either look it up in an antiques reference book or online, or you can look for the following characteristics:

Furniture. All old wooden furniture can be identified with simple examinations.

- Size and shape of dovetails on drawers. Dovetails on old furniture are always larger and less symmetrical than those on modern pieces.

- Wood grain. Furniture makers about one hundred years ago often constructed tables, dressers, and such, of quarter-sawn wood. This wood was cut to produce a distinctive wavy pattern, sometimes called tiger oak. This cutting method was extremely wasteful and isn't used today.

- Saw marks. Before the advent of modern machinery, all wood was cut by hand. Whereas cabinetmakers would take great pains to sand and smooth the exterior surface of a piece of furniture, they often left concealed areas quite rough. You can frequently see obvious saw marks on the underside of tables and the backs of case pieces.

- Shrinkage. All wood shrinks in time. With enough time, shrinkage becomes obvious. You'll sometimes see enclosed panels that have split because the cabinetmaker glued the panels into the surrounding framework. The thin panels eventually shrank and the tension caused them to split. Round tables made of a softwood such as pine can become slightly oval in time as the wood shrinks across the grain.

- Normal wear. Any piece of furniture that's been in use for three or four generations is bound to show some wear. The back legs of chairs may be worn where people have leaned back on them. Many case pieces made of softwood will have definite gouges around knobs and handles caused by fingernails hitting the wood. Kneehole desks and dressing tables nearly always have worn areas around their inner edges from chairs being pushed in and out.

Silver. Because silver is a soft metal, the patterns on antique silverware are often slightly blurred from use and polishing. Old silver also has a soft glow, a patina, rather than the brilliant, hard finish of newly made silver.

Glass. A great deal of old pattern glass is being reproduced today, and sometimes it's very difficult to tell the old from the new. However, when a present-day manufacturer produces glassware from old molds, sections of the design will be missing or quite faint. Also, as a rule, the quality of old glass is superior to that of new glass. If in doubt, hold the glass lightly in one hand and tap it with a pencil. Listen for a clear bell-like ring, which indicates that the piece is lead glass. Newer lime glass will thud instead of ring.

New, finely cut crystal, however, is almost indistinguishable from antique crystal. The only clue might be a slight etching of the lower surface from repeated scraping across tables and shelves.

China. As with crystal, fine old china that's been cared for is extremely difficult to distinguish from modern pieces of the same quality. Again, you'll sometimes find a slight roughness on the lower surfaces, which indicates where the piece has been moved back and forth across tables and shelves. Hold a plate at right angles to a strong light, too, and you might see faint lines in the finish caused by the hundreds of times hungry diners cut their meat there. A sure sign of age, though, is the brown tint and crazing that occurs on much old china and pottery, the result of repeated warming in brick ovens or woodstoves.

Here's one problem you're almost sure to run up against in carrying reference books: Many of them are fairly expensive, so some of your customers will ask if they can simply browse through a book, looking for a bit of information they need. Be polite, but refuse the request. If you allow this practice, the books will become dirty and dog-eared, and you'll never sell them.

The best solution is to keep the books in a closed glass case where the dustcovers and titles are clearly visible but where customers can't get to them without your permission. You can put a small notice on the shelf, informing your customers that the books are for purchase only and not for browsing.

Plate and Cup-and-Saucer Holders

These inexpensive items, usually retailing for $3 to $5, are popular with plate and cup-and-saucer collectors. Keep a few holders on display, and always ask the customer who has just purchased a fine plate or cup and saucer if he or she needs a holder. Often, customers will purchase as many as five or six at a time.

Furniture and Metal Polish

Furniture polishes and silver creams are also good sellers. Don't carry ordinary grocery-store brands, but the ones used most often by professional restorers.

After purchasing an antique, a customer will often ask, "What do you recommend I use to clean and care for this walnut chest (or silver vase, or whatever)?" Bring out a bottle or jar of one of your special cleaning or polishing products, and she's almost sure to buy it. The customer will thank you for helping to keep the antique beautiful, and you'll make a few dollars profit. You'll find many of these creams and polishes advertised in the antiques trade journals. Van Dyck's Restorers (www.vandykes.com) offers a good selection.

> Tip: Consider creating a one-page flyer with tips for maintaining antique furniture and the like. Eventually, make up a separate sheet for furniture, porcelain and ceramics, and silver. Give the appropriate flyer to customers when they purchase one of those items.

Handcrafted Accessories

You can add color to your shop *and* your profits by carrying, on consignment, a few handcrafted, old-fashioned-looking decorative accessories. These can be embroidered linens, rag dolls, quilted pillows, pot holders, and so on. One dealer always stocks charming Christmas stockings around the middle of November. The person who makes them for him fashions them to look as if they're made from old crazy quilts.

Whatever you decide to carry, be careful to accept only top-quality crafts, the type you see in the best shops, and beware of loading your shop down with too many artsy-craftsy items. The "old country store" look turns off many customers and detracts from your main purpose—to sell antiques.

Potpourri

Few things are as nostalgic as fragrant potpourri, and the ambience is perfect for an antiques shop, but don't overdo it. Place a basket filled with little bags of potpourri on your checkout counter, priced at $4 or $5 a bag. The bags sell quickly, and they add a pleasant aroma to your shop. Potpourri is a breeze to package too. Just place about one-half cup of prepared potpourri on squares of colorful net, gather the net up, tie with a pretty ribbon, and you're in business. You'll find directions for making potpourri and some recipes on the following pages.

Traditionally, people make potpourri from summer garden flowers, dried, then mixed with spices and aromatic oils. Even if you don't have a green thumb, there's an easy way to get literally armfuls of colorful roses and other flowers at absolutely no cost from your local florists and morticians. These people discard thousands of flowers every year, and most of them are more than happy to let you cart the surplus away. Be sure to call the day after a special day like Mother's Day or immediately following a funeral.

Florists, for example, have to stock large quantities of flowers for Valentine's Day, prom nights, Easter, and Christmas. Often on the day following the event, they'll have buckets of flowers left over that are a trifle past their prime and can't be sold. These blossoms are perfect for potpourri. All you have to do is make arrangements in advance to pick up these leftovers.

After many funerals, the family doesn't want to take the flowers home or to the cemetery. Ask the mortician to call you if the flowers from a funeral are to be discarded, not donated to a hospital or nursing home. All you have to do is go there and load them into your vehicle.

Making and packaging potpourri can be a fine activity to keep you busy in the shop during slow periods. (See pages 126-127 for ideas.)

Gift Certificates

Gift certificates made out on little pieces of paper can provide you with a welcome source of income. So often your customers will come into the shop, browse around, and then say in desperation, "I want to get a gift for my _____ [fill in the blank—son's teacher/mother-in-law/boss/secret pal/next-door neighbor, or whatever], and I have no idea what she would like." That's when you suggest a gift certificate, a guarantee of a future sale. Some office supply stores carry generic gift certificates, or you can have custom ones printed at a copy center. You can also

Potpourri is a mixture of five basic ingredients: dried flower petals or other natural material, herbs, spices, essential oils, and fixatives. The resulting fragrance, whether spicy or delicate, woodsy or tangy, depends on the dried materials used and the aroma of the oils blended into the natural materials. Roses, lavender, and tuberoses are the only flowers that retain their natural scent when dried. You'll use other flowers to add bulk to the mixture, and the oils to provide the fragrance.

People enjoy the best potpourris for their color almost as much as for their scent. The drying process nearly always softens the natural color of flower petals— strawflowers are a major exception—so choose the brightest flowers for your own mixtures. Other than strawflowers, some of the best for color are roses, hollyhocks, larkspur, cornflowers, marigolds, heather, purple violets, lilacs, blue delphiniums, and lavender.

Basic Potpourri Mixture
4 quarts dried flower petals

4 tablespoons dried herbs

4 tablespoons crushed spices

2 teaspoons essential oil

4 tablespoons fixative (orrisroot or ground coriander)

(The ingredients listed above are only approximate and may be varied according to what you have available. However, follow the mixing and storage directions as given.)

You can adapt this recipe to almost any combination of flowers, herbs, and oils:

Mix dried flowers and herbs gently in a large plastic bag. Add crushed spices and mix gently. Sprinkle essential oil over mixture and blend gently with dry ingredients. Sprinkle fixative over mixture and toss lightly to blend. Place potpourri in a crock or plastic bag and seal tightly. Mix gently from top to bottom and side to side every three or four days to help the fragrance develop and blend. The potpourri will be mature and ready to use in about one month.

Here are some sample mixtures:

Summer Rose Potpourri

4 quarts dried rose petals and other flowers

4 tablespoons rosemary

2 tablespoons crushed cloves

2 tablespoons crushed cinnamon bark

2 teaspoons essential oil of rose

2 tablespoons orrisroot

2 tablespoons coriander

Happy Holidays Potpourri

4 quarts dried pine needles, finely chipped pine bark, and dried berries

2 tablespoons dried mint or eucalyptus leaves

2 tablespoons crushed bay leaves

2 tablespoons marjoram

2 tablespoons crushed nutmeg

2 teaspoons essential oil of pine or sandalwood

4 tablespoons orrisroot

Lavender Lace Potpourri

4 quarts dried lavender and other flower petals

2 tablespoons thyme

2 tablespoons dried mint

4 tablespoons dried orange peel

2 teaspoons oil of lavender

4 tablespoons orrisroot

print them yourself using your word processor by downloading templates for them from the Internet.

An attractive sign that says GIFT CERTIFICATES AVAILABLE on your checkout counter will encourage your customers to purchase them, putting money in your pocket.

Working with the Seasons

Surviving the Slow Season

As mentioned before, your sales will probably fall off during January and February. This is just a normal phenomenon of the antiques business. People will come into your shop, of course, but not many of them will be looking for high-ticket antiques. You can help bridge those slow months, however, by stocking and displaying a large supply of low- to medium-priced antiques and collectibles. A sterling silver coffeepot may sit on the shelf gathering dust during those months, while you sell many souvenir spoons, prints, linens, and kitchen collectibles.

Taking Advantage of the Tourist Season

Do you have a steady tourist clientele during a particular time of year? Those visitors can be excellent customers, since they're in a spending mood, so cater to their needs and wants. I've found that many tourists will buy small or flat antiques without a qualm, because these things fit easily into a suitcase or carry-on bag. On the other hand, they hesitate to buy a large or bulky antique even if they genuinely want it. In most cases they'd have to ship the antique home, adding substantially to its cost or the chance of damage.

With this in mind, a couple of weeks before your tourist season starts, you might remove many of your bulkier antiques from the shelves and replace them with smaller items. Remember, that tourists love to buy souvenirs, even older ones. Cater to those souvenir hunters by stocking items such as: paperweights, ashtrays, salt and pepper shakers, pens, sterling silver spoons, ruby stained-glass pitchers and glasses, cups and saucers, and small dolls. And don't forget to place a box of old photographs or picture postcards of nearby attractions on your checkout counter.

## 06

Buying and Selling Antiques on the Internet

The Internet has become not only a viable market for antiques and collectibles but, for some, a profitable one. You, too, can cash in on this bonanza, either as a supplement to your shop sales or as an independent source of antiques income.

The condition of the antiques market has changed radically since eBay opened for business in late 1995. Until then, collectors built their collections over time. In fact, creating a sizable collection required hours visiting yard and garage sales, flea markets, antiques malls, antiques shows, and auctions. Most collectors frequented shops and malls close to home because they didn't have the means to travel all over the country searching for pieces to add to their collections.

Today, the Internet offers a vast national and international market—eBay, alone, offers hundreds of thousands of antiques and collectibles—that collectors can access from their home computer anytime day or night. Thanks to eBay and online antiques malls, buying and selling antiques online offers a world of possibilities. Created to sell Pez dispensers, eBay controlled the online antiques market for a while, but the concept caught on and now there are many Internet auction sites, although eBay is still the largest.

The popularity and success of online auctions create opportunities for you. You can use software tools to create eye-catching advertisements, have counters to keep track of how many visitors look at your page or site, and search for the best deals among several sites if you're buying.

If you're already using the Internet, you can skip the following section and go straight to the Advantages of Buying and Selling section on page 131.

Getting on the Internet

While most home-based antiques dealers today connect to the Internet through a high-speed broadband connection provided by their phone or cable television company, you can also access it through a dial-up modem using your home telephone line. A dial-up connection will work just fine to buy and sell online. Of course, you'll need to be computer-savvy. If you're one of those people who have avoided computers like the plague, perhaps it's time to take a continuing education course in basic computer operation from a local college or at your public library.

Before you begin to use the Internet, you'll need to sign up with an Internet Service Provider (ISP). While there are many choices out there, you need to select one that fits your budget. Unlimited dial-up connections cost approximately $25 per month through Verizon, AT&T, and Earthlink. You'll pay more—anywhere from $30 to $60 per month—for high-speed service which comes in three varieties: DSL, Wi-Fi, and cable modem. Of the three, cable modems provide the highest speeds, but they are also the most expensive at $60 per month. DSLs (digital subscriber lines), at $15 to $20 per month, require that your computer be within 18,000 feet of the transmission tower. If you're not, you can't get connected. And Wi-Fi, the latest innovation at a minimum of $30 per month, requires that your computer be set up for wireless transmission. As of this writing, Verizon offers what it calls its FIOS service. But this is not only a very expensive option but also requires that all your phone lines be replaced with new fiber optic ones—a messy process. Many people sign up with America Online (AOL), but because there are so many people using it, getting online can be a problem at times.

If you choose a dial-up connection, be sure your ISP offers local dial-up numbers. Check with the company about this before you sign up. You may find yourself paying hefty long-distance charges over and above your monthly Internet charge.

You'll also need software called a browser that opens to the Internet. Microsoft's Internet Explorer, which comes included with any version of Windows, and Mozilla's Firefox are the two most commonly used. Once you open your browser window, you can point the browser where you want to go by typing the Internet address or URL (uniform resource locator) into the browser's address line. Every site on the web, as the Internet is commonly known, has its own unique URL.

Web designers use HTML (hypertext markup language) to create web pages and sites. These hypertext links allow you to go from one site to another or one page to another or one part of a page to another. Every website also has a domain name preceded by www, which stands for World Wide Web. Most of the domain names of the antiques sites you'll be visiting end in dot-com, which stands for "commercial." For instance, the URL for The Antiques Almanac, an informational antiques site, is www.theantiquesalmanac.com.

But the Internet is huge, with several billion sites and growing. So you'll need to use what's called a search engine to find what you're looking for. One of the best search engines is Google (www.google.com). By typing a keyword—that is, a word or phrase that directly represents what you're looking for, such as "Parian Ware"—into the Google keyword space, then clicking on "Google Search," you'll be given a list of sites that match your search. You can search either for websites themselves or the images on them.

Advantages of Buying and Selling on the Internet

Buying and selling antiques and collectibles on the Internet does have its advantages:

- *It eliminates time-consuming shopping for stock.* Locating salable stock can take you hours each week attending auctions, estate sales, responding to "for sale" ads in the newspaper. Sometimes you come back with a car full of quality stock, sometimes it's time totally wasted. But shopping for stock online is fast. All it takes is just a few clicks of your computer's mouse.

  A big problem faced by most dealers who manage their shops alone is even being able to scout out the estate/garage sales and auctions. The best buys at estate and garage sales are always on Fridays. Auctions are nearly always held on Saturdays. Yet weekends are the times your antiques shop should be open with you there to attend to customers. If you don't have a savvy friend, willing spouse, or excellent part-time help, you simply can't attend those weekend sales.

  Online selling, though, goes on twenty-four hours a day, seven days a week so you can buy when it's convenient for you.

- *Is ideal if you live in an out-of-the-way location.* Many small towns offer few consistently reliable places to buy a wide variety of stock. However, every day the Internet lists thousands of antiques for sale—all prices, all periods, all descriptions. At online auctions, you can find everything from an Elvis record going for $5 to an emerald and diamond necklace listed for more than $5,000.

So if you buy on the Internet, you can stock a wide selection of salable inventory—funky fifties memorabilia, trendy Art Deco accessories, and genuine quality antiques. Your customers will return again and again because they know they'll always find new and interesting items to purchase. This isn't the case in shops managed by dealers who rely only on local or area sources for their stock. Too often the choice in one shop is almost identical to that in another shop because all the dealers buy from the same sources and from each other.

- *It helps you if you're a part-time antiques dealer.* Perhaps you decided to keep your regular job until you build up a reliable antiques clientele, and so open your home-based shop only during certain hours or on weekends. You can buy and sell on the Internet whenever you have a free hour or two.

  Or perhaps you live in an area where you make a substantial part of your income from the tourist trade. In that case, you'll stay open long hours seven days a week during the summer, but close up for two or three months midwinter. During those same months few locals will brave a raging blizzard to shop for antiques. But you can sit home on cold, snowy days, relax by the fire, and through the Internet buy enough stock to carry you for months once you open in the spring.

- *It eases shopping for special orders.* Few things can do more to inspire enthusiasm among your customers than for you to be able to fill special orders. Yet, this can be a genuine problem if you have to rely on traditional buying sources.

  How often, for example, can you locate a cup and saucer of an obscure pattern to fill out a customer's china set? Yet, if you closely watch items listed on the Internet, the chances are good someone out there has just that cup and saucer for sale. One more sale made. One more happy customer.

- *Reaches customers worldwide.* No longer do you have to depend upon customers in your own area. By using the Internet, you can be anywhere and can sell to customers anywhere in the world.

- *The Internet offers unique items for sale.* You may someday come upon an especially unique antique or collectible, one perhaps desired by only half a dozen people on the planet. Most dealers who maintain shops would pass that item up, knowing the chances of one of those six people coming into the shop are virtually impossible. Yet, the very collectors of those unique items scan the Internet regularly, searching for one more piece to fill out their collections.

A dealer at an estate sale discovered, along with a few other items, two strange brass tubes that contained an apparatus he didn't understand. His instinct kicked in, though, and he paid $5 for the two. He did some research and discovered the tubes were two of the earliest calculators, invented in Germany sixty years ago—a rare find indeed.

The dealer immediately listed them on eBay. Within the week he sold each tube for a hundred times that $5 to a fellow in Tokyo who collects just such devices.

■ *The Internet develops regular customers for certain collectibles.* Every shop-based antiques dealer tries to cultivate regular customers by searching for items that will fill out their collections. Dealers on the Internet do the same. The difference is that the Internet dealer has a vastly larger audience than the dealer who only maintains a shop.

One dealer specializes in selling collectible books and cameras. Now that he's expanded to selling on the Internet he has more than doubled his clientele list. He has a loyal following of buyers there who look for his unique username among the dozens of dealers selling on the Internet. They know the items he lists will be of top quality and well worth the asked price.

Disadvantages of Buying and Selling on the Internet

And just as there are plenty of advantages to buying and selling on the Internet, there are a couple of disadvantages.

■ *Prices are not wholesale.* Remember that many, if not most, of the buyers on the Internet are collectors, not dealers who plan to sell everything they buy there. Collectors are usually willing to pay a reasonable retail price for any item that will help fill out their collections.

With that in mind, the final bid for any desirable antique or collectible is almost bound to reach that reasonable retail price. Often it will go much higher, just as happens at a traditional auction.

You can hardly pay that high a price and still expect to resell the item for a profit. The profit has already been made by the seller of the item, who purchased it at a much lower price somewhere else, then offered it for sale on the Internet, figuring to make the usual profit when it sold. You would have to factor in your own overhead to the purchase price, plus add a percentage for profit. (See chapter 7 for a discussion on markup as it relates to profit.) The resulting figure—auction purchase price + overhead + profit— you'd have to list as a *minimum* starting bid for the item would be more than most collectors would pay. For that reason, many dealers don't buy on the Internet.

■ *There's no place for socializing.* Another, more personal, disadvantage of buying and selling on the Internet is the lack of one-on-one contact with customers. One of the reasons most people enjoy dealing in antiques is the personal contact they have with their customers. Lovers of antiques get just as much pleasure talking about their collections as they do bragging about their children or relating the latest antic their cat pulled.

There's little of that on the Internet. Regular dealers on the Internet do develop a few customers who contact them personally by e-mail, but the number is negligible.

In most cases the relationship between sellers and buyers remains purely business—you offer an antique or collectible, some faceless buyer makes a high bid. Money arrives in your bank account. You ship the antique to the buyer. You and the buyer know no more about one another after the transaction than you did before. And you have no more intimate association with the items you're selling than mere household goods.

The issue of fraud on the Internet is discussed on page 136.

Selling through Internet Auction Sites

Several sites on the Internet now hold either auctions or outright sales of antiques for dealers. You'll need to register with them before you can buy or sell, but there's no fee for registration. The process is quite simple and easily handled with simple directions online.

The largest of the online auction sites, with tens of millions of registered customers, is eBay.

To register with eBay, go to the website at www.ebay.com and click on the "sign in" link. You'll be asked to "click here to register." After you answer a couple of questions, the registration form will come up on the screen. You'll fill in your name, address, phone number, and e-mail address. After you choose a unique username and password and click submit, you'll be registered to buy and sell on eBay.

Once you're registered on eBay, you may list one item or a dozen, but to be successful, you'll need to list dozens of antiques and collectibles for sale at any one time. Although you may be a dealer on several auction sites, you shouldn't ever list the same item on any two at the same time.

> **Tip:** You'll have better luck starting out with a low opening bid. This encourages buyers to bid against each other. If you're afraid you won't get enough for an item, you can list it as "Buy It Now" or a combination of an auction bid and a "Buy It Now" price.

To list an item, you'll fill out a short on-screen form that asks you to describe the item, tell which category it should be in, state the minimum bid you'll accept, and determine how long you wish it to be listed.

Since eBay contains thousands of listings on any given day, most serious buyers click directly onto the specific categories that interest them. One buyer may only want to bid on Civil War memorabilia, so he'll go directly to that site. Another may be trying to fill out a set of Haviland china, so she goes to that site, ignoring all others. For those reasons, you should be quite specific when listing the category of any antique or collectible.

EBay requires you to include a clear photograph along with your antique's description and offers instructions on how to do this. You can use a scanner or a digital camera to transfer an image to the screen. With the cost of a good compact 4.0 to 7.0 -megapixel digital camera, which is sufficient for taking photos to be used online, at $150 to $200, many antiques dealers choose to take their own photos.

Since this is an auction, not a retail shop, is there any way to determine what the eventual high bid on an antique might be? Sometimes. You can set what's called a "reserve" when you list the antique. This reserve is the minimum price you would accept as a final bid. If that minimum is not met, the auction site will pull the item from the auction. However, the site will often list it again at no cost to you.

Instead of setting a reserve figure, you can simply list the antique with no minimum bid. You'll take a chance that the final bid will be high enough for you to make a profit on the antique. But that can be risky. Study the auction sites carefully and watch for final bids on antiques. In your opinion, are the purchase prices in line with the value of antiques? Could you have made a profit on similar items selling them at those prices?

You must also list a closing date for bidding on any item. Most eBay dealers list items for seven days from the time the antique comes up for auction. The bidding for that item will end at a specific time on that date exactly 168 hours after the auction began, and the person entering the highest bid by that time wins the item. Bidding sometimes becomes hot and heavy as the time runs out on a particularly desirable antique.

Once a bidder wins the item, the auction site notifies both you, the seller, and the buyer. You then send the buyer an invoice, including shipping fees, by e-mail requesting payment. In eBay's case, this all happens within their messaging system because eBay frowns upon sellers and buyers communicating privately.

Many antiques dealers who sell online accept money orders, cashier's checks, or personal checks as payment for an antique. Some accept MasterCard and Visa. In the case of personal checks, the dealer waits until they clear before shipping the item. However, the most popular and safest method of payment is through PayPal (www.paypal.com), through which a buyer can send cash directly from his or her bank account or alternatively use a major credit card. This eliminates all the risk for both parties.

Buyers over the Internet can be incredibly trusting of the dealers. One dealer said he had sold a rare manuscript for $455. The buyer said payment would be coming immediately. It arrived in cash within three days. He had stuffed the bills into a plain envelope that didn't even have a security lining.

How Reliable Are Internet Purchases?

If you haven't bought or sold anything on the Internet before, you may be inclined to ask, "How can I be sure the purchased item will be as described? Suppose it's damaged? Cracked? Chipped? Torn? Or even worse—a reproduction?" And if you're selling, "How can I be sure I'll be paid for the antique?"

Both the auction site and the buyers rate dealers who sell on the Internet. Each dealer's identifying username accompanies every offer to sell.

The auction sites encourage buyers to report their experiences with individual dealers by leaving feedback. Did the dealer ship promptly? Did the seller pack the merchandise well? Was the antique exactly as described and as pictured? While one or two poor ratings might simply be sour grapes, more than that usually means the dealer isn't legitimate. If complaints continue, the auction site could drop them.

Buyers are also rated—by dealers. Each buyer also has an identifying username that comes up on the screen whenever the buyer makes a high bid for an item. If for any reason the purchase doesn't go through, the dealer makes a complaint to the site. Maybe the buyer's check wasn't good. Maybe she backed out after the bidding closed and reneged on the purchase. Dealers know then to avoid taking bids from that person.

Regular professional buyers and sellers understand this rating system. It helps them make businesslike decisions about their transactions. You'll quickly catch on to the system, too, once you start buying and selling on the Internet.

The vast majority of sales on the Internet go through with no problems. Getting paid for an antique you sell is seldom an issue. If the winning bidder backs out and doesn't send payment, you can always contact the person who was the next highest bidder in the auction and see if he or she wants to buy the item.

But suppose you have a complaint about something *you* buy. Perhaps the item became damaged in transit or isn't as represented. What do you do? If you feel you've been defrauded, you do have resources. First, contact the seller through the auction site using official channels. If this direct method doesn't resolve the problem, file a formal complaint with the auction site which will intercede on your behalf. Though sometimes problems occur from lack of communication, sometimes it's an unscrupulous dealer who has built up a history of such problems. Try to resolve the problem yourself with the seller.

The Better Business Bureau is also a resource if the seller is a business. Mail fraud issues can be addressed to the United States Postal Service or the U.S. Attorney General.

Now, what is it going to cost you to sell your antiques on the Internet? Registration with the auction sites is free. However, there are selling charges. At this writing, eBay charges an Insertion Fee that ranges from free for items starting at 99 cents up to $200 for those listed over $200 for an auction-style listings. If you choose to sell an item with a "Buy-It-Now" fixed price, you'll pay 50 cents for prices of 99 cents

Sign Up with eBay

_____ Become a registered eBay seller.

_____ Let eBay know how you would like to pay your seller fees.

_____ Set up an eBay seller's account.

_____ Select the methods of payment from buyers—PayPal, credit card, or personal or cashiers check.

_____ Make sure your Feedback profile is on public view.

_____ Sign up to accept PayPal.

Research Your Item

_____ Look for similar items that have recently sold on eBay to help you select the best category and price.

_____ Plan your pricing by checking completed listings to see what similar items have sold for and visit other dealers' eBay stores to find out what price to begin with.

_____ Learn your item's true market value and how it compares to similar ones.

_____ Select a selling format—Auction-style or Buy-It-Now fixed price.

_____ Calculate shipping costs and look at other ways you can optimize your shipping.

Create Your Item Listing

_____ Include important details about your item, based on the category you've chosen.

_____ Fill in item specifics such as its style, size, and condition.

_____ Compose a clear and descriptive title for your listing in fifty-five or fewer letters and spaces.

_____ Take one or more digital photos of your item in a well-lit area. Avoid using a flash.

_____ Create a detailed description of your item, including what it is, who made it, what material it's made of, and its condition, as well as any special history or how you took possession of the item. Provide as many details as possible.

_____ Decide which shipping method you'll use. Pack your item, weigh it, and measure its height, length, and width.

_____ Decide if you want to sell your item nationally or internationally.

_____ Decide on the terms of your return policy.

_____ Review your listing for accuracy.

Set Up Your Seller Contact and Question & Answer Page

_____ Set up the "Ask a Question" link in your listing.

_____ Create a "Contact Seller" button.

_____ Respond quickly to buyers questions before, during, and after the sale.

Manage Your Listing

_____ Answer all questions you receive from potential buyers quickly.

_____ Send the buyer an invoice.

_____ Respond quickly to payment notification and ship the item using the method you specified in your listing.

and above. And if you choose to set a reserve price on your item, you'll pay $2 up to $200 and 1 percent of the reserve price above that amount.

If your item sells, you'll be charged a Final Value Fee of 9 percent of the sale price for an auction listing and 12 percent of the price for a fixed-price "Buy-It-Now" listing. If the item doesn't sell, you're charged nothing.

EBay and other auction sites offer listing upgrades, such as extra pictures, bold-face type, subtitles, and so on. These range from 10 cents to $2 for auction listings and 10 cents to $4 for "Buy-It-Now" fixed-price listings.

Selling through Internet Antiques Malls: TIAS

TIAS is an online site that's quite similar to a traditional antiques mall. Instead of putting antiques up for auction with no real guarantee as to the final selling price as with eBay, TIAS places them in an online catalog from which collectors buy. The dealer sets a firm price on the item and lists it at that figure.

Though small compared to the auction sites, TIAS now offers more than 800 dealers, but it has one advantage for those of us who are antiques dealers: TIAS lists *only* antiques and collectibles in traditional categories, instead of a wide variety of merchandise. So, theoretically at least, it's easier for collectors to locate the items they want.

As a TIAS dealer, you'll be required to maintain a minimum of at least one hundred items for sale at all times, and the combined value must be at least $5,000. Each item must be illustrated with a photograph. Unlike the auction sites, TIAS dealers must maintain some sort of physical address—either a street address or a post office box number. They must provide a minimum of a seven-day return policy on anything sold through the site.

TIAS offers its dealers a choice of two packages: a 10 percent commission on the antiques sold or a flat fee based on the amount of space used on the site by the dealer. Most dealers choose the first option since they pay nothing if nothing sells.

If you don't already have a merchant credit card account, TIAS will provide one for a onetime fee of $100. For more information about becoming a TIAS dealer, go to the website at www.tias.com. Click on the "sell" link. You'll be given complete information about TIAS, then asked for your e-mail address. Within minutes you can be registered and ready to begin listing your antiques for sale.

You may remove an antique from the TIAS site anytime or keep it listed as long as you like. Is there a disadvantage to this policy? Some dealers think so. Some sell only through the auctions, not through TIAS. To make a living as an antiques dealer, you must have a fast turnover of your merchandise. That turnover averages about six to seven days from the time you list an item on eBay until it sells. On TIAS, you might keep your merchandise listed for much longer before finding a buyer. Only you can decide if you can afford to do that.

Selling through Your Own Website

Perhaps you've thought about the possibility of selling antiques through your own website. While this may work well for experienced dealers looking to promote themselves as high-end antiques dealers, it's not such a good idea when you're just starting out.

Sure, you'll find plenty of website host companies offering website builders, such as Website Tonight by GoDaddy.com (www.godaddy.com). Unfortunately, these utilize easy-to-use pre-designed templates to maximize efficiency and keep costs either free or low. As a new business, you need to not only sell antiques but make a good impression. That means your site needs to look as professional as possible. Premade templates just don't make the grade in most cases.

To create a professional site, one that not only shows off your merchandise but also has the necessary tools to make it easy for customers to buy and pay for your items—you need to hire a professional web designer. A professionally designed site will cost you between $1,500 and $2,500—and that's only to get it up and running. Chances are you won't have the technical expertise to maintain it, so you'll have to pay the designer an additional fee each time you add more items.

You'll also need to promote your site through the online search engines, namely Google. Customers won't come to it unless you tell them about it and make it easy to find.

Are eBay and TIAS looking better? For most dealers, especially ones selling smaller antiques and collectibles, selling from one of the existing auction sites or antique malls is much more practical than going it alone. The auction sites and malls do all of the above for you.

If you've decided that you really want your own website, you'll need to choose a domain name. After determining that the domain name you choose is available, you'll register it online. You'll pay a small fee of $10 to $15 that will cover the use of that name for a year. You'll have to renew this annually or purchase it for multiple years at a time. You can then design your own website.

Some points to remember:

- Make the design attractive with pleasing graphics, *but* keep it simple and easy to navigate—no irritating flashing lights or loud music.
- Choose a website address that will be easy for your customers to remember and spell, preferably one containing your shop of business name, such as www.alexandersantiques.com.

While thousands of businesses now have their own websites, home-based antiques dealers are more likely to sell through eBay or one of the online antiques malls. But even a simple site will give you a presence on the web where you customers can find out more about you and the kind of antiques and collectibles you sell.

Eliminating the Home Shop

If you aren't able to or don't want to maintain an antiques business in your home right now, but think you might in the future, you could start out selling online.

This way you can sell on your own time schedule, especially if you're still employed elsewhere.

Another option is to rent space in a local antiques mall where someone else takes care of the selling. You'll search for antiques and collectibles on weekends during your days off, then take them to the mall. While this can work out well and you can make some money, you may discover that you can make more by selling those same items on the Internet, saving the time needed to set up and maintain your booth for other pursuits. After successfully selling antiques and collectibles online, you can establish yourself as a dealer and set up an online shop.

Selling Antiques Online

Begin by selling individual items on eBay, for example. Set up a routine for posting your listings, then packing and shipping them. You might want to designate a room in your house as you staging center, with inexpensive steel shelving to store items until they're sold. You'll also have to stock packing material—Styrofoam peanuts, bubble wrap, air-filled plastic cushions, and plenty of boxes and manila envelopes of various sizes. Save money by recycling all of these supplies. Let your friends and family know you're selling online, so they can give you the packing materials and boxes from shipments they've received. Your staging room should also contain your computer. Arrange everything in efficient order, so you'll be able to fill orders in as little time as possible.

> Tip: Many eBay sellers post their listings on a particular day of the week with Saturday and Sunday being the most common. You have the best chance of getting a good price if an auction closes over the weekend when most people shop online. Also, start out with a low bid such as 99 cents. This encourages buyers to bid against each other and bid the price of the item up, bringing in a higher amount for it. (See Checklist for Selling on eBay earlier in this chapter.)

07 Overhead, Pricing, and Markup

While profit may not be your only reason for opening an antiques shop, you wouldn't be in the antiques business if you didn't expect a reasonable return on your financial investment, even though you enjoy working with antiques. You also expect to be compensated for your time spent in researching current values, studying trends, and locating the antiques you'll sell.

To achieve a good return, you need to know more than antiques, themselves. You need to understand how to price them to make a profit. The Small Business Administration suggests you take three main things into consideration as you price your merchandise:

1. your overhead in operating your shop
2. your time and research involved in buying the antiques
3. the demands of the market

The Realities of Overhead

Some first-time dealers in antiques have trouble factoring the operating expenses or the overhead of their shops into the prices they place on their antiques. Too many of them underestimate the amount of money it will take to keep the doors open, so they underprice their stock. They think that if they buy an antique for $25 and sell it for $50, they've made $25 profit—not by a long shot. Don't fall into this trap. Out of that $25 must come a portion of all your overhead expenses.

Your overhead is the non-merchandise expenses as listed in the chart on pages 88–89, and also includes a percentage of your rent or mortgage payments, taxes, utilities, and home insurance. You'll also have to include your shop telephone, insurance on your stock, professional services from an attorney and accountant, advertising, employees' wages (if any), professional books and subscriptions, vehicle expenses, supplies, and maintenance on your home/shop.

Some of your expenses—mortgage or rent payments, supplies, and so forth—will remain pretty much the same from month to month. Others, however—taxes and insurance for example—will be paid quarterly, not monthly. Attorney fees may occur only two or three times a year. The cost of utilities varies widely from midwinter to midsummer.

As a result, a record of expenses and income for one month, such as those listed on pages 90–91 is not really indicative of your overall overhead and profit. Although these monthly figures are certainly valuable in helping you know early on whether you're heading in the right direction, they reflect your overhead and income *only for* that one month. To arrive at realistic figures for your overall overhead, you must calculate your expenses and income on an *annual* basis. Your cash flow statement is a big help in doing this.

In chapter 4 you saw how to figure your non-merchandise expenses per month and how to forward the expenses from one month to the next, resulting in an annual total of expenses. At the end of the year, you'll divide that annual total of expenses by 12 for a rough estimate of your overhead per month. As noted in chapter 3, you should review and adjust your business plan at the end of your first year in business. This figure—average overhead per month—will be one of those adjustments. To make a profit, you have to price your antiques to cover their initial costs, plus your average overhead per month.

Calculating the Overhead per Antique

To be honest, as an antiques dealer, you cannot add a specific, preset percentage above cost to each antique. Although most other retail business owners do follow such a plan, they buy their merchandise from wholesalers at standard prices, add a standard markup percentage, and then sell the merchandise at standard prices.

For example, the owner of an auto parts store will buy a carton of twelve dozen spark plugs from a wholesaler for a standard catalog price, add his own specific markup, and then sell each spark plug for a standard price. He'll add the same markup percentage to batteries, radiator belts, and windshield wipers. The vendors he buys from will sell the same spark plugs, batteries, radiator belts, and windshield wipers to other auto parts dealers for the same wholesale prices, and the dealers will retail them to the public for approximately the same prices. So, the prices of those items will be fairly consistent throughout an industry.

You won't buy your antiques in large lots from wholesalers at standardized prices. You may come upon a great bargain and can easily price an antique at 200 percent, 300 percent, or even a higher percentage above its cost to you. At other times you'll be lucky to get 75 percent above your costs. Consequently, don't figure on adding a preset percentage to each antique to cover your overhead. It just doesn't work that way. Simply try to price each antique so that the average markup will cover your overhead and give you a profit. Somehow, the ability to do this just seems to come naturally after a while. It's a combination of careful buying, research into current values, and experience in selling similar antiques.

In spite of this imprecise pricing system, you'll be in complete control of the prices you place on your stock, something that makes antiques dealers the envy of other retailers. No manufacturer sets the prices you must charge. Your antiques don't arrive on the shelf in a shiny cardboard box with a preprinted price and a bar code. Just as important, virtually everything in your shop is unique, one of a kind, so it's highly unlikely that any other shop in town will have an identical piece. To make a profit, you'll need to keep a close watch on your expenses, then price your individual antiques so that overall you'll show a profit.

Tip: In setting your policies on prices, consider the following:

- what services you're offering

- what your customers expect to pay

- what your competition is charging

- the area in which you live

Prices for the same antiques vary from town to town, region to region, and state to state throughout the country. Supply and demand play an important part in how much you can charge for any antique.

Setting Your Prices

Economists, when counseling novice retailers about pricing, mention three philosophies open to them:

1. They can sell below the prevailing market prices for similar merchandise.
2. They can price their merchandise at approximately the same level as that of other dealers.
3. They can sell at prices above those of most other dealers.

So how can you, a home-based antiques dealer, apply these philosophies to your shop?

Pricing below the Competition

This is a difficult policy to maintain for long and is seldom successful. If you work on a low profit margin, you must make up for the dollar loss by a high volume of sales combined with low overhead. To consistently follow this policy, you'll have to operate in the following way:

- Own your home outright and have no mortgage payments. *Problem:* You may someday want to use your property as collateral for a loan to expand your selling area. Then you would have payments to make. So it's best to figure a mortgage payment into your overhead right from the start.
- Advertise only on special occasions such as annual sales. *Problem:* This is not good marketing. Statistically, the shop that advertises consistently draws customers. The one that doesn't advertise loses them.
- Plan on a fast turnover of your merchandise. *Problem:* This would be great if you could count on it. But weather, a sluggish economy, changing tastes, or any number of other factors can mean occasional slow months for even the most successful shop.
- Buy only at very low prices. *Problem:* This is a fine practice if you can keep it up. Consistently paying rock-bottom prices, though, almost guarantees that you'll carry only low-grade antiques and collectibles. Customers looking for quality antiques won't waste their time coming to your shop.
- Carry only low-priced antiques and collectibles. *Problem:* As above, you'll attract only customers looking for low-quality merchandise. In the antiques

business, most dealers feel they must sell a few high-ticket antiques regularly to make a profit.

■ Offer few or no services. This is not really a problem, as most customers of flea-market-type shops don't expect services.

Competitive Pricing

Competitive pricing means pricing at around the same level as that of other dealers in your area and is the policy most antique dealers follow.

As a home-based dealer, you need to be constantly alert as to what other dealers *in similar locations and offering similar services* charge for their antiques. Visit other shops in your area regularly and check out their price tags. If you charge about the same prices, you should be able to maintain a steady clientele.

Pricing above the Competition

Pricing above the competition can be justified only when *non-price* considerations are as important to your customers as quality merchandise. Here are some ways to attract customers willing to pay premium prices:

■ Locate your shop in a relatively upscale neighborhood or give it the appearance of being exclusive. You can achieve an ambience of exclusivity with manicured landscaping and expensive exterior details, such as fancy brass light fixtures, brick walkways, and unusual building decor. Once inside your shop upscale customers may expect pleasant background music on a CD sound system, crystal chandeliers, uncrowded display areas, and a general sense of low-key merchandising.

■ Stock antiques of exceptional quality and not usually available in other area shops. This means that you'll have to venture far beyond the sources—local auctions, estate sales, and so forth—that other local dealers use to purchase their stock. You also probably wouldn't stock as many items as does the owner of an average shop. Instead of ten $50 antique dolls, for example, you might display one $500 doll.

■ Offer above-average services. Men and women who customarily patronize the finest shops expect leisurely assistance as they shop, free delivery, free trial-in-the-home, fine gift wrapping, colorful bags in which to carry their purchases home, off-street parking, and so forth. They're quite willing to pay premium prices to receive these services.

Regardless of which type of pricing schedule you plan to use, one rule is critical: The slower the turnover of merchandise, the higher your markup must be.

Figuring Markup Percentages

To calculate markup percentages (as shown on page 150), just divide the dollar markup on each antique by its selling price and multiply this by 100, and you'll get the markup percentage. Using the first item in the chart on page 150 as an example:

$$\$55 \text{ (selling price)} - \$25 \text{ (cost)} = \$30 \text{ (dollar markup)}$$
$$\$30 \text{ (dollar markup)} \div \text{ by } \$55 \text{ (selling price)} \times 100 =$$
$$55\% \text{ (markup percentage)}$$

As long as the figures in the right column of your inventory records remain fairly consistent, you'll know that your buying and pricing practices are in the ballpark.

Why should you calculate percentage of markup rather than actual dollar markup? Because in many cases, percentages give you a better picture of which items will allow the largest markup, more so than simple dollar amounts. A quick glance down that column can show you almost immediately that you're making a better ratio of profit on pitchers and creamers than salt and pepper shakers, for example. If this scenario is consistent, page after page in the record, you know not to go overboard in buying salt and pepper shakers and to put more of your money in pitchers and creamers.

The percentages in the right column are not percentages of *profit*. They're *markup* percentages which is a different story. Most dealers are happy to make a *profit* of 15 or 20 percent, which is what's left after all expenses or overhead are paid.

Successful Pricing Comes From Good Research

To be a successful antiques dealer, you'll need to spend many hours every week researching current values so you'll know, almost instinctively, that an antique you come upon has the potential of making a profit. You'll pore over the annual price guides that list the selling prices of certain antiques nationwide. Like any annual reference book that's in use for an entire year, however, these guides list information that can easily go out of date if prices on certain antiques rise or fall drastically during that year.

Annual price guides usually reflect average prices on a *national* basis. To more accurately understand the trends, you'll also need to subscribe to and read *regional* antiques papers. As often as possible, you'll visit other antiques shops and attend shows to determine how other dealers are pricing their merchandise. You'll sit through hours of auctions, watching what other dealers pay for antiques, knowing that those dealers will set prices of three, four, or five times their bids.

Here's an example of how you can make easy research pay off in a fast and profitable sale. Let's say you buy a Griswold iron pan at a yard sale for $1, knowing that Griswold is a hot item in the current collectibles market. Had you not, prior to the yard sale, studied the sections on Griswold ironware in your price guides, you might easily have overlooked the mark on the pan's bottom and passed it by. Once you have the pan home, you take a couple of minutes to research its specific current value. After checking the *Garage Sale & Flea Market Annual*, you find this particular pan listed at $75. So you place the pan in the shop at that price, and a collector snaps it up a few days later. This is a typical example of how constant study and research pay off in knowing not only what to buy but also how to price antiques.

Early on in your career as an antiques dealer, you'll probably miss some good buys simply because you hadn't done your research. For example, a dealer arrived at a yard sale just seconds ahead of another dealer, who was also a friend. As they browsed the tables of items, the first one passed by a small figurine, but the second quickly picked it up. The first dealer went on browsing. It wasn't until later, as they sat drinking coffee, that the second dealer asked the first, "Didn't you see that Goebel?"

"Goebel?" the first one asked.

The second dealer reached into her bag containing her purchases from the yard sale and brought out the figurine.

"This is a Goebel, made by the same company that produced the Hummel figurines. It's worth at least $60." She turned the little piece over and showed her friend the identifying mark. Needless to say, the first dealer went home and read up on Goebel pottery.

Code	Item Description	Cost	Price	Sold At	Date	% Markup
G71	Cut glass compote	$25	$55	$55	3/12/2010	55%
G72	Pressed glass cake plate	$6	$26	$26	5/17/2010	77%
G73	Set of Bavarian wineglasses (6)	$60	$150	$145	4/21/2010	60%
G74	Set of cut glass goblets (6)	$45	$175	$160	6/15/2010	74%
G75	Pressed glass water pitcher c.1910	$10	$95	$92	6/15/2010	89%
G76	Medicine bottle, c. 1895	$3	$15	$15	5/18/2010	80%
G77	Cut glass decanter	$25	$135	$130	8/10/2010	81%
G78	Vaseline glass vase, 14 inches	$35	$125	$123	5/14/2010	67%
G79	Stained-glass lamp	$75	$225	$220	5/3/2010	67%
G80	Ruby stained-glass pitcher	$15	$48	$45	5/16/2010	69%
G81	Aberina glass vase, 12 inches	$25	$58	$58	3/20/2010	57%
G82	Depression glass luncheon plates (6)	$12	$65	$63	4/14/2010	82%
G83	Set of ruby glass tumblers (6)	$30	$95	$65	5/8/2010	68%

Planning Your Pricing Policy

One rule of thumb among most antiques dealers is that you never buy an antique unless you can *at least* triple its cost to you when you place it in your shop. Some dealers insist on paying no more than one-fifth of a reasonable selling price. A markup of 65 percent is what it usually takes to cover overhead, markdowns, and mistakes and still make a profit.

A gentleman entered an antiques shop one spring day, wanting to sell a pair of especially nice mother-of-pearl opera glasses. The dealer offered him $50 for the glasses, knowing that she would probably be able to sell them for $150 when the fall theater season began. Until then, they would most likely sit in a display case, and the dealer's $50 investment would be tied up for six months. The man refused the dealer's offer, saying he'd seen a pair of opera glasses in a nearby shop for $125, and they were nowhere near the quality of his glasses. He thought the dealer should give him at least $125. So the dealer politely explained the realities of markup to him, and he said he understood. The dealer suggested that he try to sell the glasses to an individual. So the man walked out of the shop with the opera glasses in his pocket.

You'll encounter the same situation over and over as people bring you antiques they want to sell. Some will be as pleasant as the gentleman with the opera glasses. Many won't because of television shows like the *Antiques Roadshow*. Ever since the hit program hit the airwaves, people seem to think that everything that's old has value and that they'll get that full value if they try to sell their antique or collectible.

You can suggest they run a classified ad on Craigslist or sell their item on eBay, for that's the only way they'll recover a price that's close to retail.

The exception to the rule of a minimum tripling of cost is with high-priced antiques. You can then settle for a lower markup and still make a decent profit, especially if you know that one of your customers is a collector of that antique. For example, suppose you find an exquisite Persian carpet for which the seller wants $1,000. You know there's a collector in your town who will pay you $1,750 for it in a heartbeat, but he wouldn't pay $3,000. You buy the rug at $1,000, sell it two days later for $1,750, and make a tidy $750 profit for virtually no work.

What it boils down to is that antiques dealers set prices based on what's termed *demand-oriented pricing*, which means setting prices based on value, not cost, tempered by the tastes of local collectors. Demand-oriented pricing with antiques works for two reasons: Antiques are unique, and they have intrinsic value, which is often in the eye of the customer. They're not standardized merchandise, identical tubes of toothpaste that can be found in every drugstore in town.

You may have three customers, for instance, who each desperately want a walnut spool bed, but you can't simply pick up the phone and place an order with some distributor or wholesaler for three antique walnut spool beds. You'll be lucky to find even one such bed. When you do come upon that one bed, which is a highly desirable antique, you'll price it accordingly, because you have three customers waiting for it. The demand is high.

This same principle keeps the prices of fine gems high. If diamonds were as common as rhinestones, the prices would be as low as those for rhinestones, but because diamonds are scarce and the demand for them is high, prices for diamonds are high, and people willingly pay those high prices.

Experienced dealers use four elements to help them set prices: authenticity, demand, condition, and restoration.

Authenticity. You should never take the authenticity of an antique for granted. For better-quality antiques, you should have a provenance or history of the piece, including who made it and who owned it, as well as notes on repairs or restorations. For more common pieces, marks or signatures will be enough, but furniture often doesn't have any. In establishing the authenticity of antiques that have been reproduced, like brass, china, glass, and furniture, much depends on your knowledge. You should closely examine any piece you buy for resale. Not only will this help you in deciding whether to buy it, but this will also help in pricing. The more knowledge you have about a particular piece, the more valuable it becomes to the collector. The more you know, the less danger there will be of your being taken in by a newer item being passed off as old.

Demand. As mentioned elsewhere in this book, buyers in different parts of the country look for and buy different types of antiques. An eighteenth-century French armoire that commands respect and a high price in New England might be passed up in New Mexico, where collectors usually look for antiques reflecting that area's Spanish heritage. Dealers consider the demand for an antique among local buyers.

Condition. Casual shoppers may not be too particular about a few scratches or a bit of rust on an antique. In contrast, serious collectors—those willing to pay the highest prices—demand top condition in the antiques they buy. For instance, assume that you have two plates of flow blue china in a desirable pattern but one has many knife scratches across its surface and the other is virtually scratch-free. The price tag on the second plate should be at least 30 percent higher than that on the first plate.

Restoration. Restored antiques and collectibles are pieces that have had breaks or lost parts repaired or replaced. This applies to furniture, china, and pottery, and sometimes to silver. To remain an antique, a piece should be 60 percent original. A "married" piece, made up of parts of two or more similar old pieces, is acceptable if the customer knows what he is buying. Any piece newly made of "old wood" or parts is still a reproduction. It's important that you take the amount or type of restoration into consideration when pricing your antiques.

The "You-Get-What-You-Pay-For" Syndrome

If you began selling antiques and collectibles at garage sales or flea markets, you may acquire a flea-market mentality. That is to say, you're afraid to mark up quality items because no one will buy them, since patrons of these types of sales are looking for bargains. But professional antiques dealers, especially those who sell top-quality items, have a different philosophy. They believe that most customers won't respect an antique unless it has a decent price on it. If a dealer prices an item too low, the customer may think it's inferior or that it has a defect and will start looking for cracks or chips. Customers don't come into a nice antiques shop looking for great bargains. That's for flea markets. Collectors expect to pay a reasonable price for quality antiques. If you know this, you'll be able to sell to most collectors and still make a profit, but this is only if the price is not equal to or higher than the published value of the piece. A good collector knows to buy low and sell higher.

You'll most likely become accustomed to buying low-priced collectibles and selling them at correspondingly low prices. And you'll be afraid to invest your money in better antiques that would bring higher prices, so you'll fill your shelves with merchandise that will bring only modest profits. Sooner or later you'll stumble upon and buy some excellent and highly desirable antiques. Even if you price them at their current high prices as listed in the antiques price guides, you'll be surprised at how fast they sell. At the same time, your inferior merchandise may sit on the shelves gathering dust. The lesson here is that customers will pay for quality. If you cull the poor items and stock only antiques that bring decent prices, your profits will be correspondingly higher.

However, you have to be careful not to price yourself out of the market. The area in which you live determines to a large extent how much you can charge for your antiques. The owner of a shop in the trendy Old City neighborhood of Philadelphia, for example, will be able to charge far more for a large stained-glass window than a dealer in Austin, Texas, can, regardless of how many people in that lovely western town want the window.

Your Services

Another element to consider when planning your pricing policy will be the services you'll offer. You'll have to factor many extras into your pricing system. One of the most valuable services you can give your customers actually costs you nothing—your extensive knowledge about antiques and the willingness to share that knowledge with them.

A recent survey by a New York public relations firm discovered that the shopping habits of many customers are changing. Fifteen or twenty years ago, price and quality influenced their purchases. Today's shoppers put more emphasis on service. They want to receive extensive information about their purchases from cheerful, well-informed salespeople. One executive put it this way: "People are no longer looking at price, price, price. Price was once the only criterion. Now it's not. They're looking for service."

You can put this trend in your favor if you develop a reputation for being the most knowledgeable and helpful dealer of antiques in your town. Take the time to educate your customers about styles of earlier periods. Show them how to gauge an antique's age. Share little anecdotes about history as it relates to antiques. These very personal services cost you absolutely nothing, but they're almost guaranteed to bring the customers flocking to your door.

Many other services you offer definitely will mean more expense for you and will have to be passed on in higher prices.

Delivery. Will you deliver furniture without charging for the service? Or will the price of the antique include delivery within a certain area, but you charge extra for delivery outside that area? Or will you have a flat no-delivery policy on everything, even a 10-foot-long dining table? With today's high gasoline prices, which most likely will never go down, can you afford to offer free delivery at all? Most retail furniture stores, for example, charge a minimum of $25 for delivery.

Layaway Plan. Will you have a layaway plan? You'll almost have to offer this service, since many customers simply can't pay the full price of an antique right up front. The figure on page 156 is typical of a layaway contract. You keep a copy of this contract in your files and give the customer a copy. Note that each subsequent payment, after the down payment, is entered on the contract. Remember, if you offer such a plan, you'll have to store the items until your customers pick them up.

Any dealer who has a layaway plan learns pretty quickly the advantages and disadvantages of offering this service. First, the bad news: You won't lose any income by allowing a customer to pay off an antique in installments, but it does delay your receipt of the full amount of the purchase. Your money will be invested in the item, yet you don't realize your profit on it for perhaps ninety days. In the meantime, the antique is off the selling floor and you're losing the potential of selling it for immediate cash.

On the positive side, you'll increase your sales volume many times over by allowing customers to make a down payment on an antique, then pay off the balance in, say, three installments, which is the usual arrangement. The world is full of people who love antiques and sincerely want them for their homes but who must budget every dollar of their income. A layaway plan allows these people to allocate a few dollars every month in their budget to antiques. You'll make loyal customers of anyone who buys an antique from you on a layaway plan.

Checks. While it may seem obvious that if you're in business, you will accept checks for payment, many smaller antiques dealers are wary about accepting them. Though a check, even with proper identification, may seem like a sure method of payment, it's possible it will be returned unpaid for insufficient funds. The only hedge against this is either to not accept checks or to accept only those drawn on local banks.

Credit or Debit. Will you give credit—that is, allow a customer to take an antique or collectible and pay for it in monthly payments? Not unless the customer uses a credit card you accept. While you'll have to pay a small percentage of each purchase to the credit card company, this amount is worth it to let them handle any problems that may arise from nonpayment. Also, in today's retail market, accepting credit cards will attract more customers. By accepting credit cards—you must have a separate merchant account for each type of credit card you accept—you'll also attract your share of impulse buyers, who wouldn't make a purchase if they didn't carry a credit card. The same applies to debit or bank check cards.

Gift Wrapping/Elegant Packaging. Will you gift wrap? Few antiques shops offer this service, even for purchases that are intended as gifts. Will you have pretty bags printed with your shop's name, or will you use inexpensive plain ones from a wholesale paper firm? Plain bags will do nicely. After all, you're not competing with Tiffany—at least, not right now.

Think carefully about just how much you can afford to spend on anything except more antiques for your shop, especially in your first year as a dealer. Each expense must be passed on to your customers in higher prices.

Name _____

Address _____

Phone _____

Date _____

Antique to be put away on layaway _____

_____

Purchase price of antique _____

Down payment (minimum 1/3 of purchase price) _____

Note: Balance must be paid within 90 days. No refunds.

Purchaser's Signature _____

1st payment _____

Amount paid _____

2nd payment _____

Amount paid _____

3rd payment _____

Amount paid _____

Discounts

You also need to take into consideration the fact that most antiques dealers expect to get a 10 percent discount on anything they buy in the shop of another dealer. This is the usual courtesy dealers extend to one another. Many savvy customers who aren't dealers will also ask for a 10 percent discount on their purchases. Unless buyers have a state tax number or other business identification, you're not obligated to give them discounts. Many dealers automatically add 10 percent to the price they expect to get for an antique. But, remember, pricing up and then offering a discount, especially a substantial one, is dishonest. For example, take one dealer who constantly has 50-percent-off sales, but, in reality, has increased her prices over her already set ones before the sale. While some customers are naive enough to think they're getting a deal, they're actually paying full price for the item.

What about additional or larger discounts for special groups such as students and seniors? Few dealers regularly extend special discounts to such groups.

What do you do about the aggressive customer who picks up a pair of candlesticks you have priced at $79 and offers you $50 cash? It will happen. Do you stand firm at $79 or give in to make the sale, knowing you'll make some profit, even at $50? To be honest, this is demeaning. Would your customers go into a fine clothing shop, try on a half-dozen expensive gowns, and then haggle over the price of the prettiest one? Of course not. The shop owner would be horrified at such behavior. The reality of the antiques business, though, is that some customers will press you to lower your prices, even though you're not running a flea market, where they expect to haggle. Unfortunately, they equate "bargaining" with "antiques" and think they can bargain with any dealer.

Your policy about lowering prices should depend on two things:

1. How long has the antique been in your shop? Has it been sitting there for a year with virtually no interest from customers? In that case you'll probably be glad to get your investment back, plus at least a little profit.

   Let's say you bought a framed needlework piece for $6 and placed it in your shop with a $39 price tag. Even though you thought it was well worth $39, it hung there on the wall for months. No one even looked at it. Finally, a customer offered you $25 for it. Without hesitation, you sold it to her. No, you didn't get its full value, but you then had an extra $19 plus the item's original cost of $6 to invest in antiques that would move quickly.

2. How high was your original markup on the antique? If, after checking your records, you discover that you still will make a decent profit, even at the reduced price, you should go ahead and sell it. That was the case with the needlework piece. If you had paid $20 for it, you would not have let it go for $25, but at a cost to you of $6, you'll still come out ahead.

Odd-Ending Prices

Almost every drugstore, department store, and discount store uses the odd-ending pricing system—that is, merchandise is priced at $3.98 or $3.95 instead of $4.00. The reason is psychological. Many customers tend to mentally round down a $3.98 price tag to $3.00. However, just as many others round it up to $4.00. Odd-ending, though, has never been a practice in most quality antiques shops.

Some dealers feel that odd-ending of pennies cheapens the value of an antique. After all, you're selling investment, beauty, and pleasure, not cornflakes. Yet odd-ending of dollars doesn't seem to have the same devaluing effect. Pricing your antiques at $19, $39, $149, and so forth can be quite effective. Some dealers round their prices off at $15, $25, $100, and so forth. There's no right or wrong here. Just make your own decision based on your own feelings about pricing.

Multiple and Individual Pricing

How do you price antiques that come in sets: chairs, crystal and china, sterling silver flatware, and so forth? Do you write one price tag that covers the entire set, or do you price each unit individually? It depends.

Chairs. If you have a set of six matching chairs, for instance, price them at six for one figure. The reason is that most people will want all six chairs. Very few customers will be trying to find one chair to complete a set they already own. Craftspeople of generations ago used literally thousands of patterns in the furniture they constructed, so the chances of your having duplicates of a customer's chairs are almost astronomically impossible. Besides, if you sold one chair from your set, you'd be left with just five chairs, a partial set.

Crystal and China. Crystal and china, especially if they're of a fairly popular pattern, are a different story. You'll seldom find a complete set of crystal or china. The very nature of old china and crystal is that a few pieces would have been broken through the years. As a result, many of your customers will own partial sets, and they're always cruising the antiques shops looking for an odd piece or two to help fill out the set.

What if you found a set of antique china? Though it was originally a service for twelve, plus covered tureens, platters, a gravy boat, and vegetable dishes, when you bought it, it also contained twelve berry bowls and twelve soup plates. However, it had only nine dinner plates, eleven luncheon plates, ten bread-and-butter plates, and nine cups and saucers, two of which were chipped. You would be constantly on the lookout for odd pieces to bring it back to its original service for twelve. If by some miracle you came upon a full set in a shop, you certainly wouldn't want to buy the whole thing, but you would buy individual pieces in a minute.

Most dealers find it simply easier to sell each piece of a partial china set separately rather than as a whole. In the end they'll make more profit. But this is limited to only certain antiques and collectibles, such as pottery, porcelain, and silver. You can certainly extend this policy by offering a slightly discounted price to a customer who buys all of the pieces of a certain pattern in your shop. If there are only a few pieces of a pattern, you should price them individually, especially if the pattern is difficult to find.

> Tip: Another alternative to selling a partial set of china is to create a "complete" set of six or eight place settings, using the better pieces, then sell the remaining ones individually. This arrangement will suit someone looking for an antique set of china they can use today. Most antique sets of china came with twelve place settings, plus serving pieces.

Sterling Silver Flatware. If you're lucky enough to obtain a complete set of antique sterling silver flatware, never break it up because collectors highly value a complete set.

Don't hesitate to buy and display odd pieces of the more popular patterns, though. As with crystal, many people are always searching for a spoon here, a fork there to fill out a set of a particular pattern.

Groups of Odd Items. Many times you'll have small items in your shop that simply don't warrant your time in pricing them individually. That's when you group them and sell them as one unit. For instance, a dealer bought three big fruit jars full of old marbles. About twenty of the marbles were valuable enough to be priced separately at $5 each. The remaining ones were worth from $1 to $2 each, so he placed twenty-five of these in each of eight plastic bags and priced them at $29 a bag. This saved him the time he would have spent pricing each marble separately and the trouble of selling them one or two at a time. Buyers got a bargain in that they received twenty-five collectible marbles for less than the cost of buying them separately.

Hard-to-Price Items. As time goes on, you may acquire a library of reference books on everything from autographs to zithers but still not be able to locate a reasonable selling price for an unusual antique you come upon. In that case you call a local dealer who handles current merchandise similar to your antique and ask him the price of a top-of-the-line piece. Use that figure as your guideline.

> **Tip:** Some dealers of lesser-valued antiques and collectibles have been using eBay to help set prices. This is the lazy way out and not particularly accurate. You cannot decide upon a retail price of an antique by using just one or two final auction bids as a reference. If you do use online prices, choose several from the antiques malls instead. While winning bids from regular antique auctions are what appraisers and price guide publishers use to find the average price of an antique, using the results on eBay will give you a false price because of the competition/entertainment factor among bidders. Some buyers bid the price of an item higher just so the other bidders don't win it, not because they want it to add to a collection.

You may have to use this technique when you come across an item, say, a 1930s Wilson tennis racquet in superb condition that you can't find in any of your reference books. In this case you need to call a local sporting goods shop and ask the price of its best Wilson tennis racquet. Usually, the shopkeeper will cheerfully give you the figure, and you'll be able to price your racquet accordingly, since highly collectible items often sell for as much as new ones of the same type.

This technique also comes in handy when you need to identify the pattern of a particular piece of sterling, crystal, or china. Whenever possible, you'll find it to your advantage to list pattern names on your price tags because many patterns are incredibly similar. No customer wants to buy a wine glass or sterling fork, for example, and then discover, once he gets home, that it's similar to but not exactly his pattern.

One way you can identify a pattern is to take the piece—whether it's sterling, china, or crystal—to a local jewelry or china shop and ask the manager if it is illustrated in one of the shop's catalogs. You may find a photograph of the piece there, along with the pattern name and retail price.

Using Price Tags

You'll need many thousands of price tags, even in your first year of business. Small stringed tags are fine for small items such as cups and saucers, but you may tag your medium-to-large antiques using your business cards. Since you're going to buy business cards anyway, simply increase your order to 5,000 or so.

Any good copy center can print 5,000 business cards for about a penny each. Order them in a color and type style that coordinates with your street sign and advertising. Include on the cards the name of your shop, your address and phone number, and your logo, if you've chosen one.

To convert these business cards into price tags, first punch a hole in the upper-left corner of a card, using a standard hole punch. Cut about a foot of yarn or narrow ribbon in a coordinating color and thread it through the hole. Write the price of the antique on the card below or to the side of your shop's name or on the reverse side, and tie the card, using the attached yarn or ribbon, to the antique. You now have an attractive price tag that's highly visible and that remains as an advertisement of your shop after the customer takes the antique home.

You're probably thinking, *"Punch holes in thousands of cards? Cut and tie yarn through thousands of holes?"* The secret is to start as early as possible, building up a supply before you ever open your shop. Draft your friends and family to help. You'll need a continual supply of these tags after you open the shop, too, so just prepare a few more every day during slow periods. You'll always have plenty of attractive price tags on hand this way.

> Tip: If you're selling more valuable antiques, you might want to invest in top-fold business cards, printed with your shop name and information on the front card and blank on the inside one. Here, you can write a more detailed description of the piece along with its price and code number. Some dealers at higher-end shows prefer this method because it gives their customers more information and looks more professional.

Some of your antiques, such as bowls, vases, and most china, won't lend themselves to tie-on tags. For those pieces most dealers just use the self-adhesive labels that come in packages of 1,000. Don't buy any labels smaller than 1/2 inch by 3/4 inch. You need room to write the antique's code number along with its price, and the very tiny ones aren't large enough.

Never stick an adhesive price tag on paper goods. This includes prints, sheet music, books, postcards, playing cards, and so forth. Old paper is fragile, and many adhesive tags will effectively remove printing or even the paper itself when the tag is removed. Far too many holes in paper goods are made when some dealer had stuck a tag on them, essentially ruining the collectible.

The best solution is to drop the item into a plastic sleeve, then stick the price tag on the sleeve. You can purchase plastic sleeves in many sizes, ranging all the way from some large enough to hold sheet music down to little ones just right for the smallest postcards. You'll find standard sizes in office supply stores, but for more of a variety, go online to EverydayPlastics.com (www.everydayplastics.com).

To a certain extent the same caveat about sticking adhesive labels on paper goods holds true for linens. Many times an adhesive tag will leave a residue on a fine linen handkerchief, for example, that's almost impossible to remove. Write the price on a small string tag, then pin the tag to the linen with a tiny safety pin. Buy little brass pins in bags of one hundred at a crafts store.

It isn't practical to put books in plastic bags since customers like to browse through them, and you can't stick safety pins in books. But you might want to try this: Open the book to its approximate center, then place a piece of yarn about 21/2 feet long along the channel between pages. Close the book; then take the two ends of the yarn and tie them securely along the book's outer spine. Tie a string tag to the knot in the yarn, tie the ends of the yarn into a bow, then cut off all excess yarn. This creates a secure and attractive price tag that won't come off even when customers flip through the book.

Sold Tags

Every once in a while you'll sell an antique, usually a large piece of furniture, that the customer can't take home right away. It has to stay on the sales floor for a while. That's a perfect time to make a real statement to your other customers about the salability of your antiques. All you have to do is tie a large red tag that says "SOLD" onto the antique and let it sit there in plain view. This not only informs customers that your antiques are selling, but it lets them know that they shouldn't hesitate if they're genuinely interested in a particular piece. It might not be there when they come back.

A dealer once had for sale a late-nineteenth-century secretary that carried a fairly high price. One day a woman and her husband came in his shop, saw the desk, and fell in love with it. They came back several times, examining the piece, measuring it, discussing how it would fit into their home. She really wanted the secretary but just couldn't make up her mind to buy it. Early one Saturday morning, someone else purchased the secretary, but the customer had to leave it in the shop for a few days. So the dealer put a SOLD tag on it. That afternoon the woman's husband came in with a fistful of hundred-dollar bills, ready to buy the secretary as a surprise birthday gift for his wife. He almost went into shock when he saw that SOLD tag. Unfortunately, that's how the antiques buying game works. Since a dealer usually has only one of the item, when it sells, it's gone. As the old saying goes, "He who hesitates is lost."

Try to impress this thought on your customers: If they see an antique they like, they should buy it right then (or put it on layaway), because it may not be there when they come back. Those red SOLD tags are all the evidence you need to make your point.

Employing Markdowns and Sales

In certain types of businesses, retailers price their merchandise high enough to accommodate substantial markdowns at the end of a season. They plan ahead on taking reductions because they know that statistically they'll have leftover merchandise then. They also know that they may overbuy on certain items or sizes—too many size 40 jackets or purple bikinis, for example. They may stock up on flowered sheets just before the decorating magazines begin promoting striped sheets.

These problems don't exist in the antiques business, which is not to say you won't ever reduce the price on an antique. You just won't do it very often and certainly not on the scale of most retail shops.

There isn't an antiques dealer who hasn't paid too much for an antique or bought something that turned out to be a real dog in some way. If you find yourself with such an antique sitting in your shop for a year or more with absolutely no response from customers, the only solution is to reduce the price, sell it, and get it out of your shop. Better to take a loss than to have your customers become bored looking at the same tired merchandise.

Many shops do have regular sales, though, usually in early spring and late fall. Some do quite well with this practice. Of course, you'll always have customers who wait for these sales. They've had their eyes on certain antiques for weeks or months, hoping to get the piece at a reduced price. That's okay. You'll still make a decent profit on those sales.

Instead of marking new prices on existing tags, however, you can place several signs around that state 15% OFF EVERY ANTIQUE IN THE SHOP. This way, when the sale—usually of two weeks' duration—is over, you won't have to write and attach new tags. Everything just automatically goes back to the original price.

Other dealers prefer to lower the prices on certain antiques but not on others. They either mark sale prices on the old tags or group the sale antiques on specific tables or in specific areas.

You might decide to hold an annual yard sale of marked-down antiques and collectibles. Close your home-based shop for a Saturday morning and put all your sale items out on the front lawn. This keeps customers from thinking everything in the shop is on sale. At noon close out the yard sale, open your shop, and you're right back in business.

Is there a flea market in operation anywhere near your home? If so, selling off your mistakes there is another way to recoup some or all of your investment and get the unsalable items out of the shop. Hundreds of bargain-hunting men and women crowd the aisles of these open-air markets. The exposure is terrific, so the effort put into hauling the leftovers there and spending a day selling them can pay off handsomely. The rent for tables at flea markets is usually quite reasonable, so even though you reduce the prices on your mistakes to rock-bottom, you'll still come home with money in your pocket to invest in new stock.

Markdown Inventory

One way to avoid making future mistakes in buying is to keep a running record of every antique whose price you must reduce (see the following page). This record is in addition to your inventory and sales records. Record each marked-down antique, what you paid for it, the original tagged price, and the final selling price. By studying this record, you'll know either not to buy such antiques in the future or not to invest too much money in them. A blank copy of this form is in the appendix.

For Midwinter Sale

Code #	Item Description	Purchase Price	Original Price	Sale Price
C12	Yorktown Souvenir plate	$35	$65	$52
F38	Mission-style armchair	$28	$75	$60
F66	White corner shelf	$10	$35	$28
F52	Small iron woodstove	$50	$125	$100
C22	Pr. Royal Copley vases	$10	$42	$34
C18	Bean pot	$6	$12	$10
F44	Oak captain's chair	$125	$185	$148
G33	Pressed glass punch bowl/glasses set	$45	$95	$76
F21	Victorian marble top Eastlake washstand	$125	$385	$308
F08	Black and white enamel top kitchen table 1930	$25	$375	$300
G11	Glass sugar and creamer	$6	$15	$12
C20	Cup and saucer 1950s	$2	$5	$4
P10	Stereopticon	$16	$65	$52
F32	Painted poplar pie safe	$125	$375	$300
K16	Coffee grinder box mill	$18	$95	$76
F45	Pr. Bentwood side chairs	$185	$350	$280
C34	Napco ceramic head c.1950	$50	$165	$132
K28	Kim-bo tobacco tin	$8	$96	$75
M13	Ebony walking stick	$28	$135	$108
T36	German cuckoo clock	$45	$225	$180
K23	Toleware coffeepot	$37	$300	$240
K11	Advertising iron	$15	$45	$36
G06	Monopoly Game c.1935	$10	$85	$68

08 | Display and Merchandising

Good planning, an attractive shop, salable merchandise, and well-planned marketing act as a team with one goal—to bring customers to your shop. Once they're in the door, you'll use two additional powerful aids—*enticing displays* and *effective merchandising*—to make them say, "I'll take it!"

The way you display your antiques and the way you present them to your customers are crucial to your success as an antiques dealer. They're the little extras that are like icing on cake, whipped cream in Irish coffee, that special topping on pizza. The good news is that it's easier to master creative display techniques and skillful merchandising than just about any other facet of managing an antiques shop.

Displaying Your Antiques

Creating an Image

The research you conducted for your business plan helped you understand pretty well who your customers will be as well as their income level, shopping habits, and preferences as to the types of antiques they might choose for their homes. You used this information as you stocked your shop. Now you'll use the same information for displaying your antiques. Since you know what merchandise your customers expect to find when they visit your shop, you'll create and maintain an image in your displays that harmonizes with their expectations. With one big exception, which you'll read about it in chapter 10, the customers who enter your *home-based antiques shop* aren't expecting to walk in under Waterford crystal chandeliers and to be offered a glass of fine champagne to sip as they shop. They'll probably be more comfortable in a casual, informal atmosphere, one that feels like home.

That's a big advantage you have over owners of shops in commercial spaces so play the home ambience up every way you can.

Types of Displays

Displays usually fall into one of three categories: open, closed, or ledge. Each of these categories has a specific use.

1. *Open displays* are those that are scattered throughout the shop and are easy for the customer to inspect. They include furniture, small antiques displayed on furniture, and open shelves. Most dealers consider this the ideal type of display. It's just human nature, of shoppers, anyway, to want to inspect any item that interests them. The very act of reaching out to an antique, picking it up, looking underneath, holding it to the light, and then reading the price tag often leads to the decision to buy. You can't discount the value of easy access in merchandising antiques.

    This same easy access, however, can lead to breakage or damage. Some parents don't watch their children as closely as they should, and every antiques dealer alive has cringed as an overexuberant child knocked a piece of fine porcelain into history.

2. *Closed displays,* the alternative to open ones, are usually locked glass cases. They're the place for valuable, fragile, or small antiques. Do antiques sell as well in closed displays as on open shelves? No. Somehow, a pane of glass creates a psychological as well as a physical barrier between the customer and the antique. It intimidates all but those who are seriously interested in a piece. Customers who are only mildly interested in antiques displayed on open shelves will still pick them up to read the price tag. However, they usually won't ask you to unlock a case to inspect the same pieces. Nevertheless, this is the only reasonable alternative for some antiques, especially very small items.

    Aside from breakage, you have to consider the possibility of theft. *Never* display genuinely valuable small antiques or any type of jewelry, even marginally collectible pieces, on open shelves. Unfortunately, shoplifters find it too easy to scoop them into a pocket or shopping bag. Such pieces must go into a closed and locked case.

A dealer learned this lesson the hard way after a shoplifter made off with two sterling silver souvenir spoons she had placed in a spoon rack hanging on a wall. He also stole several pieces of 1940s jewelry that were lying on a velvet-covered tray on top of a case. Better to miss a few marginal sales than lose good merchandise to shoplifters. Any customer who is genuinely interested in an antique will ask to have a case opened.

3. *Ledges* are windowsills, the tops of cabinets or dividers, or any flat surface other than a shelf, where you can display merchandise. Ledges are great areas for relatively inexpensive but attractive antiques and collectibles. They're the ideal places to put pieces that will draw customers from one area of your shop to another, often out of curiosity.

Perhaps you have twenty-five or thirty unusual purple and blue bottles that you can cluster on a sunny windowsill grouped by color. On a bright day this display can be most attractive, both from the inside of the shop and from outside. Or maybe you have some dainty handkerchiefs that you can arrange in a small basket to set on a table in your shop. Customers will pause in their browsing to look through the basket. If they decide to buy one, fine. The important point, though, is that they stopped in that area for a few minutes.

The most valuable ledge is the top of your glass case. You could place an attractive teapot, small lamp, or colorful cup and saucer there to attract attention. Customers will be drawn to the antique on top of the case and may stay to investigate the sterling silver, perfume bottles, and miniatures displayed inside the case. But try not to obscure too much of the view down

Tip: As a precaution against shoplifting, offer to hold items on or behind your checkout counter while customers continue to shop. Many will pick up a small antique or two and carry them around with them as they shop. You don't want to offend perfectly honest customers by implying that they're about to shoplift something, and in most cases, they're simply holding on to the pieces while they decide whether to buy them. Yet some dealers have lost a few valuable antiques to shoplifters who'll do just that, then drop it into a handbag or pocket when the dealers are not looking and leave while they're busy with other customers.

into the case. Consider using a low glass case as your checkout counter. Your customers might just buy one or two additional small items as they check out.

Effective Lighting

Take advantage of light to help display your antiques. You can add a romantic, old-fashioned charm to your inventory by placing several lamps, fitted with decorative iridescent flamelike 40-watt bulbs, throughout the shop. Your customers, who use incandescent bulbs in their own homes, will find the pools of warm golden light from these bulbs cheerful and inviting as they brighten dull corners and highlight choice pieces of furniture. This light is also flattering to a woman's complexion—especially important when she's trying on jewelry or vintage clothing—and is perfect to illuminate the patina of your antique furniture. To save energy, you can mix energy-efficient screw-in fluorescent bulbs with the decorative ones.

Standard lightbulbs, however, use lots of energy and are more expensive to buy and operate. Unless you use a great many high-wattage bulbs, they won't keep your shop effectively illuminated. Plus the heat from many 100-watt incandescent bulbs can be disastrous if your shop isn't air-conditioned. An alternative solution is to use a combination of low-energy screw-in fluorescent bulbs for ambience and high-wattage fluorescent tubes for light. Fluorescent tubes are highly energy-efficient and give off a great deal of light per dollar spent. Considering the current cost of electricity, they're a bargain. On the downside, however, long, industrial-looking tubes don't do a thing for the ambience of an antiques shop. In fact, they can make it look more like a bathroom or a factory. The secret is to hide them.

When you remodel your home to accommodate your antiques shop, you might consider having valances built around all the walls at the ceiling line. An electrician can wire the wall for fluorescent tubes, which can then be hidden behind the valances. The light from the tubes will be directed up and onto the ceiling, where it will diffuse and spread around the room. The light will illuminate the entire room

Tip: Consider installing strips of energy-efficient adjustable spotlights—the type often used in today's kitchens. By adjusting the spots, you'll be able to highlight an area of your shop or specific antiques.

with no sharp shadows. Fluorescent tubes come in several tones, ranging from cool to warm. Be sure to buy the warmest ones. Their color will blend nicely with the warm tones of any incandescent bulbs you have.

Do you have large windows facing the street? If so, keep some of your lamps lit during the evening hours so that your showroom is visible to passersby. Many times customers will return to inspect antiques they glimpsed through a window previously.

Make Color Work for You

There's a psychology to color that can't be denied. Using it to its best advantage will increase sales.

- *Red* is exciting, powerful, sexy, patriotic. It can also be disturbing. Use it in moderation.
- *Yellow* is cheerful and happy, signifying youth and energy. It's great when used against a dark background.
- *Blue* symbolizes water and sky, peace and serenity. It's also men's favorite color, so use it wherever you want to attract male customers.
- *Green* is fresh and cool, like forests and the great outdoors. When teamed with yellow, it says "Spring."
- *Pink* is sweet and lovely, innocent and young. Coordinate pink with lace and ribbons for Mother's Day and June brides.

Many people dislike purple and become depressed by gray, so you might think twice about using them in your displays. Orange, too, is disturbing to some people, so avoid it, except for Halloween.

Keep color in mind as you set up your displays. A few pieces of colored glass scattered around a room won't attract much attention. *Group* them by color, however, and you multiply the impact many times over. For example, place a half-dozen blue canning jars on a Hoosier cabinet, a collection of green Depression glass on a dining table, and several pieces of ruby-colored glass on a white marble-topped table.

Display Props

Props are any physical objects that you use to display an antique but that aren't salable merchandise in themselves. Employ props to make an antique more visible, to enhance its color or style, or to draw attention to it. A prop doesn't overshadow or detract from the antique. It enhances the antique without drawing undue attention to itself. You'll find excellent commercial props—plate holders, cup and saucer holders, doll stands, and such—advertised in antiques trade papers. The most interesting props, though, are those you'll find for little or no cost. Going to the coast on vacation? Look for pretty shells to display your pearl jewelry. Interesting driftwood is great to use around any nautical antique. A battered bucket that surfaces behind a relative's barn could be scrubbed, painted, and used to hold piano rolls. Old bricks, with their soft rust color and appealing texture, might serve as a base for antique tools. You could use old crates to hold used collectible magazines or small prints. Many dealers display odd plates and platters in folding wooden dish drainers.

Of course, you can also use antiques or collectibles to display other antiques. For instance, hang an embroidered tea towel on the upper bar of a little washstand or stack old spice cans on top of a bread box or rest an old doll or teddy bear on a high chair. These aren't really props, though, since you intend to sell them.

Positioning Your Antiques

Think Proportion and Balance. Before beginning any work, artists first consider proportion and balance—how the various elements will relate to one another. You should do the same before positioning your antiques. Here are some general rules:

- Curving or diagonal lines are more interesting than straight lines.
- Asymmetrical groupings are more interesting than symmetrical ones.
- Elements of varying sizes are more interesting than those of identical sizes.
- *Three* seems to be a magic number in design, one that implies harmony. These three elements might be three different sizes, three different heights, or three different colors.

As you position your antiques, look for ways to use curving or diagonal lines, elements of different sizes, and units of three elements in your displays.

You don't have this much freedom when displaying antiques on a bank of shelves, of course. Even so, you can create interest by using antiques of differing sizes or by placing some things close to the wall and others forward.

One dealer set up a special display of about thirty-five sets of cups and saucers in preparation for Mother's Day. He placed them on two glass shelves, then stood back to evaluate the display. It was awful! The dealer thought he had done it properly because he used a zigzag pattern, placing one set forward and the next set back. The display was totally boring because there was no variation in height. Fortunately, the solution was easy. He placed the sets that were in the rear on cup-and-saucer holders. This arrangement gave some height to the display, as well as making the sets in the rear more visible. He could have also used small boxes wrapped in plain dark-colored paper.

Group Your Antiques for Maximum Effect. The way you group your antique furniture can help your customers visualize it in their own homes. Many people who come into your shop will be searching for a specific item. They may need a table to place beside a couch, a pie safe to hold their VCR and tapes, or a floor lamp to use as a reading light. Arrange your antique furniture in casual groupings, just as they might be in a home, so that your customers can actually see, for example, the way a low table might serve as a coffee table, especially if you place an attractive candy bowl or a few books on it.

If you specialize in one period, such as eighteenth century, Victorian, Arts and Crafts, or primitive, you'll have no trouble displaying your antique furniture in such groupings. If, like most dealers, you carry antiques of several eras, try not to display, all in one corner, a turn-of-the-century Bible table with an Art Nouveau floor lamp and a red velvet sofa right out of *Gone with the Wind*. This creates instant confusion.

The trick is to group antiques of specific eras together. In one room or alcove, you might place formal, English antiques, along with appropriate accessories. In another section of the shop, display antiques of another style or period. This system not only adds to the harmony of your decor but also helps customers as they search for that special antique. The person who wants a Hoosier cabinet will be immediately drawn to your "country" display, whereas the one looking for an Eastlake table for her late-nineteenth-century bedroom will gravitate quickly to the area filled with Victorian antiques.

The same theory holds true for collectibles. Group them according to category. If you have several nice Coca-Cola pieces, for example, display them in one area. Then, if a collector comes into the shop searching for Coca-Cola items, she'll be drawn immediately to that display. If you scatter a Coca-Cola tray here and a bottle carrier there throughout the shop, intermingled with every other kind of collectible, she could easily overlook a few choice items—and you might miss a sale!

Tip: Use the elements of proportion and balance to highlight a large piece of furniture. For instance, you might hang a large picture on the wall above the left end of a sideboard. That's the first element in height and size. Then you could stand a few old 8-inch-high books in the center of the sideboard. That's the second. On the far right side of the sideboard, you could place a 12-inch-high chocolate pitcher surrounded by a few cups. That becomes the third element.

This arrangement uses the curving line principle, from top left down to center and up to the right. The grouping is also asymmetrical, since the picture is larger and higher than the chocolate set.

Keep 'Em Moving!

One final word about displays: Rearrange your antiques regularly. Shift furniture from one side of the room to another. Put cookie jars in a bookcase one month and on a library table the next. Move cups and saucers from a shelf on one wall to a shelf on another wall. This is one of the best ways to keep your regular customers from becoming bored with your stock.

Sometimes an antique will look completely different in one setting from the way it does in another. You'll be amazed at how rearranging your stock can create interest and generate sales. Even regular customers can walk right by an antique a dozen times and never see it. Move it to another location, and they may instantly purchase it.

Suppose you have an antique that hasn't sold despite moving it all over the shop. You feel strongly that the piece is worth the price you placed on it, so you don't want to mark it down. In this case it's time to remove it from the shop for a breather. Take it off the shelf or floor, store it for three or four months, then bring it back out. Chances are that even your regular customers will think it's new stock.

A dealer had a problem selling an old Raggedy Ann cookie jar. At the time she first placed it on a shelf, she priced it as listed in all the reference books. For some reason it didn't sell, even though it was a desirable collectible and fairly priced. After six months, she took it down and stored it. Once back on the shelf, *at the same price*, that cookie jar sold within a week.

Merchandising Your Antiques

Hard Selling Is for Used Cars—Soft Selling Is for Antiques

Antiques buyers are browsers. Unless they've been in the shop before and have already chosen a particular antique, they like to wander around at their leisure. Most of them sincerely resent having a salesperson on their heels, loudly heralding the value of every antique that even casually catches their attention. This is the fastest way to antagonize potential customers and chase them out of the shop. The soft sell—low-key, laid-back, friendly but not aggressive—is the most effective way to sell antiques.

This isn't to say that you should ignore your customers. Far from it. Greet them with a friendly "Hello" or "Good morning" or "Good afternoon" as each walks into your shop. You can follow that with "Let me know if I can answer any questions or help you with anything." If your customers indicate that they're looking for specific items, you should try to find what they're asking for among your inventory. However, if they say, "I'm just looking around," you can smile warmly and say, "Go right ahead." Then make yourself busy with some small task, while staying alert to any questions they might have.

Be sure to acknowledge each customer, even if you're busy with one person when another enters. You can still glance in the newcomer's direction, smile, give them a pleasant greeting, and then go back to helping the first person.

Should you be suddenly rushed with a half-dozen or more customers, announce in a voice just loud enough to be heard by all, "Look around, folks; I'll be with you in a minute." This announcement makes them all feel welcome, and they'll most likely stay in the shop until you can get to them. Otherwise, they might walk out, sensing that you're too busy to wait on them.

Most successful dealers wait until a customer shows a real interest in a specific antique before making an effort to sell it. At that point, though, you can begin merchandising. "The inlay on that cabinet is so delicate and intricate. See how the cabinetmaker used ivory and mother-of-pearl to create the pattern?" Or "I see you're interested in the Frankoma pottery. Are you a collector? If you'll notice the color of the clay on the bottom of these pieces, you'll see they're all from the first firings."

If customers leave the shop without buying, send them on their way with just as much warmth as you showed when they entered. "Thanks for stopping by! And please visit us again." Encourage all customers to sign your guest book. You'll want those names and addresses for your mailing list. Also, ask them if they'd like to be on your e-mail list, so you can notify them of special seasonal promotions or sales.

Sell the Sizzle, Not the Steak

All right, you know you're not in the restaurant business, but when Elmer Wheeler, a very cagey fellow, told a group of salesmen, "Don't sell the steak, sell the sizzle," he made merchandising history. That truism works in any business, including antiques. You sell the *benefits* of owning an antique, not the antique itself.

After all, a table is a table is a table, to misquote Gertrude Stein. A table is four legs and a flat top. As an antiques dealer, are you selling your customers four legs and a flat top? No. You're selling beauty, prestige, investment, pleasure, and pride of ownership.

Show a customer how the deep patina on an Empire-era table enhances the wood, and she'll immediately see it glowing in her own home. Explain how the table's lines reflect Napoleon's influence on French architecture and furniture, so she can relate the table to that period in history. Show that such a table is quite rare, and she'll realize she's buying a piece of furniture that's one of a kind, a genuine asset to her collection. Let her see how the table's simple yet elegant lines will complement the other furniture in her living room, creating an arrangement that will evoke admiration from all who see it.

In other words, get your customers' *emotions* involved. Instead of seeing merely a set of pretty Meissen china, let a woman visualize how she might set her table with the china, then invite friends over for a festive dinner. Let her imagine the pleasure she'll derive every time she looks at the lovely pattern. Maybe she'll even be able to pass the set on to a daughter or son. That's selling the sizzle, not the steak.

And don't overlook your male customers. Men are most often interested in the craftsmanship that went into a piece of furniture, as well as its history.

Look for the Stories behind Your Antiques

As you buy stock for your shop, try to find out whether an antique has an interesting history. This isn't always possible, of course, but surprisingly often when you buy from individuals, they can tell you fascinating stories about their marble-topped tables, cut-glass cruets, hobnail perfume bottles, or whatever. Maybe it's a canteen carried by a soldier during the Spanish-American War. Or it might be a Bible brought through Ellis Island by an immigrant from Ireland. It could be an old maple rocking chair that survived the long trek on the Oregon Trail. Perhaps it's a fanciful cane that once belonged to your state's most revered governor.

Any such history adds much to the value of an antique when you describe it to a customer. Stories are also *invaluable* to someone who collects that particular type of antique. Suppose someone comes into your shop asking for button hooks that carry advertising slogans from shoe shops. If you happen to have an advertising-related button hook that you can pretty well document as having belonged to Lizzie Borden, Emily Dickinson, Annie Oakley, or some other famous woman, you can be certain that a collector will pay you a premium price for it. For this reason, ask the seller of an especially interesting antique, "Can you tell me something about this?"

Granted, you have to take some tales with a grain of salt if they sound too fanciful. After all, what are the chances of a sea chest that came over on the *Mayflower* being found in a rancher's tack room in Wyoming? Pretty slim. Just use your judgment, based on the credibility of the seller.

Accentuate the Positive

No one likes a Gloomy Gus, yet too many dealers can't resist peppering their conversation with dire comments about the state of the economy, the world, and everyone in it. They don't like the politicians in Washington or the way the last election went. According to them, their competition is selling inferior merchandise. On and on and on. Who can blame a potential customer for getting out of that shop as quickly as possible?

Enthusiasm and a positive attitude have to be two of the greatest assets you can have as an antiques dealer, and the enthusiasm you feels for your profession is contagious. When you act as though each antique in your shop is a thing of joy and beauty, your customers will begin to see them as such, and they can't help but respond. Your happy attitude will rub off on your customers, and they'll be much more likely to buy.

Caring for Your Antiques

A great deal of the stock you acquire for your shop will be in need of a little TLC before it can be put on display. While you don't want to take away all signs of age—after all, a few beauty marks of wear are what make an antique more valuable than a new piece—the antiques you sell should be clean, polished, and ready for use.

Silver

First, don't wash either plated or sterling pieces in your dishwasher. Some automatic dishwashing detergents contain chemicals that can darken silver. Just wash it in warm water with mild detergent, then rinse and dry quickly with a soft cloth.

Second, *never* use one of those products where you dip silver in a chemical solution. It'll remove the tarnish, all right, but along with it will go the oxidation (the dark accent deep inside patterns) that identifies antique silver.

Silver that is mildly tarnished needs only a gentle polish with a high-quality, brand-name product such as Wright's Silver Polish.

Every once in a while, you'll come upon an interesting piece of silver, though, that is so badly tarnished its surface is a solid dark gray. Try one small area with a standard cream polish and plenty of elbow grease first. If you get zero results, dampen the piece with white vinegar, sprinkle with salt, then gently, ever so gently, rub it with a sponge thoroughly dampened with vinegar. The chemical action of the salt and vinegar should dissolve the tarnish pretty quickly. Rinse, then polish with your regular cream silver polish.

> Tip: This technique won't work on plated silver that's so badly worn the base metal shows through. In this case you might consider replating the piece, the cost of which you can work into the price. Replating makes silver-plated pieces more attractive, so they're more likely to sell.

Copper and brass

You can resurrect many a tarnished copper teakettle and brass dresser handle with a similar routine.

Scrub the piece first to remove surface grime. Make a paste of equal parts salt and vinegar, thickened with flour to the consistency of thick cream. Spread a layer of this paste onto the tarnished item. Wait a half hour or so, then rub briskly with a soft cloth or sponge dampened with more vinegar. Very badly tarnished metal may require a second application. Rinse, then polish with a good brass polish like Brasso.

Another version of this method requires dipping the cut surface of a half lemon directly into salt, then scrubbing it across the tarnish. This works equally well as the salt-vinegar technique.

Chrome

Chrome in an antiques shop? Yes, chrome. The enormous popularity of Art Deco today and the growing nostalgia for the fifties, primarily among today's younger consumers, mean there's a real market for chrome collectibles. Such "antiques" as the chrome-edged dinette sets that served half the kitchens of America a few decades ago command high prices today.

You can use any of several methods to clean chrome that's just mildly dirty. Rubbing alcohol on a soft rag will work. So will a mixture of ammonia and hot water. Baking soda on a damp rag is a good cleaner. Chrome that hasn't been cleaned in fifty years is another story. It will probably require stronger measures. Try rubbing it with wood ash from your fireplace on a damp cloth.

Once the chrome is clean, polish it with wadded newspaper.

Most of those chrome-edged kitchen tables had glossy laminated tops, and many acquired stains through the years. In all honesty, you may not be able to remove every fifty-year-old mark. Some stains will respond to treatment, though.

Try soaking a sponge or cloth with PineSol and covering the stain for a half hour or so, then rinsing. Repeat the process, using household bleach instead of the PineSol.

Once you're satisfied you've removed as much stain as possible, clean the top with an ammonia-water mixture, then dry and polish with a good furniture polish.

You can often remove tiny rust spots from chrome with the cola-foil technique. Crumple a small piece of aluminum foil into a ball and dip it into regular cola. Rub briskly on the spots.

Crystal

Delicate antique crystal must be treated with the greatest care. Wash it, one piece at a time, in a basin of lukewarm water and gentle dishwashing detergent. Line the basin and surrounding countertop with a terry towel to ward off chances of nicking the crystal. Rinse with lukewarm water; dry; and polish with a soft, lint-free cloth.

Glass

Even glass that isn't crystal-quality must be cleaned carefully. Be especially wary of sudden temperature changes. A dealer bought an expensive Depression glass bowl on one of the winter's coldest days. He left the bowl in the car while he carried other items into his house. Before returning to the car, he filled the sink with warm, sudsy water. He brought the bowl inside and immediately placed it in the sink. Within seconds the bowl cracked right across the middle, a victim of the rapid, seventy-degree rise in temperature.

Many old small-necked bottles and vases become discolored in time, and cleaning them requires some special techniques. The first is to fill the vase to the stain line with lukewarm vinegar and let it soak for a few minutes. Insert a narrow bottle brush into the bottle or vase and scrub the sides, then rinse with warm water and air-dry.

You won't be able to get the brush into the bulbous bases of many vases, however. So, the second treatment is to pour in a handful of dry white rice, then fill the vase to the stain line with warm, soapy water. Swish the water around gently. The mild abrasive action of the rice will often remove stubborn stains.

Another method, a favorite of many dealers, is to fill the vase to the stain line with warm water, then drop in a denture-cleaning tablet. The tablet's effervescent action is a great cleansing agent.

Finally, if all else fails, you can try this treatment for stubborn glass stains. This usually works on heavy bottles or low-quality glass, but shouldn't be used on delicate or expensive pieces. Fill the piece to the stain line with warm, soapy water and pour in a handful of coarse kitty litter or fine sand. Swish the piece around and around, up and down.

Stained-glass panels

Most modern stained glass is as tough as window glass and needs very little special care. Just spray on glass cleaner and polish with newspaper. Polish the leading with a soft cloth.

Antique stained glass is another story, especially if it has painted sections. These painted areas are extremely fragile. Dampen a soft artist's brush with a mild ammonia-water mixture and clean the panel very gently, working from top to bottom. Let it air-dry out of the sun. Don't polish the leading. The dark gray tones are perfectly acceptable in antique glass.

Artwork

An oil painting that's sound, no cracks or loose paint, and not really dirty, can be freshened by dusting with a wide, soft brush. Working from top to bottom, use gentle, light, short strokes.

A grimy oil painting, if it's sound, can be cleaned with distilled water on cotton swabs. Dampen the swabs with the water and, very gently, work from top to bottom. The optimum word here is *gently*.

Before you do any cleaning of art such as watercolors or prints that are on old paper, however, be very sure that the paper is sound. Fragile antique paper can literally fall apart in your hands if you're not careful. Dust it, using that soft-brush technique, only. Never put water on paper art.

Frames

Old frames abound at yard sales, auctions, and flea markets. They're often a good buy, to sell individually and to showcase antique art. Cleaning a frame in good condition is easy.

First, wipe it with a rag wrung out in warm, soapy water, then rinse. That'll remove most dirt. If a layer of grimy residue remains—perhaps pollution from smoke—dampen a rag with mineral spirits and go over the frame again. That should do it.

More often than not, however, the frames that you find will need some TLC to make them salable. Should you be interested in doing this, you'll find an entire chapter devoted to refinishing frames in *How to Recognize and Refinish Antiques for Pleasure and Profit,* also published by Globe Pequot Press.

Books

Old books are always more valuable if their dust jackets are intact. But dust jackets don't always protect old books from dust.

If you need to clean the books in your shop, use the techniques favored by museums and archivists at large libraries. To remove dust from backs, place a layer of cheesecloth over the brush attachment of your vacuum hose, turn the power to low, and sweep front and back carefully.

The same caveat about old paper exists here as it does with old art on paper. Don't take a chance on damaging book pages if they appear to be fragile. Just leave them alone. Smudges on book pages in good condition, however, will respond to a special pink eraser, sold as Pink Pearl or Opaline that you can buy at an artist's supply store.

Linens

Many old linens will arrive in your hands embellished with brown stains. Most of these stains won't disappear with regular washing, since they've been there for generations. You can, however, sometimes remove an old stain with a method used by savvy antiques dealers. Dampen the piece, then make a paste of your regular laundry detergent and color-safe bleach. Rub the paste into the stain, apply more paste on top of the stain, then place the fabric in the sun for a few hours. A gentle washing will then often remove all or most of the stain.

Ink spots, if not too old, can usually be removed by applying a dab of toothpaste, rubbing gently, then rinsing.

Scorch marks, if not too dark, will lighten when rubbed with white vinegar.

You can't avoid having to iron most old linens before placing them in your shop, but crocheted doilies are another matter. After you wash old doilies, you can give them a fresh, just-ironed look by dipping them in liquid starch, then spreading them on a terry towel that's laid on a carpet or rug. Stretch the doilies out, then anchor the edges with pins. Once dry, the doilies will be very salable.

China

Old china cups often have an undesirable brown tea-and-coffee stain. Remove this by rubbing with a mixture of salt and vinegar.

Another type of brown stain on china occurs simply from age. You'll see this often on platters, bowls, plates, and so forth. One of the best and safest ways to remove this stain is with household bleach. Fill or immerse the piece in bleach and let it soak for a few hours. In most cases the stain will disappear.

Tiny brown hairline cracks often respond to bleach too. Soak the piece in bleach, or if that isn't practical because of the piece's size, dab bleach on the line with cotton swabs. Repeat the dabbing every few hours until the line lightens.

An alternative method is to dissolve two or three denture cleaner tablets in a dishpan filled halfway with hot water. Immerse the stained china, especially stoneware pieces, into the solution and let them soak for twenty-four hours.

Candleholders

Glass, silver, brass, or china candleholders can be cleaned and polished with any of the above methods. You must remove any residual wax first, though. The easiest way is to soak the piece in warm water until the wax softens. You can pick out most of it, then wipe off any remaining wax with a paper towel. Candleholders that can't be dunked in water, such as wooden ones, require different treatment. Just put them in your refrigerator until the wax becomes brittle. You can then carefully chip it off with a blunt knife.

Leather

The best cleaner for leather is usually not saddle soap but a mild solution of warm water and a gentle, nonacid-based, clear facial-quality soap (Neutrogena). Most genuine leather has a faint grain, which was the direction in which the hair grew on the hide. Always wipe along the grain if you can find one.

Try not to spot-clean leather. The best results occur when you work on entire sections. Clean quickly, trying not to soak the leather. Wipe with clear water, and dry with a soft cloth.

Marble

Even though marble appears to be rock-hard, it actually has enough porosity to absorb dirt. You can clean mildly dirty marble by scrubbing with a regular household cleaning brush and dishwashing detergent.

If the marble is really grimy, you'll have to get a bit sterner with it. Make a paste of household bleach or hydrogen peroxide and flour to the consistency of heavy cream. Wet the marble with either bleach or peroxide and spread a thick layer of the paste over the entire piece. Cover the marble with plastic wrap and seal the edges tightly. This will keep the paste from drying out.

Place the marble in a cool area, out of the sun. Allow the paste to work for several days, then rinse it off.

You'll often find more stubborn stains on antique marble that tops old dressers, commodes, and small tables. Organic stains (tea, coffee, tobacco, ink, and the like) that didn't succumb to the first bleach/peroxide-flour treatment will usually respond to an additional remedy. Buy whiting from the hardware store and mix it and hydrogen peroxide together into a thick paste, add a few drops of household ammonia, and layer onto the stain. Place a bowl over this mixture to retain moisture and let it sit for a couple of days, then rinse.

This method has little effect on rust stains from metal. To eliminate them, you'll have to use one of the rust removers sold at hardware stores. Once the marble is free of dirt and stains, polish it with a heavy-duty floor wax.

> Tip: You can even sand away rough edges on marble. If the marble is in good condition except for generations of dirt and some small chips around the edge, use fine-grain sandpaper and plenty of elbow grease to smooth off the irregularities, then clean it.

Christmas ornaments

Antique Christmas ornaments are fast sellers, bringing in high prices, but they're one item you should never make any attempt to clean. The finish on these ornaments is extremely delicate and can rub off at the slightest touch.

White rings on wood

As a rule, these rings, caused by moisture, are easy to remove. Try any one of these remedies:

- Dip a rag in light oil or softened petroleum jelly and rub the ring lightly.
- Dip a piece of fine steel wool in denatured alcohol and rub very gently.
- Dip a rag, dampened in light oil, into cigar or cigarette ash and rub the ring gently.

Decals

Some fifty or sixty years ago, mothers lovingly embellished virtually every high chair and crib with decals of cute little ducks and rabbits. You can remove these decals by soaking them in white vinegar, then scraping gently with a dull table knife.

Stuffed animals

Cornstarch is the best medium for cleaning old stuffed animals whose pile is dirty. Rub it gently into the pile with your fingers, then let it rest overnight. The next day shake the animal gently, then carefully brush out any remaining cornstarch with a soft brush.

09 | Promoting Your Business

You know you have a good selection of antiques and collectibles, well displayed and realistically priced. You know your antiques are just what the men and women in your area need and want for their homes and offices. But how are you going to get the word out about your shop? Certainly, your friends and neighbors know of your new enterprise. And you can't depend on just a sign out front to draw customers in. You need more than that. You need good marketing.

A good marketing plan will spotlight your shop to the community with all the pizzazz of a Hollywood klieg light, as well as establish you as a knowledgeable and valuable source of information on antiques. It will also help you determine how much money to allocate to your advertising budget, select the best media for advertising, then evaluate the results of that advertising.

You'll acquire and keep your customers by creating an image for your shop through careful and consistent marketing. What is marketing? Marketing is, plain and simple, a means of letting the world know about your shop. For you, as the new owner of an antiques shop, marketing will encompass paid advertising, free public-relations-type publicity, direct mail, social networking, and a big grand opening. Your success as a home-based antiques dealer will come from a combination of many forms of promotion, each one reinforcing the other.

Do you need any special training to do all this promotion and advertising? No. No one knows your business as well as you do, and no one can promote it as well and with as much enthusiasm as you can. You know the antiques business and the type of people who buy antiques. You know your inventory. You understand that this is a cyclical business with high and low months.

The buying and selling of antiques is different from almost any other form of retailing. Above all, it's one where creativity and an eye for value constitute the pillars of success. You'll use these same two attributes in your marketing.

As the owner of your antiques business, you're in a much better position to promote your own shop than any professional publicist could. Allocate a few hours every week to doing your own marketing. Once you get into it, you'll probably discover that marketing is actually pleasant and quite creative.

Creating Your Marketing Plan

Your first marketing task will be to create a plan to guide you through your promotional efforts for your first year in business. You'll evaluate and adapt this marketing plan, just as you do your business plan, every year. You'll quickly discover that this marketing plan is as important to your business success as is filling your shop with beautiful antiques.

Just as your business plan is a guide to help you think through and resolve the overall conduct of your antiques business, a marketing plan will help you bring customers in and keep them coming back. It's an ongoing process that continues for as long as you remain in business.

Once in place, your marketing plan will act as a road map to guide you, month by month, through both your short-term and your long-term promotion plans. It will help you coordinate your various promotions for the most effective use of your hard-earned dollars. Your plan will spur you to start organizing, well in advance, special events to coincide with holidays and community affairs. You'll always have the money in your budget for a big spring mailing, for example, because you planned for it in January.

To begin your marketing plan, break it down into sections, as you did your business plan. Adapt the following to suit your needs:

Start off with a few statements that define your annual goals—weekly and monthly media advertising, special promotions, image-enhancement plans, networking plans.

Create a month-by-month breakdown of your marketing efforts, based on the answers to your questions and your statements of goals. This section becomes your specific guide for the entire year.

You'll notice that the sample marketing plan for Alexander's Antiques on the pages 191-194 schedules a grand opening celebration, which will probably be the

Research for Your Marketing Plan

The research you did before preparing your business plan gave you lots of demographic information about your community and the customers of other antiques shops in your area who may soon become your customers. Using this information, answer the following questions:

1. Who is the typical antiques buyer in my town? (Male? Female? What age?)
   _____

2. What is the median family income of this person?
   _____

3. What radio station is this person most likely to listen to?
   _____

4. What newspaper is this person most likely to read?
   _____

5. Roughly, what percentage of my customers will be retired?
   _____

6. Will most of my customers live within a thirty-minute drive of my shop?
   _____

7. How many tourists visit my town every year?
   _____

8. How do most of these tourists travel (car, plane, train)?
   _____

9. Where do most of these tourists stay while in town?
   _____

10. During which months do most tourists visit here?
    _____

Once you've thought through the answers to the preceding questions, you'll have the information you need to make an effective marketing plan.

biggest promotion of your first year in business. All the information you need for writing the backgrounder, press releases, and so forth, mentioned in this first-year plan follows the plan.

Before you can begin formulating your marketing plan, you'll have to do some research. What type of people live in your community? What types of customers patronize other antiques shops in town? What is the socioeconomic level of your community? What's the median income per household?

Your plan should be flexible enough to allow for additions or alterations as the necessity arises. Note that in March and August, Eliel Alexander markets himself as a speaker at civic clubs. He obviously is successful, because he's actually presenting talks in May and November. He added the two lines in May and November mentioning the talks after he received the go-ahead and scheduled the talks.

> Tip: Buy a large wall calendar that has 2-inch-square blank spaces for each day. Transfer all your planned advertising, promotions, contacts, and the like to the appropriate days. You'll then see at a glance what needs to be accomplished on any specific day.

Sample Marketing Plan

Here's how a typical first-year marketing plan for Alexander's Antiques might look. Note that this plan begins in March, when he opened his shop. In succeeding years the plan will begin in January. A blank copy of the plan is in the appendix for you to photocopy and use.

At first glance, all this promotion may seem like a lot of work. After all, you're selling antiques too. By breaking the tasks down into weekly increments, you should be able to handle a similar marketing plan in a few hours each week. Use early mornings, slow hours during the day, or evening hours, whichever suits your schedule and personality best. The reason you have a plan is to help you schedule your time so that you can take advantage of every possible promotional opportunity.

The marketing plan illustrates the two major divisions of marketing. The first, and the one most familiar to many new retailers, is *paid advertising*. It's easy to believe that ads in newspapers, for example, are the best way to publicize a

Alexander's Antiques

Goals:

- to hold at least three sales or special events during the year

- to speak to at least two civic groups during the year

- to establish a mailing list of at least 400 past and present customers

- to develop business among summer tourists

Month	Campaign	Budget
March	Purchase weekly ads in *Fraser News*.	4 x $55 = $220
	Call program chairpeople of local civic clubs to offer self as speaker.	
	Call director of Washington County Community College continuing education program to offer myself as an instructor for antiques courses.	
	Join chamber of commerce.	$125
	Begin plans for May Grand Opening.	
	Set up Local Search Page on Google, Yahoo, and Bing.	
	Register on Facebook.	
April	Purchase weekly ads in *Fraser News*.	4 x $55 = $220
	Attend Lincoln City Antiques Show.	$15
	Write backgrounder and press releases for Grand Opening.	
	Make preliminary contacts with newspaper editors, radio, and TV program directors for Grand Opening publicity.	
	Send backgrounder and press releases to editors and program directors via e-mail.	
	Prepare talk for Lincoln City Women's Club on Arts & Crafts Movement.	
	Contact editor of *Washington County Magazine* about feature story in summer issue.	

Design flyer for Grand Opening.

Have flyers copied. $30

Distribute flyers.

Post Grand Opening announcement to my Facebook page.

Send out e-mail invitation to family and friends
    about Grand Opening.

May   Purchase weekly ads in *Fraser News,* plus   4 x $55 = $220
            display ad the week before Grand Opening.   1 x $400 =$400

Purchase 10 spots on WABC radio. $200

Grand Opening – May 17–22.

Buy stamped postcards for Summer Sale. $100

Have print shop print cards. $40

Buy box of address labels and print some for cards. $15

Present speech to Lincoln City Women's Club
    on Arts & Crafts Movement at luncheon on May 27.

June   Purchase weekly ads in *Fraser News.*   4 x $55 = $220

Mail postcards.

Create and print "15% OFF" signs for summer sale.

Post summer sale announcement on Facebook.

Send e-mail announcement of summer sale to family
    and friends, plus registered customers.

July   Purchase weekly ads in *Fraser News.*   4 x $55 = $220

Hold summer sale through the month of July.

Begin plans for Fraser Days promotion.

Contact persons asking to borrow items for Fraser Days
    exhibit.

August   Purchase weekly ads in *Fraser News.*   4 x $55 = $220

Call program chairpeople of civic clubs again.

Write press release for Fraser Days promotion.

Call *Fraser News* editor about feature for Fraser Days.

Send backgrounders and releases to *Fraser News*
   editor and radio stations.

Firm up plans for Fraser Days exhibit.

Post announcement about Fraser Days exhibit
   on Facebook.

Send e-mail announcement about Fraser Days
   exhibit to family, friends, and registered customers.

September	Purchase weekly ads in *Fraser News*.	4 x $55 = $220
	Fraser Days exhibit on view from September 19–25.	
October	Purchase weekly ads in *Fraser News*.	4 x $55 = $220
	Begin plans for Holiday Open House and Sale.	
	Update e-mail and regular mailing list.	
	Buy stamped postcards for Holiday Open House and Sale.	$100
	Have postcards printed.	$40
	Print address labels for postcards.	
November	Purchase weekly ads in *Fraser News*.	4 x $55 = $220
	Prepare talk for Collector's Club on Rookville Pottery.	
	Present talk to Collector's Club on November 22.	
	Mail postcards for Holiday Open House and Sale.	
	Attend Lincoln City Antiques Show.	$15
	Decorate shop for the holidays.	
	Post announcement about Holiday Open House and Sale on Facebook.	
	Send e-mail announcement about same to family, friends, and registered customers.	

December	Purchase weekly ads in *Fraser News.*	4 x $55 = $220
	Post holiday greeting on Facebook.	
	Send e-mail holiday greeting to family, friends, and	
	registered customers.	
	Hold Holiday Open House and Sale from Dec. 6–11.	
	Close for the holidays from Dec. 25 to Jan. 2.	
	Contact web designer about building a website for	
	the shop in the coming year.	

business—and they can be during the first months. In the long run, however, paid advertising is usually less effective than the second type of marketing known as *public relations* or *publicity,* which is free advertising you generate in the local media, on the Internet, and through personal contacts.

Paid versus Free Advertising

You'll have to include money in your budget for paid advertising. There's no way around it. Right at first, when all the money's going out and little's coming in, you may cringe at the thought of paying for advertising. The fact remains that advertising is essential, especially during the first months of business, when your visibility as an antiques shop in the community may be slim. Paid advertising is a guaranteed way to get your name before the public to let them know you're there. Later on, after you've established yourself, you'll be able to gather quite a bit of unpaid promotion. But first, how do you get the most bang for your advertising buck?

It doesn't make sense for the owner of a small home-based antiques shop to use what's termed the shotgun approach to advertising, which means spreading your money and efforts like buckshot over a huge area. This type of advertising works only for very large general-interest firms that appeal to a wide variety of customers—old, young, men, women, low-income, high-income, and so on. You're better off to use the rifle approach, which aims directly at your target market, which is, of course, your customers.

Newspaper Advertising

The shotgun approach to newspaper advertising would be to buy ads in a big metropolitan newspaper, one with a circulation of 500,000 or so and read by practically everyone in the city. Keep in mind that the majority of its readers would be unlikely to become your customers, and your little ads would be lost among the huge discount-store ads. The rifle approach narrows down your target area. Buy ads in the local paper that services your small town or in the community paper distributed in your section of the big city. Your ads will show up in its less crowded pages, and its readers will live close enough to your shop to be logical customers.

Paid newspaper advertising comes in two types: display and classified, otherwise known as the "want ads."

Display Ads. Display ads are the large boxed ones scattered throughout the main sections of the paper. They can be highly attractive, especially if they contain graphics, but they're extremely expensive. Your grand opening is the one time you should spend the hundreds of dollars to place a display ad in your local paper. For that one-time-only special event, you'll get results from such an ad, and it will reinforce the free publicity you get, doubling the impact.

You may have had some training in graphics and layout in one of your business courses. If not, this is one time you should spring for professional help in preparing that all-important grand opening ad. The cost won't be prohibitive, and professionals know how you can get the most value for your advertising dollar. Just be sure your ad follows the tried-and-true format used by every good advertising writer—the AIDA formula.

What is the AIDA formula? It's the specifics used by professional advertising people to create professional-quality ads and flyers. Here's how it works:

- The A stands for ATTENTION.
- The I stands for INTEREST.
- The D stands for DESIRE.
- The A stands for ACTION.

To begin using this formula, write a headline at or near the top of your ad or flyer. This should contain some lively text that will attract the reader's *attention* to the ad by announcing your newsworthy event. Follow the headline with more text that creates *interest* in your shop or the event. Halfway down write text that will stimulate the reader's *desire* to know more about your shop or to attend a special event.

Finally, near the end, place some short, punchy text that will motivate the reader to take *action*, to come into your shop.

Below is a typical display ad for an antiques shop grand opening. Can you see how this ad uses the AIDA formula? Do you see how this formula works? Does this format seem familiar? Probably so, because you see it every day in ads, brochures, flyers, and other promotional material created by public relations and advertising professionals. You can't go wrong with the AIDA formula in display ads.

Display Ad

ALEXANDER'S ANTIQUES
Specializing in Arts & Crafts Furniture and Accessories

Mission Oak and Late Victorian Furniture

Old Toys

Late 19th and Early 20th Century Pottery & Art Glass

Antique Clocks

Art Deco Collectibles

Stained-Glass Lamps

Early Advertising Prints

Estate Jewelry

Kitchen Collectibles

Bentwood Chairs

Early Photographic Cameras

WE BUY ESTATES
OR SINGLE ITEMS

Antiques Valuations · Estate Sales
Consignments · Antiques Reference Books

494-555-6938

Tuesday–Saturday
10 A.M. – 5 P.M.

123 Chestnut Road, Fraser
(Three blocks from downtown)

> **Tip:** Be wary of spending any advertising money on an ad that's simply one of fifty or so other small, similar ads covering an entire page in the paper. These pages usually promote a town's annual event, such as Good Neighbor Days, a German Oktoberfest, or a Chili Cookoff Weekend.
>
> A representative from your local newspaper may approach you to buy such a display ad, saying it'll be good advertising for you. It won't because again you'll just be one of many. You need to stand out from the crowd. This type of ad is slightly larger than a business card and contains scarcely more information than a business card does, yet you have to pay the same high display-ad rate. Unfortunately, these ads just don't carry their weight, especially for a new business.

Classified Ads. The best advice is to forgo display ads except for your grand opening and stick with regular ads in the classified section of the paper, where prices are more affordable. To be honest, ads for antiques in the classified section are, in most cases, actually more effective than display ads, since many people who are searching for antiques read the classifieds, especially the subsections headed Antiques, Auctions, Furniture, and Garage Sales. Place an ad in the Antiques category, and they can't miss it.

For $55 or $95 a week in many smaller newspapers, you can purchase a substantial classified ad that will really stand out. Don't hesitate to pay a small additional fee to enclose your classified ad in a strong, decorative border.

The best classified ads are those that highlight a few specific antiques rather than trying to catalog a whole laundry list of items. Just be sure the name of your shop is in bold type, along with your address. The following might be a typical classified ad for a home-based antiques shop:

Consistency is the key to successful classified advertising. Don't place ads a couple of times, then decide they're not paying off. Set up a regular schedule, preferably weekly, and run your ad regardless of any obvious results. Many people will see your ads with the name of your shop the first time or two, and it won't register. But as they read them, week after week, in the same section of the classifieds, they'll begin to notice. Many papers will give you a special rate, too, if you sign a contract for a specified number of insertions. Talk to the advertising manager to receive such a reduced rate.

NEW THIS WEEK AT

ALEXANDER'S ANTIQUES

Mission oak dining table and 6 chairs

Fine roll-top desk, c. 1900

Tiffany-style stained-glass lamp

Wicker fern stand

Plus hundreds of other quality antiques

Stop in for a look at our collection of Arts and Crafts pieces

And have a cup of coffee while you shop

123 Chestnut Road

494-555-6938

Open Tues.–Sat. 10 A.M. – 5 P.M.

Radio Advertising

Radio is not usually the best advertising medium for a small antiques shop, but you may want to run a few spots for your grand opening. The rifle approach works well here, also. Let's assume that the initial research you did for your business plan indicated that your average customer is probably a thirty-nine-year-old married woman with an income of $45,000 per year. Your shop/home is in a suburban community of a large metropolitan city, and this customer lives in that community.

You decide to advertise your grand opening on local radio. Instead of buying time on all three local radio stations, you call each station and ask for the demographics of its listeners. You may discover that one station appeals mostly to teenagers and young adults, and it plays the music they enjoy. Another station plays mostly oldies-but-goodies favored by the over-fifty crowd. The third station plays contemporary jazz and pop. This information tells you to concentrate your radio advertising money with station number three, the one your *average* customer is most likely to listen to.

> **Tip:** *Never* read your weekly classified ad over the telephone to a clerk at the paper. Always type it and take it in or send it by e-mail or fax. Ask how much it will be to run it either by the week or longer. Then insist that it be printed exactly as you wrote it. This alone will save you money because your ad will cost exactly what the clerk quotes you.
>
> A novice dealer phoned in an ad that mentioned, among several other antiques and collectibles, an Art Deco vanity bench. When she opened her paper two days later, she hit the roof when she saw the vanity bench described as "Art Decoration." She raced to the paper, located the employee who'd taken her ad over the phone and demanded to know why her ad didn't read as she'd called it in. The employee, who'd never heard the term Art Deco, answered in all innocence, "Well, there was a little space left at the end of the line, and I didn't see any need to abbreviate the word decoration when I could spell it out!"

You'll discover, when talking with the radio's advertising account person, that the station charges a different rate for slots aired at different times of the day. As a rule, the most expensive slots are those aired during what's termed "drive time"— that is, weekdays from 6:00 to 10:00 a.m. and 4:00 to 7:00 p.m. The least expensive slots are often during the middle of the day.

You'll get the most coverage for your money by scheduling those midday slots. Anyone who is at home during the day—retired people, housewives, shift workers— will hear them. Add to that the many people who listen to radio at work, and you come up with a large portion of the population.

Most advertisements for radio fit into ten-, thirty-, or sixty-second slots. A ten-second spot consists of approximately twenty words. A thirty-second spot is about sixty words, and a one-minute spot runs around 120 words. You can pack a surprising amount of information into those few words.

The easiest way to write radio spots is to begin with a sixty-second one because it allows you the most space to get your message across. Even so, avoid meaningless words. Try to use only those words that carry your message. Once your sixty-second spot is complete, go back and eliminate words until you've reduced the spot to thirty, then ten seconds.

Here's a typical sixty-second spot for radio:

Alexander's Antiques is the newest antiques shop in town, and we're having our big Grand Opening May 16 through 21. Alexander's Antiques is the shop in Fraser for primitive furniture, fine nineteenth-century pieces, and those popular collectibles from the turn of the century. At Alexander's Antiques you'll find Belleek, Shelley, Limoges, Haviland, and Wedgwood china. We carry reference books on antiques for you serious collectors. Looking for an inexpensive gift? Check out Grandma's Corner in the back room. Nothing there is more than $25. During our Grand Opening we'll have free flowers for the first fifty ladies, and we'll give away two gift certificates worth $50 each. Don't miss it, the big Grand Opening at Alexander's Antiques, 123 Chestnut Road in Fraser, where the coffeepot is always on!

Now let's take that sixty-second spot and delete enough words to bring it down to thirty seconds. Here's what we might come up with:

Alexander's Antiques, at 123 Chestnut Road in Fraser, is having its big Grand Opening May 16 through 21. Alexander's Antiques is the shop for fine Arts and Crafts and Mission Oak furniture, early twentieth-century collectibles, beautiful china and pottery, plus reference books. Register for $50 gift certificates during the big Grand Opening, May 16 through 21, at Alexander's Antiques, 123 Chestnut Road, where the coffeepot is always on!

Okay, so your budget is pretty thin and you can only spring for a few ten-second spots. You can still let people know you're in business. Here's how:

Alexander's Antiques announces its gala Grand Opening—May 16 through 21. Antiques, collectibles. Register for free gift certificates. Alexander's Antiques, 123 Chestnut Road in Fraser.

Amazing, isn't it, the amount of information you can squeeze into twenty short words?

Did you notice how many times Eliel Alexander repeated the name of his shop? That's very important in radio advertising. The more times a business's name can be repeated, the more likely the listener will remember it.

Television Advertising

Forget paid television advertising. It's far too expensive for the average small business. You may be able to get complimentary spots on local television for your special events, however. More about that later.

The Yellow Pages

It used to be that everyone "walked their fingers" through the Yellow Pages. It was the fastest, easiest way to locate almost any product or service. Until recently, a listing in the Yellow Pages was the best way to draw customers to a business. In fact, it was the best way to attract new and out-of-town customers who didn't see a business's ads in the local newspaper.

But that's all changed since the emergence of Local Search on the Internet and social networking sites like Facebook and Twitter.

Today, the high monthly cost of a Yellow Pages ad doesn't justify its relatively low return rate. And the proliferation of online promotional methods will only improve with the smart phones on the market. Another downside to the Yellow Pages is that you have to commit to a full year of advertising. Compare that to all the free promotion available to you on the web.

That's just about all the paid advertising you, as a home-based antiques shop owner, should consider. For more information about Internet website advertising, see chapter 6. Now let's look into all the free promotion you can get for your shop.

Free Advertising: Publicity (Public Relations)

One of the biggest mistakes you can make as a first-time owner of a small business is to depend solely on paid advertising to promote your shop. You just pay your money, get some coverage in the local paper, then sit back and wait for customers to stream into your shop. But that's just the beginning. There's a whole world of promotion out there just waiting to be tapped if you're willing to spend time and energy on *publicity*.

Many dealers are totally unaware of the incredible amount of publicity they can get—thousands and thousands of dollars worth—and not pay a dime for it, other than the time and minimal costs necessary to prepare releases.

Free publicity can take the form of feature stories in newspapers, complete with big photographs of you and your shop. It can be lively spots on radio and even announcements on local and cable television. And even more effective are mentions in people's blogs and on their social networking pages. Being in the antiques business puts you in a special position in that you can even get other *businesses* to help you to promote your shop. According to many surveys, the beauty of *public relations* or unpaid publicity, is that *consumers respond to it three times more often than they do to paid advertising*.

Think about it. Your neighborhood movie theater might run a weekly ad listing the current movies it's showing and call each one "best of the season," "a must-see," or "heart-wrenching drama." You've seen, heard, and read the same hype so often about so many movies that you seldom pay much attention to it. Yet if you read reviews of the same films, written by a well-respected critic, and the critic highly recommends the films, perhaps using the same words that are in the ads, you'll sit up and pay attention. The implication is that the critic made an unbiased judgment of the movies, where the theater would say anything to get moviegoers to plunk down our cash for a ticket. The ads are paid advertisement. The reviews are unpaid publicity. See how this works?

The same holds true for you and your shop. People read ads, certainly, and you almost have to run them, but your customers will give more credibility to *feature stories* written by a newspaper reporter or editor than they will to the ads. This coverage has the appearance of being a genuine news story. Readers naturally feel it's objective and unsolicited, yet you actually are the originator of the stories.

To generate this free publicity, you'll need to prepare press releases, backgrounders, public service announcements, and flyers. But remember, each announcement or release must be newsworthy. Whatever you're writing about must be news, otherwise editors will ignore it.

Press Releases

A press release is a one- to two-page document that describes a special event you plan to hold, plus information about your shop. It's the accepted method of making contact with the media—print or broadcast—and a well-written release will get a busy media person's attention. Many of these people have few or no support personnel, so to catch their eye a release should follow specific guidelines and a particular format.

Guidelines for a Perfect Press Release

- *Keep the release to one page.* Media people don't have time to read more than that. If they want more information than you can place on one page, they'll ask for it.
- *Place a release date on the first line in the upper-right corner.* If you'd like the information to be released immediately, type For Immediate Release. Or you can type what's termed an "embargo" by specifying a certain date: release between May 8 and May 15, for example. However, media people are under no obligation to abide by your release date and will run the story whenever it fits their publication or broadcast schedule.
- *Using bold, capital letters, write a one-line headline that accurately describes the subject of the release.* The headline should be catchy and enticing enough to get the media person's attention. This isn't the time or place to be cute. Just tell it like it is.
- *On the first line of text, write the name of your city and the date you plan to deliver the release.*
- *Double-space all text, and use either 12-point Times New Roman or Arial as the font.*
- *Make sure to include the five Ws of journalism—who, what, why, where, and when—in the first paragraph or two.* This is the place for your first mention of the event you're promoting.
- *Use simple language, short words, short sentences, and shorter paragraphs when you compose the text—the same type of writing you find in your daily paper.* Media people dislike flowery language and overblown adjectives.
- *Be enthusiastic but objective when describing your shop.* Don't call it the "best antiques shop in the county." This could be a matter of opinion. Instead, say it's "the newest antiques shop" or "the only home-based antiques shop in town," both of which are newsworthy, and this is what media people, especially newspaper editors want—news.
- *Get as much solid information as you can on one page.* Remember, the person reading it probably knows nothing about your shop. You must tweak their curiosity and interest with facts, facts, and more facts.

- *Include a quote or two from yourself in the text.* Editors, especially, like quotes as they help personalize what might otherwise be a dry story. You'll probably be the source for this quote, so make it lively and usable.
- *Print your release on good-quality, 24-pound, 8 1/2-by-11-inch paper.* Businesses usually print their releases on white paper, so why not print yours on ivory or light gray? It'll stand out in that sea of releases and just might get the attention of a harried editor. Just don't use any bright colors or decorative margins.
- *Place your name, daytime phone number, and e-mail at the end of the release so that the media person can call you for more information.*
- *Call each media outlet and ask for the name of the person who handles the department that would logically run your release.* Then send your release to that person.

Page 205 shows a typical press release for a special exhibit for the antiques shop and page 211 shows one for the grand opening of the shop. With a little luck, such a release should result in at least a short news story or a mention in a community-events-type column, whether in print, on the air, or online.

Backgrounders

You probably can get much more than short notices in your local media by including what's called a *backgrounder* with your press release. A backgrounder consists of one or more printed pages, giving background information about you, your new shop, and any especially interesting or unusual things about you and your shop. This is the information the media person will use to determine whether your shop is interesting enough to warrant running a feature story—and you want that feature story.

A backgrounder includes statistics about you and your shop, such as your name, your shop's name and location, the types of antiques you sell, and so forth. It may also have one or more quotes from you as the owner and some interesting information that won't fit into the press release. If the media person decides to run a feature about you, the reporter assigned to the story will receive a copy of your backgrounder and will bring it with her to use during the interview. The backgrounder helps the reporter come up with enough questions and information to write either an article or do an on-air interview. Pages 206-207 shows a typical backgrounder.

FOR IMMEDIATE RELEASE

For more information contact:
Eliel Alexander (494) 555-6938

ALEXANDER'S ANTIQUES CELEBRATES FRASER DAYS WITH HISTORICAL EXHIBIT

Fraser, Pennsylvania, August 9, 2011 - Alexander's Antiques will celebrate Fraser Days for the first time with a special historical exhibit showcasing memorabilia and household items used at the time of the founding of the town in 1902.

Shop owner, Eliel Alexander, a member of the Washington County Historical Society and currently serving on its Board of Directors, is planning a unique exhibit in his shop for the duration of the Fraser Days Celebration, featuring pieces from his own collection and shop inventory combined with borrowed items from some of Fraser's oldest families. On display will be an antique crazy quilt that once belonged to Sarah Johnson, wife of Fraser's founder, Seth Johnson, a ledger dated 1902 from Brown's General Store, early twentieth-century appliances, early readers from Fraser's original one-room schoolhouse, as well as a writing lap desk, old photographs of the town, and many other items.

"I love history," said Alexander. "And this exhibit gives me the chance to show off my collection and my new shop."

The exhibit will be open during regular business hours, Tuesday through Saturday, from 10 a.m. to 5 p.m., plus Sunday and Monday, September 18 and 19, from 1 to 4 p.m.

Only three blocks from the Main Square, the center of the Fraser Days activities, Alexander's Antiques is within easy walking distance of Fraser's business district. As the only home-based antiques shop in town, it offers the warm ambience of a private home.

# # #

Name of new shop: Alexander's Antiques
Location: 123 Chestnut Rd.
Telephone: (494) 555-6938
E-mail: ealexander@webservices.com
Owner: Eliel Alexander
Hours of operation: 10:00 a.m. to 5:00 p.m., Tuesday-Saturday

Relevant information:

Alexander's Antiques, Fraser, Pennsylvania's newest antiques shop, is in owner
Eliel Alexander's home and is the only home-based antiques shop in the area.
Alexander converted the front three rooms of his home into a 600-square-foot shop
that faces Chestnut Road. During the week of May 16 to 21, 2011, he will hold a
gala Grand Opening celebration of his new shop.

Eliel Alexander has lived in Fraser the last twenty-six years and has been an
avid collector of antiques for the last thirty. His own collection includes fifty pieces
of fine Rookville pottery, which he has acquired over the years while traveling
America. From time to time, Alexander plans to exhibit pieces from this collection in
a special glass case in his shop.

Alexander is active in community affairs and is a member of the local Rotary
Club, the Chamber of Commerce, and is on the board of the Washington County
Historical Society.

Born in Philadelphia, Pennsylvania, he spent his childhood in a home filled with
Victorian-era antiques. It was then he developed a love for and appreciation of
antique furniture and accessories. At the same time, he developed a dislike for the
ostentatious ornamentation of some Victorian pieces. This is what led him to study
Arts and Crafts furniture designers such as William Morris and eventually to specializing in this aesthetic style.

According to Alexander, "Many collectors consider fine antiques one of the
best investments because statistically they increase in value over time. In most
cases the construction of antique furniture is superior to that of modern construc-

tion methods. In addition, antiques bring beauty into a home and pleasure to their owners. Many people today mix a few antiques with their contemporary furnishings, whether they've been passed down from members of their families or have been purchased."

The unique aspect of this shop is an area called "Collector's Corner," which displays moderately priced collectibles—none over $25. No other antiques shop in this area has such an exhibit.

In addition to selling antiques and collectibles, Alexander gives valuations of individual antiques, as well as conducts estate sales for Fraser residents in the homes of their relatives, offering them an alternative to placing their antiques in auction houses.

You will notice in the backgrounder the mention of Eliel Alexander's extensive collection of majolica pottery. Can you see how such a collection could make an excellent photograph or video clip, perhaps with him holding, and perhaps talking about, a particularly unique and valuable piece? Media today demands illustrations to get the attention of readers or watchers.

When you write your backgrounder, be sure to include anything about you or your shop that would create a good image. This information will greatly help your chances of receiving free coverage in your local media.

Public Service Announcements (PSAs)

You can use the same press release and backgrounder to generate free public service announcements on local radio stations, in addition to the paid announcements you might buy. Some program directors at smaller local stations will also tape an interview with you and run it many times prior to your grand opening. They use these interviews to fill in spots where their advertising representatives weren't able to sell paid ads. You might be able to get such a tape about your grand opening aired during locally produced home-type shows, too.

Some local television stations have what they call "Community Bulletin Boards" or similar programs where they announce community events. You might be able to get some very short announcements about your grand opening on these programs.

Don't count on it, though, as most of these announcements concern nonprofit events since the television stations know businesses have larger budgets to pay for ads.

A better alternative is to hook up with the producer of a local cable TV home show. Send them a copy of your release and backgrounder and invite them to tape a show at your shop. People do watch these programs, even though they may be on at odd hours. Home and Garden shows are extremely popular, and you'll surely find one that might even like an occasional segment on antiques and collectibles. The next time a show which might be just right for you is on, jot down the name of the producer, then call the cable company and ask how you can get in touch.

Flyers

Attractive, colorful flyers can be a great way to get the word out about your shop at very little cost. Any copy center can print a flyer, in large quantities, on colored paper for about 5 cents a sheet. Assuming that you order 1,000 flyers, your cost will be only $50. However, you must have the flyer all prepared, that is "camera-ready." With 1,000 flyers in circulation, potentially 1,000 or more people will learn of your shop or of a special promotion. That's a lot of promotion for so little money. Radio and television ads disappear and can't be recalled the second after they're aired. Newspaper ads must compete with perhaps hundreds of other similar ads, and a newspaper is usually discarded after one reading. Online ads have an even shorter life span. A flyer, however, is a highly visible and portable advertisement. A well-composed flyer can contain a wealth of information that simply can't be included in any other type of advertisement. You can easily create a flyer in Microsoft Word or, better yet, in Microsoft Publisher, that simply gives general information about your shop, which you'll place in bed-and-breakfast inns, hotels, chamber of commerce information centers, and other places frequented by tourists. Flyers can also be used as direct-mail pieces to announce special promotions. You can distribute your flyers at antiques shows and flea markets as well.

Most people will stop to glance over an attractive flyer. Then, if the subject interests them, they'll pick it up and hold it for study later, perhaps even attaching it to their refrigerator doors with a magnet. Use bold type that's easy to read, and include at least one graphic that represents an antiques shop.

Now take another look at the newspaper display ad on page 196. Do you see how this ad for Alexander's Antiques' grand opening could be used just as well for a flyer? The advertising or public relations agency that prepared this ad for Eliel Alexander

> **Tip:** Create a flyer that measures 5½-by-8½ inches, then print it out twice. Paste the two flyers side by side on a full sheet of paper to create your master copy. Take this to a copy center to be reproduced on attractive, brightly colored paper. Producing half-size flyers offers two advantages: The size is convenient to take along, and you'll get twice as many for the same price. Consider offering 5 to 10 percent discount to new customers if they bring the flyer with them to your shop. This is a great way to track the flyer's effectiveness.

would give him the master copy. He could then take it to a copy center and have as many flyers as he wanted printed to promote his grand opening.

Regardless of who prepares your flyers, just remember the AIDA formula on page 195, which works equally well in laying out flyers. Get people's <u>A</u>ttention with a smashing headline, capture their <u>I</u>nterest with compelling text and graphics, instill <u>D</u>esire with alluring descriptions, then move them to <u>A</u>ction with a forceful suggestion.

Preparing for Your Grand Opening

Your grand opening is your first and best opportunity to make an impression on the antiques-buying public in your community. So make it good and promote it as much as you can.

Publicizing Your Grand Opening

All of the above examples of advertising and public relations devices can be used in one way or another to promote your grand opening. Ideally, you should hold this event for at least a week, beginning on a Friday or Saturday. Don't choose a holiday weekend, as most people are too busy having fun on Memorial Day, July Fourth, and Labor Day weekends to generate much enthusiasm for visiting an antiques shop.

Preparing a Publicity Campaign

Whether it's for your grand opening or some other event, you'll need to prepare a publicity campaign. Before trying to promote your event, you need to create a list of media outlets. This list should include the outlet's name, contact person's name, mailing address, phone, fax, and the e-mail address of the person you're contacting. Do this for all sorts of media—newspapers within a 50-mile radius, local radio, television and cable television stations, local websites and online bulletin boards. Your media list will become your most valuable promotional tool. Update it regularly.

Begin your publicity campaign three or four weeks before your event.

Contact each media representative and introduce yourself as the owner of a new antiques shop in town. Explain that you're planning a grand opening that should be a fun event for the community. Ask whether you can e-mail a press release like the one on page 211 and backgrounder for the person to read. Make your shop sound so interesting that the person will want to know more about it. Be sure to follow up in a few days with a second phone call or a second e-mail.

The time of day you make your phone call is important. Media people frequently work right up to the deadline before a newspaper goes to press and before a show goes on the air, and they have no time to talk with anyone then. For a morning paper the best time to call them on the phone is usually early morning. For an afternoon paper the best time is usually early afternoon. Call early in the week for Sunday edition editors. However, e-mail is the best method of contact since most media people read it when they have a free moment.

You must convince the media person that both you and your new shop are interesting. If you succeed, either the editor or a reporter from the newspaper or the program director from the radio or television station will invite you to come in for an interview or will make an appointment to visit you in your shop, the most likely scenario. Radio talk show hosts will usually set up an appointment with you and will then conduct the interview over the phone. A TV station will usually have a reporter and a news van stop by your shop to get some live video to be shown on the nightly news.

Be sure your shop is in top-notch shape. At the interview, the reporter will ask you about yourself, specifically how you got into the antiques business, and your shop. Be sure to give the reporter all the details about your grand opening, and be enthusiastic. In all but large cities, the opening of a new shop is genuine news that the paper wants to mention. The paper may assign a photographer to take pictures or the TV station may send a cameraman to shoot video clips during the interview, so dress appropriately. Any printed or aired feature story with any sort of images will definitely result in new customers. Let the photographer or cameraman know about any sorts of antiques in which you specialize or some that are particularly unique.

FOR IMMEDIATE RELEASE

For more information contact:
Eliel Alexander (494) 555-6938

FRASER'S ONLY HOME-BASED ANTIQUES SHOP TO HOLD GRAND OPENING

Fraser, Pennsylvania, May 4, 2011 - Eliel Alexander, owner of Alexander's Antiques, announces the Grand Opening of his new antiques shop during the week of May 16 through 21 at 123 Chestnut Road.

Only three blocks from the Main Square, it's within easy walking distance of Fraser's business district. As the only home-based antiques shop in town, it offers the warm ambience of a private home. According to Alexander, "I chose to open my shop in my home because I want to create a homelike atmosphere where my customers can easily visualize the antiques in their own home."

Alexander has long enjoyed the antiques of the late nineteenth through the early twentieth centuries and so chose to specialize in antiques and collectibles of this period. Here, customers will find fine examples furniture, ceramics, and other accessories of the Arts and Crafts period, as well as furniture in the Mission Oak style. Electric stained-glass lamps from the same period will add to the atmosphere. Art pottery and glass came into its own during this time, so Alexander believes examples of Rookville pottery and amberina glass, among others, will enhance his offerings. He plans to display these accessories and the furniture they complement in warm homelike groupings to help his customers get decorating ideas for their own homes.

On May 21, the last day of the Grand Opening, Alexander will hold a drawing at 4 p.m. for two $50 gift certificates, good toward any antique in the shop. Parking is available on Chestnut Road and in the city parking lot on Main Street.

# # #

Most newspapers, television and radio stations won't run a free story about a commercial enterprise if you don't buy an ad occasionally—that's life in the media world. If you've bought some advertising spots for this event, you'll probably get free publicity spots, too.

You can count on a positive response from colorful flyers, though. Take flyers announcing the grand opening to every hotel, motel, bed-and-breakfast inn, and information center in your area. Ask to have the flyers displayed on a table or counter where people can pick them up. Travelers often have a free hour or two on their hands, and many would like to know of some interesting local place to visit.

Distribute your flyers anywhere people interested in antiques might gather—thrift shops, auction houses, flea markets, decorating shops. One way to show your gratitude to the owners or managers of these places is by giving them your business card with a handwritten note on the back saying "15% discount on one purchase anytime during _____." (Fill in the calendar year for which the discount will apply.) Not only is this a courteous gesture, but it'll bring them into your shop, too.

Make sure that all your advertising and publicity mentions some sort of incentive for customers to visit the shop during the grand opening.

Preparing Your Shop for Your Grand Opening

Make your shop as festive as possible for this event. Place bouquets of flowers throughout the shop and on your checkout table. Use flowers from your garden or pick up several bouquets at the supermarket. Have soft, lively music playing on a radio or CD player. Fill antique bowls with mints or wrapped chocolate candies and place them on several tables. Decorate potted trees, either outside or inside, with tiny, twinkling white lights. Meet each person who enters the door with a pleasant greeting and an invitation to sign a guest book and register for free gift certificates or any other promotion you're using during the grand opening.

Plan to provide some light refreshments, such as cookies and bridge mix (nothing too messy), accompanied by hot coffee and hot or iced tea or lemonade. Although refreshments involve some extra work and expense, they're worth it.

Try to get a relative or friend to help out on the first day or two of the grand opening. Chances are you'll have a crowd, and you, as the shop owner, should be available for pleasant chatting and discussion about your antiques. Your helper can fill in at the checkout table by handling money and wrapping purchases.

You can get additional after-the-event media coverage by calling newspapers to announce winners of the gift certificates. Even a brief mention in the paper will be worth far more in publicity than the value of the certificates. Should have someone take a photograph of the drawing and the people who win the certificates and offer the photograph to the paper. Make sure its an action shot showing you congratulating the winners while handing one a certificate—all this against a background of antiques.

You'll derive additional value from your gift certificates if you have those who register for them fill out small forms with their name, address, phone number, e-mail address, and any preferences they have for specific types of antiques or collectibles. Provide an attractive jar or bowl in which they can deposit their forms. These will also provide you with an instant mailing list for regular and e-mail.

Think how often you've seen the same type of device used by large companies. You sign up for a chance at a free trip to Hawaii, a new car, or some other prize, and pretty soon you're receiving promotional mail or phone calls asking you to buy life insurance, aluminum siding, cemetery plots, vacuum cleaners, or whatever. In your case you'd use this list, along with the names in the guest book, later to send announcements of sales or some other promotional event. It's a perfectly legitimate marketing strategy.

Using the Internet to Promote Your Antiques Business

The Internet has become an integral part of everyday life. If you're one of those people who has your head stuck in the sand and thinks that it's strictly for geeks and students, you better think again. More and more people are turning to the Internet to find what they need, whether it's information or items they want to buy and collect. It's fast becoming one of the most effective ways to market a business—even an antiques shop.

It took until 1997 for the Internet to gain more than 50 million American users. But it only took twelve months for Facebook, the leading social networking site, to top 100 million users in 2009. Now more than 300 million people have pages on this super successful social network.

It's for this reason that it is extremely important to get your shop's name out there in Cyberspace before you have your Grand Opening. Today, the right type and amount of Internet promotion can mean the difference between a successful business and mediocre one.

Developing a Strategy for Online Promotion

Before doing anything, you need to plan out how you're going to make the best use of the Internet given the amount of time you have to spend on it and your computer expertise.

You have several alternatives to help you promote your shop on the Internet:

- Registering for Local Search
- Publishing a blog
- Registering on a social network site
- Creating your own website

While you may choose to use all or just some of the above suggestions, each interlinking with the other for the best result, it's important to keep things simple, or you'll end up spending more time on the Internet than you do selling antiques.

Local Search

The first and easiest method of Internet promotion is to register for one of the three major Local Searches—Google.com, Yahoo.com, and Bing.com. Registering on these sites doesn't require much computer know-how, and you'll see results in two to four weeks.

What exactly is Local Search? Each of the above search engines—the services people use to find what they want on the Internet—offers you a page that includes your shop's name, address, phone, e-mail address, website, and a map to show customers how to get there. In addition, you can also post digital photos of your shop and add online coupons for special discounts. But the most important part of Local Search is the reviews, posted by satisfied customers. Today, many people rely on online reviews by ordinary people like themselves before purchasing anything. For a potential customer to find you, all they have to do is type in the word *antiques* and the name of your town and a list of all the shops registered will appear. If you get lots of good reviews, your listing will eventually migrate toward the top of the list.

To get started using Local Search, go to http://GetListed.org. Click on each of the three search engines and fill out the form for each. It's that simple.

Publishing a Blog

If you're especially knowledgeable about a particular group of antiques or collectibles, you may want to consider publishing a blog, otherwise known as a web log.

While many bloggers—the people who write blogs—post messages to their blogs daily, you may want to publish yours weekly. And instead of just chatting about this and that in your blog, share your expertise with your readers.

The important thing is to post messages regularly. If weekly, make it the same day each week, so your readers, also known as "followers," will know when to expect your next post. To get started, go to Blogger.com (www.blogger.com), sponsored by Google. If you're not already a registered user of Google, then you'll have to do that first. Just go to Google's home page (www.google.com) and click on "Sign In." This will take you to a page where you can fill in your information and create a username and password. Then go to Blogger.com and click on the bright orange "Create a Blog" button. It's as easy as one, two, three.

They let you show off your writing, and people can get to know you through your posts. It gave people an avenue to get to know me in a less formal way than my corporate brochures and other business communications. Blogs are also interactive. People post comments, and share blog posts with others. That transforms it into viral marketing.

A blog is an online journal that you update regularly. Each update, also called an entry or a post, is usually short, perhaps just a few paragraphs, so followers can read them fast and respond to them by leaving comments. Always write your blog with a specific type of person in mind. If you're writing to potential customers, think of them as antiques collectors. What information do they need? What are they searching for?

Above all, write as you talk. Pretend an antique collector is in your shop and you're having a conversation about what he or she collects.

> Tip: Before you start blogging, visit other blogs that are like the one you're thinking of writing. Go to Blogger.com and do a search for "antiques." You'll get a list of all the blogs that deal with the subject of antiques. Click on one at a time to begin your research. Note what you find interesting in the ones you visit. But to be successful, you have to update regularly and it takes discipline to do that.

Social Networking

Social networking online is a bit like attending a chamber of commerce networking event. You are introduced to someone. You shake hands, smile, make small talk. Only at the end of the conversation do you share your business card. Social networking online works the same way. Instead of a business card, you have your social networking profile. Instead of making small talk over the appetizers, you post tidbits about your day as well as make insightful comments that support your business.

It doesn't matter where you have the social interaction, online or in person. It's all about meeting people and getting to know them. The Internet just gives you access to a broader group of people to meet.

Of the four major social networking sites, Facebook, the most popular, will probably serve your needs best. Coming in second is FastPitch, a site that's great for growing businesses like yours to market themselves. LinkedIn, with more than 50 million users, is more for professionals seeking jobs or business opportunities. The network that probably is the least useful is MySpace. While it doesn't just cater to teens and college students anymore, you'll most likely not find anyone here with the interest or discretionary income to buy antiques.

The profile, common to all of these sites, is the heart of any social network. Your user profile lays the groundwork for building relationships with people who share your interests and personal contacts. Social networking also allows users to get to know you in ways traditional advertising can't. So what do you need to do to cash in on this burgeoning user base?

Before opening an account on a social network, you should consider what each site offers and how it can benefit you. Create a strategy; without one, you could end up wandering from site to site without accomplishing anything and wasting precious time that you should spend attending to your business.

Ask yourself the following questions:

- What are your needs?
- What do you plan to use social networking for?
- What is your primary goal?
- Do you want to connect to other antique dealers or to potential customers? Both are viable options.

Promoting your business through social networks isn't as much about selling antiques as engaging potential customers in open, honest conversation. In order to convert these conversations into dollars, you need to post information about antiques and collectibles. Facebook's fan pages, which act as an extended profile, are ideal for this. Here, you can discuss trends in antiques, special pieces you've seen or acquired, the latest prices at auctions, and the most popular collectibles.

Recommend antiques sites, post antiques news clips and auction results. And by posting announcements of upcoming events, such as antique shows and special sales, you can help direct more attendees to them. As users become "fans," everything you post will appear in their News Feed every time they log on.

Respond to what your followers post. Show them you appreciate their interaction. Once they have your attention, they'll return again and again. Ask questions on the wall of your fan page. Perhaps start a thread. Social network users love to give their opinions.

However, be careful not to come off like an aggressive salesperson peddling your antiques. Offer some sort of benefit to your followers. Make them feel they need to take advantage of your promotions. Is a sale on for a limited time? Are you offering an exclusive service to your followers on a particular network?

Also, always tell your followers what's new. Tell them unusual things about the antiques you carry in your shop. What new items have you discovered? What stores lie behind your discoveries? Include some discounts. If you also have a website, you can post promotional codes that users can fill in to get a special discount—perhaps 20 percent off their first purchase in your shop.

Don't forget that what you post stays out there for a long time. Watch your personal opinions, rants and raves, and sarcastic remarks. Be careful how you respond to followers' comments. They can come back to haunt you. Remember to manage your reputation by not doing anything to harm it.

Finally, don't promise your followers one thing and do another. They'll surely ignore you.

Setting Up Your Profile

Since you're most likely a sole proprietorship, you'll be the personality behind your profile, which becomes your online representation of you and your business. For this reason, it's important to know what to include and what not to include.

1. Get personal, but not too personal. Include your special interests, favorite antiques and collectibles, music, movies, books, and so on—anything you think will help you bond with your site's users.
2. Share photos and perhaps videos. Adding these to your site offers potential customers a look into your business.
3. Give the impression that you're serious about antiques.
4. Keep your page lively. Include anecdotes about antiques and insights into the antiques business.

Lack of clarity is the biggest mistake businesspeople make on social networks. You've got to be clear on who you are and why you're there.

Social networking is sound marketing using the latest technology. Focus on giving value to your followers. Eventually, they'll become fans who know and trust you. And after that it's just a hop, skip, and a jump to their becoming loyal return customers making educated decisions about buying antiques rather than purchasing on impulse.

Creating a Website

Lastly, creating a website requires a few more computer skills. You may want to hold off launching your site until your business is more established. You'll find instructions for designing and building your site in chapter 6. Whenever you launch your site, remember to integrate it with the rest of your Internet promotions. Social networking and blogs help bring visitors looking for more information to your site.

Make good use of social networking sites on the Internet. Offer tips on your website. Invite people to your special antiques events. The Internet is where it's at, and you should be there in one form or another.

Follow-Up Promotions

The fallout from the media blitz surrounding your grand opening will last for several weeks. After that you'll want to continue your publicity campaign to hold on to present customers and gain new ones. You can achieve this through direct mail, welcome services, special events, speaking engagements, public service, and networking.

Direct Mail

Direct mail is any correspondence you send your customers through the postal service or online—either regular or e-mail. For an antiques shop this usually means postcards and flyers. Direct mailings are certainly not inexpensive at today's postage rates, but they're one sure way to keep in touch with your customers, let them know you value their patronage, and at the same time inform them of special events at your shop.

You might consider getting a bulk mailing permit if you plan to send out hundreds of letters several times a year. At this writing the permit costs $185 annually and allows you to mail a letter-size envelope for 26.8 cents. Each mailing must consist of at least 200 envelopes. You can print the required postage onto the envelope with a postage meter or glue special stamps individually on the envelopes. For an additional one-time-only fee of $185, you can get another permit that allows you to have bulk-rate postage preprinted on your envelopes. This last method is a real time-saver and bypasses both the postage meter and the stamps.

You can't get any special rate for postcards, however. No matter how many postcards you send, you must stick on those 28-cent stamps or purchase them with postage affixed for about $11 for a package of eighteen. The U.S. Post Office offers a variety of stamp imprints on the cards, so pick one that's appropriate for antiques, such as one that commemorates a historic event.

Suppose your mailing list is still in its infancy, and you're not ready to go the bulk-mail route. Here's another suggestion. Did you know that you can get envelopes preprinted with your shop's name and return address *and* prestamped for little more than the cost of the stamp itself from the U.S. Postal Service?

To order these envelopes, go to your local post office and fill out a "Personalized Envelope Order" form or go online to www.usps.com, then click on The Postal Store tab where you can fill in an online version of the form. (The form is reproduced on page 220.) You'll include on the form your shop name and return address. You may even include a couple of lines of advertising if you like. At this writing, charges for the envelopes are as follows:

- #10 business envelope: $247 for a box of 500
- #10 business window envelope: $247 for a box of 500

Personalized Stamped Envelopes

Ordering Instructions

PERSONALIZE YOUR ENVELOPES with up to seven printed lines. Envelope size, fonts and/or endorsement selections may modify the number of lines available. Contact your post office for information on USPS endorsements (Return Service Requested, Address Service Requested, Forwarding Service Requested and Change Service Requested, or Temp-Return Service Requested). Please note: Nothing can be printed below the City, State and Zip Code line except official postal endorsements.

Lines may not exceed 47 characters and spaces — 40 if all uppercase letters are used utilizing Arial, 8 point type. Selecting another font style or size may modify these maximums. Each line within the return address must be the same style, size and color.

HOW TO ORDER

Online » usps.com/pse
By telephone » Call 1-800-782-6724 (between the hours of 6:00 am and 2:00 am EST)
By fax » Fax order form to 1-816-545-1201
By mail » Send order(s) to:
Personalized Stamped Envelope Program
U.S. Postal Service
Stamp Fulfillment Services
PO Box 7247
Philadelphia PA 19101-7103

* A separate order form is required for each return address ordered.
* Purchasers are responsible for their text or item errors. All claims regarding orders must be made within six months.

PAYMENT INFORMATION

You may pay for your order by credit card, check or money order made payable to U.S. Postal Service for the total amount due. All orders must be prepaid and include any prior balances. Insufficient payment will result in either reduced quantities ordered, or your order not being processed. We accept the following credit cards: VISA, MasterCard, Discover/Novus, American Express or Diners Club International.

FONT OPTIONS

Your return address will be printed with a flush left margin. USPS now offers a variety of font styles, sizes and colors to personalize your envelopes. Choose from Arial, Rockwell, Script or Times New Roman fonts; black, blue, green or red ink; sized at 8, 10 or 12 points. The default option is Arial, 8 point, printed in black ink. This selection is included in the base price for envelopes. However, for a minor additional charge, you may select from any combination of fonts, colors and sizes listed. You may also elect to uppercase all type and/or bold individual lines at no additional charge.

The default option, Arial 8 point black, will be used if no premium options are selected.

SAMPLE FONT STYLES

Sample text for 8 point Arial. (default)
Sample text for 10 point Arial.
Sample text for 12 point Arial.

Sample text for 8 point Rockwell.
Sample text for 10 point Rockwell.
Sample text for 12 point Rockwell.

Sample text for 8 point Script.
Sample text for 10 point Script.
Sample text for 12 point Script.

Sample text for 8 point Times New Roman.
Sample text for 10 point Times New Roman.
Sample text for 12 point Times New Roman.

Default Sample
8 Point Arial
Boston, MA 02129

DIMENSIONS

ENVELOPE DIMENSIONS »
10 envelope is 4-1/8" x 9-1/2"
9 envelope is 3-7/8" x 8-7/8"
6¾ envelope is 3-5/8" x 6-1/2"

WINDOW SIZE »
6¾ envelope is 1-1/8" x 4-3/8"
9 & # 10 are 1-1/8" x 4-1/2"

WINDOW LOCATION »
1-1/16" from left edge
13/16" from bottom

SHIPPING CHARGES

Please allow 2-3 weeks for delivery of telephone and fax orders. Please allow 3-4 weeks for delivery of mail orders.

*For expedited delivery, call 1-800-782-6724 **prior to placing your order** to obtain the additional shipping cost for Express Mail® or Priority Mail® service.*

BOXES OF 50 »

QUANTITY	FEE
1 box	$ 4.60
2 boxes	$ 6.00
3 boxes	$ 7.00
4 boxes	$ 8.00
5 boxes	$10.00
6 boxes	$10.50
7 boxes	$11.50
8 boxes	$12.00
9 boxes	$12.60

BOXES OF 500 »

QUANTITY	FEE
1 box	$8.60
2 boxes	$12.60

For orders greater than eight boxes of 50, a box of 500 is your best buy.

Shipping charges and premium option fees must be included for each pre-printed return address you order. Maximum shipping charge $12.60 for each printed address.

FOR INQUIRIES

Stamp Fulfillment Services
U.S. Postal Service
PO Box 219208
Kansas City, MO 64121-9208

EMAIL »
Stampfulfillment.services@usps.gov

PHONE »
1-800-782-6724

PS Form 3203-X, Oct 2009 (Page 1 of 3)

- #6 3/4 short regular envelope: $244 for a box of 500
- #6 3/4 short window envelope: $244 for a box of 500

In about four weeks the envelopes will arrive in the mail. Each envelope, regardless of type, will carry a preprinted stamp in the upper-right corner and your shop name and return address in the upper-left corner. You pay about 5 cents each, above the cost of the postage, for these preprinted envelopes. This is a real bargain, when you consider what printers charge to print envelopes with your shop's name and return address. For an additional $238 for #10 envelopes and $236 for #6 3/4 envelopes, you can add postage to your 500 preprinted envelopes.

Using an E-mail List

Mailing lists have always been a good way to keep in touch with your customers. Today, with so many people electronically connected, assembling and using an e-mail list is imperative. With this list you can let your customers know about special sales and events or when you've just acquired unique items. To create such a list, ask customers for their e-mail addresses as part of each sale

Welcome Services

Welcome services such as Welcome Wagon provide a way of getting information about your shop to newcomers to the area. Friendly residents call on newcomers, bringing along a basket full of gifts, samples, and discount coupons that can be redeemed at local businesses. Many times people moving to a new community know little or nothing about the town. They have few if any friends. They're eager to begin meeting people and learning what the business community has to offer.

As an antiques dealer, you'd probably want to offer these newcomers a discount on their first purchase at your shop. Everyone loves a bargain, and these people are almost sure to stop in to take advantage of your offer. They're prime candidates to become your customers because they're all furnishing and decorating new homes.

Here's how a welcome service works. You pay the welcome service company a fee and provide the representatives with a supply of cards and/or brochures or flyers describing your shop and mentioning the discount. You and your customers will find Welcome Wagon, for example, online (www.welcomewagon.com) and in the Yellow Pages. If you can't find a welcome service in either place, call your local chamber of commerce.

> **Tip:** To prevent becoming a constant target for donations from dozens of worth-while charities and benefits, make a substantial annual contribution to your favorite charity. Sure, it's hard to refuse anyone. After all, aren't so many organizations out there worthy of your help? Yet, as the owner of a new business, you can hardly afford to give money to others when you need every penny for maintaining your business.
>
> When charitable solicitors ask for a donation, just say, "Thanks for coming by, but I give all my charitable money to [whatever charity you support]."

Special Events

Even though your grand opening was probably your first special event, you need to plan on others throughout the year. If you make these events unique, you just might generate some free publicity in the local media.

Here are some suggestions:

- Hold a contest in your shop one weekend when people come in dressed in antique or period-style clothing. Take photographs of each entrant, then award a prize or gift certificate for the most authentic in three categories: men, women, and children. A museum curator could be the judge. Call the newspaper and request a reporter and photographer to be on hand when you award the prizes.
- If your town has an annual history-based event such as a Pioneers' Day, Gold Rush Festival, or Civil War Reenactment, have a special sale to coincide with the dates. Wear a period costume in the shop on those days.
- Arrange for your town's historian to be in your shop for two or three hours one weekend to tell stories about the town's beginnings. Request a reporter and photographer from the newspaper to cover the event.
- Plan a special display of historic artifacts or memorabilia belonging to local residents. Be sure to invite them and their friends to the event. Perhaps some will be willing to tell stories about their memorabilia. Again, alert the media.

The more you create events that are newsworthy, the better chance you have of getting free promotion. You'll gain many customers every time the media features your shop, and longtime customers will continue to look upon your shop as the most interesting in town. They'll tell their friends, who will then become customers. Remember, the best type of promotion is viral marketing—word of mouth. Friends tell friends, whether in person or through online social networks.

Speaking Engagements

You may not look upon yourself as a public speaker, but you've probably spent many hours discussing antiques trends, restoration tips, building a collection, authenticating antiques, and so on with friends and family. You can turn this natural interest in talking about antiques with friends into speaking in public about the same topics, which will quickly give you lots of visibility in your community.

The program directors of church groups, special-interest clubs, retirement communities, and service clubs are always looking for speakers who can give twenty- or forty-five-minute talks. As the owner of an antiques shop, you're an accepted authority on the subject, so volunteer your services.

Once you're scheduled to talk, ask what the main focus of the club is, then tailor your talk to fit. You might talk about the history of sundials for a garden club. An investment club would be interested in learning how antiques rise in value and how trends affect prices. Residents of a retirement community might like to know how to determine the value of antiques they own.

Perhaps you'll receive an invitation to give a thirty-minute talk at the monthly luncheon of the local retired teachers' group. Though the program chairman who called may leave the topic up to you, ask if club members are especially interested in a particular category of antiques, such as Victorian china and glass. Then put together an informal talk on the history and characteristics of various kinds of antique china and cut glass. Since everyone responds well to the "show and tell" technique, take along several examples from your shop to illustrate your talk. Be entertaining and informative and give your listeners interesting facts about antiques that will add to their pleasure in collecting them. Plus, you might also make a sale or two.

Now, as a businessperson, always try to find ways to make your talk pay off in sales. Bring along a stack of gift certificates that offer the bearers 15 percent off any antique in your shop. Give each person attending one of these certificates. You'll sell many antiques as a result, and with any kind of luck, the people who redeem the certificates will become loyal customers.

Short talks such as these are easy to present. You're simply discussing something you know very well. You'll hardly ever get paid for giving these talks—usually a complimentary lunch is usually the extent of remuneration, although sometimes you'll receive a small honorarium. Statistically, though, many of the people hearing you will visit your shop, perhaps for the first time. Another big plus is that your name will be printed in the paper as the speaker for that event, resulting in more free publicity.

If you find that you enjoy public speaking, you might want to consider presenting workshops through a college's continuing education department. Look over continuing education catalogs and you'll find dozens of fascinating courses offered, all geared toward making life more pleasant or interesting for the participants. Presenting these workshops does involve more time and preparation than the short talks. However, you will actually get paid for giving them. Generally, classes run from one and a half to two hours per week for anywhere from two to four weeks. The fee is usually $25 to $30 per hour no matter how many students, so tell the school to limit your enrollment to fifteen to twenty-five students. If you have more than that, you won't have enough time to answer questions.

Tip: Evaluate the effectiveness of your advertising and publicity efforts by doing the following:

- Ask every new customer, "How did you hear about my shop?"

- Place a coupon on your flyers that entitles the recipient to a small gift—perhaps a bag of your potpourri or a 10 percent discount on a purchase if they redeem the coupon before a certain date. The number of coupons redeemed is a good indication of the number of people who responded to your flyer.

- Watch your daily records closely to see whether sales increase substantially on days following those when your ads appear.

- Examine your records following a special in-house event to see whether sales have increased substantially.

Public Service

Most dealers feel they should give something back to the community in which they live. As an antiques dealer—and therefore an expert on the subject—you can use your knowledge in many ways. Your time would be welcomed at your local historical society in identifying period furniture and accessories. You could sponsor a student from a high school business class and act as a mentor in showing him or her the ropes of running a retail business.

Let the local amateur theater group know you'll lend pieces from your shop to be used as props in its plays. Not only will you earn the group's undying gratitude, but your shop will be acknowledged in the program. And don't forget to contact your regional film development agency. Offering furniture or accessories to be used in films is not only good publicity, but you may even be paid rental fees.

Tip: To compete with other antiques shops in your area, do the following:

1. Make yourself and your shop highly visible to the community through constant networking.

2. Stay open a half hour in the afternoon after your competition has closed its doors. If the shops in town close at 5:00 p.m., you should stay open until 5:30. If they close at 5:30 p.m., keep your doors open until 6:00. Many people browse in one antiques shop after another for hours before deciding to buy. If you keep your shop open after others have closed, you might get that last-minute business.

3. Make a special effort to draw interior decorators to your shop. These professionals often work with well-to-do clients who allow them free rein in choosing items for their homes. In most cases the decorators don't quibble about prices. You might stay open one night a month for interior decorators and serve a little wine and cheese to help them relax after a busy day. Show any unusual or decorative antiques you've acquired since the last open house. Find out what antiques they need to decorate their clients' homes and try to locate those pieces. Call a decorator if something comes in that you know she can sell to a client. Working with interior decorators is a win-win situation for everyone. You sell the antiques at top dollar, the decorators get a commission on the sale from their clients, and the clients receive fine antiques for their homes.

Networking

Make time for contacts that can result in a great deal of profitable business. Get to know the real estate agents in town and leave some of your business cards in their offices. Half of their clients are buying new homes, and they may need furniture and accessories to decorate them.

Join clubs and organizations and attend their meetings. Volunteer to work on committees. You'll quickly develop friends who may become good customers.

10 | Other Ways to Make Money in Antiques

Your home-based shop will be your primary source of income as an antiques dealer, especially during your first year in business. Later on, though, as you acquire a reputation as an expert in the field, you may want to branch out into one or more other antiques-related fields. Many antiques dealers do just that, which adds substantial amounts to their annual incomes.

Some of the related businesses you might consider are selling at antiques shows, appraising antiques, managing estate sales, selling high-ticket antiques by appointment only, and subleasing space to another entrepreneur.

Selling at Antiques Shows

Antique dealers call the practice of selling at antiques shows "working the shows," which means renting space at an antiques show and selling some of your merchandise for two or more days from that space.

Some dealers work only the shows in their surrounding areas. Others work any show within a few hours' driving time. A few dealers set up annual itineraries, usually in winter in most parts of the country, that take them around a circuit of a half-dozen or more shows.

Whether it's one show or ten, this is by far the best way to present the greatest number of antiques to the greatest number of potential customers in the least amount of time. Instead of waiting for buyers to come to your shop, you take your merchandise to them. Lovers of antiques flock to these shows because they know they can see more antiques in two or three hours than they would in days of trudging from one shop to another. As a result, at each show thousands of transactions take place between buyers and dealers.

Nonprofit organizations, such as hospitals, symphony guilds, and large service clubs sponsor some annual shows as a way to raise much-needed funds through the proceeds from admission fees and space rentals. Other antiques shows are strictly commercial affairs, managed by professional organizers, who pocket all the proceeds. As a rule, there's little difference in the types of shows as long as the sponsors know their business and manage the shows in a professional manner. What does differ is the price of renting a space. At the usually high-end nonprofit-sponsored shows, a space can rent for $400 to $1,000 for a three-day weekend. And dealers come from all over the country.

There are several variations to the large and often high-end shows held annually by nonprofits and commercial promoters who put on shows in a particular region or around the country.

The first is what may be referred to as the semiannual firehouse show. At this middle-market type of show, items usually sell for no higher than three figures, with much of the merchandise in the $25 to $150 range. Rents at these shows are moderate, with dealers coming from the surrounding region.

The second type is a lower-end show, held monthly during the colder part of the year, which actually is a glorified indoor flea market where the promoter or civic organization rents 3-by-8-foot tables for $12 to $15 each, rather than renting spaces. Most dealers rent at least two or three tables, which they cover with attractive cloths and display their china, glassware, jewelry, and so forth on portable shelves. Dealers to this type of show are more local. The promoter advertises the show in local media, as well as mails postcards to former customers on a mailing list.

The procedure for working the shows is pretty much the same, whether you exhibit at annual, semiannual, or monthly affairs. How would you, as a home-based antiques dealer, begin working the shows? Start by making an objective assessment of every show you can attend.

1. *Attend as many shows as possible throughout your state or section of the country.* Your local newspaper will run announcements of antiques shows in your immediate area. Read the various antiques trade papers, such as *AntiqueWeek* and *Antique Trader*, for dates and locations of these shows. No matter where you live—in the East or West, North or South—you'll find similar regional publications that describe area antiques shows. Pay entrance fees ranging from $5 to $15, and you'll be exposed to hours of first-hand education about how antiques shows are run, how dealers manage their booths, and what they're selling.

2. *Observe the preshow promotions.* Do they appear to be professional and well coordinated? Is the newspaper advertising backed up with spots on radio and local television, as well as announcements on local Internet sites? Do you find flyers announcing the shows at local antiques shops? Is the show venue attractive and in an easily accessible location? Does it have plenty of free parking?

3. *Once a show opens, take an hour or so to observe the way it operates.* Is it clean and well lit? (Buyers often want to examine an antique in strong light before purchasing it.) Do the people in charge appear to be cheerful and well organized? (Frazzled promoters are invariably poorly organized.) Are the aisles wide enough for customers to walk freely from one booth to another? (People don't like to be jammed, shoulder to shoulder, in a public building.) Did the promoters provide some kind of food service for customers, and does the food appear appetizing? (People will linger at a show much longer if they can refresh themselves with a soft drink and snack.) Are the antiques on display of a high quality? (You can't charge reasonable prices for antiques at a show that has a flea-market ambience.) All these factors contribute to an antiques show that will attract buyers.

4. *Check out the dealers themselves.* Happy dealers indicate well-managed shows. Approach a few of the dealers at a show and explain that you're thinking of reserving space in the next show. Don't be shy. Most dealers in antiques love to talk about their profession, and they'll be glad to chat with you. Ask them what they think of the show. Has their relationship with the organizers been pleasant? Do they feel the space rental is reasonable? Most important, ask these dealers *if they plan to rent space at the next show run by this particular group or promoter.* Dealers don't return to a show if they don't make money the first time.

5. *Check out what people are buying.* Is furniture a big seller? What about cut glass and china? Are the dealers who display jewelry and sterling silver doing a brisk business? Or do customers seem more interested in moderately priced collectibles? Does it seem that there's little pattern to what customers are buying and that almost any well-priced antique will sell? The answers to these questions will help you decide what to bring to the show yourself.

6. *Observe which areas attract the most customers.* You may notice that some areas of the hall draw a larger crowd than other areas. As a rule, experienced dealers like to be close to the hall's entrance, since customers tend to start their shopping there. Most people then gravitate to the right, so spaces on the right side of the entrance are usually more desirable than those on the left. Spaces in corners can be dark, and many people will avoid them. Dealers in balcony spaces often report lower sales volume because some people won't or can't walk up steps.

If you're satisfied with the operation of a show, ask one of the dealers to introduce you to the promoter. Introduce yourself and say that you'd like to reserve a space in the next show. Don't be surprised if you hear that the show—a year away—is already fully reserved. This isn't uncommon with some of the better shows in large cities. If the show is full, just ask to have your name put on a waiting list. I've found that, many times, a few dealers have to cancel their reservations and the promoters then rent their spaces to others. Once you're accepted for the show, you'll be asked to sign a contract. Most promoters will ask for one-half the booth fee at that time, with the balance due on the first day of the show.

As a beginner, you should start out small. Contract for the smallest booth, perhaps 10 by 10 feet. That way you'll have a chance to learn the ropes with minimal expense. Once you see how you did at that show, you might rent a slightly larger space at the next one—provided your sales warrant it.

Some promoters charge a fee for space but don't include a table in the fee. Many of them, however, will rent tables to dealers for the duration of a show, usually charging $12 to $15 per table per day. Obviously, you'd need several tables for even a small booth, and since most shows run at least three days, you can see that table rental at this type of show could be a major expense. Most knowledgeable dealers construct their own tables. A sheet of plywood with galvanized-pipe legs that can be screwed into sockets in minutes makes a sturdy table. Of course, you must cover the raw plywood with attractive fabric. Your initial expense will be about the same as renting tables for just one day, and you'll own the tables for every subsequent show. Promoters at the larger, most expensive shows provide not only carts on which you can pile your equipment and merchandise to transport it to your booth, but often they'll hire local college students to help with the loading and unloading.

You'll also need attractive shelves to display your antiques. Serviceable shelves can be made from painted shelving or plate glass. Glass shelves, however, are more costly, heavier, and are more likely to chip or break when moving from show to show. The choice is yours. Just look at what other dealers use at shows and decide what would work for you.

> Tip: You can make a very portable compact shelf system using small stepladders and some 8- to 10-inch-wide pine shelving, painted or unpainted. This system sets up and breaks down easily, is easy to transport, and is cost-effective.

Finally, even though the hall appears to be well lit, you should provide additional lamps to spotlight your antiques. One dealer didn't realize how dull and uninviting his booth was until he got it set up, then looked around at some of the booths nearby. All the other dealers had high-intensity, clip-on spots beaming on their crystal and china. Their booths looked sparkling and bright, and his looked dreary. So he bought a half-dozen spots at the nearest discount store. It made all the difference.

As we all know, every new venture takes longer to complete than planned, and setting up your booth at an antiques show is no exception. You'll need hours to unload your van or truck, unpack boxes, and arrange the antiques attractively. Show promoters understand this, so, assuming a show opens on Friday morning, they allow dealers to enter the hall on Thursday afternoon to set up their booths. Then, even though you might feel on Thursday night that your booth is ready for the first customers, always arrive early on Friday morning to dust the furniture again and perhaps rearrange a few things.

Good retailing demands that during the run of the show, you continue to rearrange both your furniture and your smaller antiques. Many people return to a show again and again on subsequent days, walking up and down the same aisles before they decide to buy. They may pass right by a pretty whatnot displayed on one side of your booth, then finally see it on the other side of the booth on their third visit.

Be careful about filling cabinets with smaller items, especially if the cabinet is also for sale. Should the cabinet sell before the items in it, you may be hard-pressed to find space to display them in your booth. Buyers will tend to pass by a full cabinet thinking it's just a prop. If you have any type of cabinet for sale, make sure it's prominently featured and only place a few things in or on it.

As your antiques sell, you'll also want to rearrange your stock so that your shelves appear full. Customers like to feel they have a good selection to choose from. They're far more likely to buy if you seem to have an ample supply of antiques, even during the last few hours of the show.

Tuck a box or two of extra stock underneath your tables. When your shelves begin to look a little bare, just dip into these reserves and restock your shelves during the show. Still you don't want your shelves to look too crowded at any time during the show. You'll sell more antiques if the shelves appear orderly and attractive, not jumbled up as at a flea market, plus if you have too many items on display, customers may miss some of the important, higher-priced ones.

While most shows provide a folding chair for you to sit on, it isn't a good idea to sit all the time. And while working a show can be tiring, psychologically, customers feel that a dealer who's sitting isn't interested in them. Also, it's a great temptation to chat with other dealers and neglect potential customers if you're seated.

Instead, chat with your customers, but don't be pushy. Nothing turns off potential customers more than an aggressive salesperson. Many dealers feel it's better to be passive, assuming that their customers already know what they want. Often collectors of antiques browse a show looking for the pieces they can't find elsewhere. If they don't see them, they don't buy. Ask your customers what they collect or if they're looking for something special. Chances are you may have something back at your shop that they may be interested in purchasing. Remember, you're in the business of selling antiques, and it doesn't matter if you sell them at the show or not. The contacts you make at the show—both customers and other dealers—are invaluable.

To keep fatigue at bay during the show, bring high-energy snacks such as granola bars, nuts, or trail mix to munch on discreetly between customers. Arrange for a friend, spouse, or fellow dealer to watch the booth for you occasionally. You can then sit for a few minutes and eat a nutritious lunch at the snack bar, take midmorning and midafternoon breaks, and visit the restroom. Some shows even provide hostesses who'll fill in for you.

Most shows run for at least two and sometimes three or four days. This time affords you an opportunity, assuming you live close by, to adjust your stock. You may find on the first day of the show, for example, that you sell a great deal of furniture but comparatively little glassware. As a result, you know to dismantle one of the tables holding glassware and fill the space with furniture you'll bring from the shop the next morning. It pays to be flexible. Display what people want to buy and you'll make money.

A real side benefit to working the shows is that you're subtly advertising the existence of your shop. Be sure to have posted somewhere in the booth an attractive sign that mentions the name and location of your shop. Many people will visit you at the shop even if they don't buy during the show. Most dealers also place business cards in little trays somewhere in the booth. Encourage everyone who comes into the booth to take a card. And when talking to potential customers, always hand them your business card.

> Tip: If the show promoter doesn't provide a sign for your booth with your business name on it—and many don't—print one on a sheet of bright-colored card stock (65–97 pound), then make a stand up "A" frame support from two pieces of corrugated cardboard and attach it to the back of the sign. Place this in a prominent position in your booth.

Working antique shows is also good for promoting your business. Often, trade magazines will send a reporter to review the show. Give those writers every courtesy because they'll talk about your booth, describing your antiques and also mentioning your shop's location. Be polite and, should they wish to take a photo or two, let them. Too many dealers at middle-market shows not only look down on the press, but are downright rude to them. This is free publicity, and you need all you can get.

Do you adjust your prices to compensate for your costs in exhibiting at the shows? No. Most dealers who work the shows build show costs into their prices. No customer wants to discover a price on an antique in a show different from the price she saw on the same piece in your shop, and vice versa. This is not good merchandising. Unfortunately, many dealers do this.

Are there any disadvantages to working the shows? Of course. You must pack your antiques and haul them in either a van or a truck to the show site. Then you have to pack up and haul back to the shop anything that doesn't sell. Some show promoters hire college students to help exhibitors unload and load their antiques. If you need such help, be sure to arrange for it with the promoter in advance.

Another disadvantage of working the shows is that you have to be there for a show's duration. If you work alone in your shop, you must either close it during the show or hire someone to work in your place. You'll also have to stay in hotels or motels if a show is more than an hour's drive from your home. Many shows don't close until 8:00 or 9:00 in the evening, and driving any distance after a full day of selling can be a real drag, especially when you have to get up early and drive back to the show the next day.

On the whole, most dealers in antiques find working the shows both profitable and fun and worth the effort.

Appraising Antiques

Many people need to have their antiques appraised for one reason or another, and you'll be asked many times to perform this service.

In all likelihood you won't qualify as a *licensed appraiser*. To become certified with the American Society of Appraisers as an antiques appraiser, you must go through a rigid application process and be employed full-time as an appraiser. Many dealers, however, perform *informal appraisals* for their customers. This is perfectly legal as long as you don't advertise yourself as a certified appraiser or claim to be one.

The main criterion of an informal appraiser is to have a working knowledge of antiques. Certainly, you don't have to possess the expertise of an appraiser at Sotheby's, but you should be able to recognize specific styles in antiques and be able to locate and reference their current values. Two incidents show how you might use your abilities as an antiques dealer to enhance your income.

A young woman came to a reputable dealer, needing an informal appraisal of an antique rocking chair that had been lost by a moving company. The moving company actually wanted to depreciate its value because it was used. She had three photographs of the chair, so the dealer could easily determine its style and relative age. She also told him the year she had bought the chair and how much she'd paid for it. All this information gave him something to go on. Then he checked the current prices of similar rocking chairs in local antiques shops. Once the dealer had this information, he began preparing a folder that he could present to the moving company. He took the photographs to a copy center and had them laser-printed onto one sheet and also photocopied a page from a book whose text said that antiques increase in value each year. Then he typed a report in which he gave his estimate of the antique's current value and listed his own credentials as a dealer in antiques. The dealer enclosed all this in a card-stock cover and gave it to the young woman, along with his invoice. The invoice covered the copy center charges and a reasonable fee for the dealer's time spent in researching the value of the rocking chair. Even though this was an informal appraisal, the moving company accepted it and paid the woman for the lost rocking chair. However, this same appraisal is not recognized by insurance companies, banks (in the case of an estate), or in a court of law.

On another occasion, a woman who had inherited a portion of her mother's considerable estate, including a houseful of antiques of every vintage, approached this same dealer. She needed an inventory of the antiques with their values for estate tax purposes. The dealer visited her home and made notes about every antique. He also took a photograph of each piece with his digital camera. After having his photos printed at a one-hour photo printing service, he reviewed his notes, using the pictures as guides. Because many of the antiques were quite old—seventeenth-century German and English—he didn't want to rely on his own judgment about them, so he reinforced his basic knowledge with information from several current price guides and came up with an approximate value for each piece. The dealer created an inventory that listed the antiques, their description, and his appraisal of their value. The woman was delighted with the photographs. She hadn't expected to receive them. They'll be invaluable to her in case of fire or theft of any antique in the collection. The appraisal, however, will not.

Certified appraisers charge exceptionally high rates for their services—up to $150 per hour plus expenses. Most antiques dealers aren't in that rarefied category and must be realistic about how to invoice for informal appraising. Some dealers base their charges on the hourly rate interior decorators receive for their services. But before doing any informal appraising, you need to check who will accept informal appraisals. It pays to research this before you do an appraisal for anyone.

While informal appraisals may be fine for small pieces, you should decline to appraise anything that you know to be of exceptional value, and instead recommend a certified antiques appraiser in your area. Your honesty will go a long way to insuring your reputation.

Managing Estate Sales

One of the fastest ways to make the most money in antiques is by selling someone else's property at an estate sale. Although these sales involve a great deal of work on your part, you'll invest none of your own money other than for advertising or temporary help. You invest your time and energy only, for which you'll receive a commission of 30 percent—the usual fee—on everything you sell.

How do you get started as an estate seller? First, have the words Estate Sales printed on your business cards. Place a sign to that effect somewhere in your shop. Mention the service below your address in every newspaper classified ad you run and in your online profile with the major search engines, Google, Yahoo, and Bing. It won't be long before the phone starts ringing with people eager for you to dispose of their belongings for them. Sometimes they'll be the children of an elderly parent who has died or moved into a retirement community or assisted living facility. Many times your calls will come from people who are retiring, moving into a condominium, and weeding out a lifetime of possessions that won't fit into a smaller home.

Once you've firmed up the dates of the sale with a client, you're ready to advertise the sale. In your local newspaper place a display ad that lists some of the most interesting items, antique and otherwise, and schedule the ad to run about one week prior to the sale. List all the interesting antiques on postcards and send the cards to everyone on your mailing list, again, about one week before the sale. The newspaper ad will bring in buyers of both antiques and related items, while the postcards will alert your regular customers to the antiques in the sale.

Obviously, to justify the expense of this advertising, any sale must consist of hundreds of items. You may, on occasion, be approached by a seller who has only a half or third as much as you need to make a sale worthwhile. There's one way to take advantage of such an offer, assuming you have a large storage space available. You simply move the merchandise to your storage space, hold it until your next scheduled sale, and combine the two. Such a procedure means physically moving many pieces of furniture and boxes from the owner's home to your storage space, then moving them again to the sale venue. This is a lot of work. Frankly, the owners would have to agree to a much larger commission before you'd pledge yourself to such an arrangement.

Don't even think about managing an estate sale alone. You need help before, during, and after the event. Otherwise, you'll be overwhelmed by midafternoon on the first day of the sale. Once you have possession of your client's home, you and your helper must sort through, organize, and price every piece the owners leave behind—every pillowcase, every pot, every box of Christmas ornaments, every pair of gloves, every potted plant, and so forth. You may have to wash a mountain of glasses and dishes too.

You'll nearly always hold estate sales on weekends in your clients' homes. Many of these homes are quite small, so experienced estate sales managers often use a take-a-number system to avoid a bone-crushing, wall-to-wall mob during the first thirty minutes or so of a sale. As customers arrive—usually long before the published time to open—they're given a number that identifies their place in line—first come, first served. Depending on the size of the home, you should allow fifteen or twenty people in at a time. Within a half hour this first crush is usually over, and you can open the door to whomever else may come.

In most cases the owners of the homes must vacate them at least three or four days prior to the sale, as you need that much time to sort, clean, and price the merchandise. Once, a friend went to an estate sale where, at the very moment buyers crowded in the front door, the owners were rushing out the back, leaving their breakfast plates, covered with bits of egg and toast, on the kitchen table. You can avoid this disaster by having a written agreement with your clients that spells out all the particulars of the sale.

All the miscellaneous household stuff you have to deal with will bring in plenty of money if you price it just a little higher than you would for a yard sale. The real moneymakers, however, will be the antiques and collectibles. You'll be swamped with both dealers and collectors at any sale where you advertise antiques. Dealers will, in fact, become your most loyal customers at estate sales. As dealers, they have to buy at prices that will enable them to add a decent markup and make a profit, so you have to price the antiques in the sale accordingly. You'll be most successful if you price antiques and collectibles at about one-third their retail values.

Why one-third of retail? Then, you'll probably say, you'd buy the most desirable antiques yourself. Yes, unless the owner specifically forbids it, you certainly can buy antiques from the sale before the door opens, but you have to be honest. Price every piece as though you were offering it to the public, then pay that price yourself. At one-third retail you'll still get a good deal. In addition, you'll also collect the commission on that sale, which is, in effect, giving you a 30 percent discount over the already low price.

Estate Sale Checklist

Prepare Your Sale Items

_____ Have the person who hired you create an inventory of the contents of the home.

_____ Have that same person sign a contract stating the date(s) of the sale, what your commission (usually 30 percent) will be as well as other costs, how much promotion you will do, your valuation of special items, and so on.

_____ Ask them to pack up all items that won't sell, such as family photos, papers, and personal items.

_____ Organize all items into categories and display them in the appropriate rooms.

_____ Place furniture in rooms where it would be used.

_____ Display holiday items in a bedroom and seasonal items on a porch or in a garage.

_____ Clean and repair items as you go.

_____ Determine the value of antique items and price and label all with a description when applicable.

Check Local Sale Regulations

_____ Check with your local government about "signage" restrictions.

_____ Find out if you need a permit to hold a estate sale in your area.

Plan Your Sale Promotion

_____ Call local newspapers for ad prices and deadlines. Don't forget "free" shoppers' papers since they often get the best distribution.

_____ Create your ad, including date, time, address, directions, and items of interest.

_____ Run your ad at least one week before and the week of the sale.

_____ Post online advertisements where possible.

Decide on Your Estate Sale Policies

_____ Decide how long your sale will run—number of days and hours.

_____ Decide if you will accept checks or hold items for people.

_____ Decide if you're going to allow other dealers to buy items before the sale.

Assemble Your Supplies

_____ Assemble your "checkout" items—cash box, extra bags, tissue/newspaper for wrapping.

_____ Assemble your "try-before-you-buy" items—extension cords, batteries, lightbulbs.

Erect Signs

_____ Hang posters at major intersections and along the road of the sale's location.

_____ Distribute flyers to local stores, churches, laundromats.

_____ Make sure each contains the address of the sale, hours, major items of interest, arrows pointing in the right direction, and, above all, the word ANTIQUES in big letters.

Set Up Your Sale Area and Your Cash Box

_____ Create a smooth traffic flow throughout the house.

_____ Display similar and complementary items together in appropriate places.

_____ Make sure everything is clearly visible and well marked.

_____ Create a list of "minimum prices" you will accept for each item, especially more valuable ones.

_____ Decide how you'll deal with items that don't sell.

_____ Get change from your bank—$20 in coins, $50 in ones, $40 in fives.

Ask for Help

_____ Recruit at least two people to work the length of the sale.

_____ Educate your helpers about pricing and negotiating.

_____ Leave a number where you can be reached should you have to step out.

Just as you use psychology when displaying antiques in your shop by putting the most popular and salable items at eye level, you'll use psychology in your estate sales by placing antiques and collectibles in the first rooms that customers enter. Normally, these will be the living and dining rooms. Display china, crystal, pottery, silver, dolls, and any other especially collectible antiques on tables where customers can see and examine the pieces quickly, and position furniture wherever it will be seen most easily. Serious buyers, including dealers, never waste a moment at estate sales. They expect to sail through the home at record speed in the hope of beating others to the choice antiques. Casual buyers, on the other hand, may spend an hour or more wandering from room to room through the home. They expect to look over every single item in their search for bargains. As a result, you can use a back bedroom to stack ordinary linens, put ordinary kitchenware in the kitchen, and put tools, outdoor furniture, and such, in the garage or the backyard.

Station your helper at a card table near the front door to act as cashier. This will free you to roam through the home, answering questions and assisting customers. Both of you should keep a sharp eye out for shoplifters. Unfortunately, this type of petty thievery does happen at estate sales.

The owners may leave some very valuable antiques with you—fine jewelry, jade figurines, complete sets of china, and the like. In all honesty, you have to ticket these pieces with high prices. Often, no one will be willing to pay those prices, yet you need to sell the antiques. The solution some estate sales managers use is to put an "Offer Box" at the cashier's table. Any customer may place a bid in the box for any item. You then open the box at a specified time, and if the items have not sold before that, you award them to the people who made the highest bids.

> Tip: If you're running an estate sale for more than one day, consider marking anything left at closing on the first day of the sale down to half-price for the second day. Then, during the last hour or so before closing, announce that anyone present can make an offer. You should do almost anything to move the last items out. Whatever you have left at closing, you can then box up and take to the Salvation Army or Goodwill for a tax credit, which the owner gets, of course.
>
> After the sale finishes, tally all sales and write the owner a check for 70 percent of the amount, keeping the remainder as your commission.

The Week Before the Sale

- Sort all items for sale.

- Put up flyers in public areas around town.

- Place your newspaper ads.

- Gather supplies, get change, and confirm "helpers."

The Week of the Sale

- Display items for sale.

- Put up directional signs around the sale's location.

- Block off any areas of the house you don't want shoppers to enter.

During the Sale

- Put one person in charge of cash box—never leave it unguarded.

- Have another person strolling around to prevent shoplifting and to answer questions.

Selling High-Ticket Antiques by Appointment Only

If you're still working full-time or have a part-time job and don't want the bother of operating a shop, you can still deal in antiques. Some dealers sell by appointment only. When selling this way, you won't maintain a traditional shop with display shelves and such, and you won't have a sign out front inviting customers to come in and browse. Instead, you'll deal only with serious collectors who are in the market for higher-priced antiques. If you decide to sell antiques this way, you won't make an appointment for anything less than three figures.

Your customers will phone and make an appointment to visit your home. This meeting may have all the ambience of a visit between two old friends who simply sit down and enjoy a cup of tea served in antique china.

You'll get most of your business through word-of-mouth referrals from satisfied customers and by placing discreet advertisements in decorating magazines that simply mention your services, not specific antiques. You may find interior decorators, who constantly search for unusual or rare antiques for their clients, to be your most consistent source.

As an appointment-only dealer, you'll buy nothing in advance for resale. Instead, you'll work with your customers to determine the ideal antiques for a certain location in their homes, then set out to locate pieces to fill that need. To do so, you'll need to spread the word through the antiques dealers' network that you're searching for certain pieces. You may haunt auctions or fine antiques galleries in your quest. Once you find the desired items, you'll purchase them, usually with the understanding that they can be returned if your customers refuse them, and have them delivered to their homes. Your customers will examine the pieces and, if they're satisfactory, they'll purchase them. Of course, you'll add a substantial profit into the final price for each piece.

You may choose to buy fine antiques without a *specific* client in mind, but, like any traditional dealer, assume that your considerable investment will eventually pay off. Since this is an extremely low-key business, you might mingle the antiques you plan to sell with your own family pieces, literally making your entire home a shop. When a pair of French chairs, a Sheraton dining table, an early-nineteenth-century sleigh bed, or a sterling silver candelabra sells, you simply replace it with another antique. In the meantime, the original piece has been a part of your home's decor. Depending on what type of antiques you choose to sell, you may go on extensive buying trips to New York, New England, New Orleans, or even Europe to select your stock.

Or you might decide to set aside a portion of your home strictly for your merchandise, but that area should never resemble a traditional antiques shop. Instead, it should suggest an elegant home, complete with fine furniture and accessories.

But don't take appointment-only selling of fine antiques lightly. To sell an item for four, five, or six figures requires extensive knowledge of and experience with fine antiques. You should be located where a considerable portion of the population has the means to invest in expensive furnishings. Your home should be as tasteful as that of your clients. Sales and turnover may be exceedingly slow in comparison to those in the traditional shop, but, as with Realtors dealing in multi-million-dollar houses, the financial rewards can be great if you're successful.

Subleasing Space to Another Entrepreneur

Do you have, or can you create, space in your home to be used by another antiques-related business, such as a secondhand bookstore or a fine crafts shop? Granted, such an arrangement would be impossible for many home-based antiques dealers.

Nevertheless, if you have a large home and minimal personal requirements, subleasing space can be an excellent way to create some extra income. Depending on the amount of extra space you have available, you could easily take in several hundred dollars a month in rents.

Naturally, any business you admit into your home would have to be compatible with antiques. Properly chosen, however, such an endeavor can actually produce business for your antiques shop, especially if there's easy indoor access from one shop into the other.

Let's visualize a scenario. Four friends browse through a bookstore searching for first editions. While they chat, they can't help but see displayed in the next room dozens of equally lovely antiques in your shop. What would be more natural than to drift over there and take a look?

The same scenario could hold true for almost any shop whose personality is harmonious with that of antiques. You could even place some of your pieces in the adjacent shop to be sold on commission. A bookshop could place a small church pew along a wall for the comfort of browsers. A crafts shop might display some of its prettiest goodies on a series of small tables. Each of these antiques would be for sale, and the owner of the bookstore or other business would receive a nice commission on any sale—a win-win situation for everyone. Persons who sublease space get the use of attractive antiques, and the owner of the antiques shop has an additional outlet for her merchandise.

A Final Word

There are no magic roads to success in this or any other business. Hard work, enthusiasm, and persistence can accomplish miracles. Calvin Coolidge's quote below says it all.

Press On

Nothing in the world can take the place of persistence. Talent will not; nothing is more common than unsuccessful men with talent. Genius will not; unrewarded genius is almost a proverb. Education will not; the world is full of educated derelicts. Persistence and determination alone are omnipotent.

—Calvin Coolidge

Appendix

Suggested Reading

The following books and magazines are a must-read before starting your new antiques business.

Books

The Antiques Handbook, Abbeydale Press, Leicestershire, England, 1998.

Antique Trader Guide to Fakes and Reproductions, 4th ed., Mark Chevienka, Krause Publications, 2007.

Fake, Fraud, or Genuine? Identifying Authentic American Antique Furniture, Myrna Kaye, Bulfinch Publishing, 1991.

Field Guide to American Antique Furniture, Joseph T. Butler, Owl Books, 1986.

How to Sell Antiques and Collectibles on eBay . . . And Make a Fortune, Dennis Prince and Lynn Dralle, McGraw Hill, 2004.

Know Your Antiques, Ralph and Terry Kovel, Crown Publishers, 1981.

Kovel's American Antiques 1750-1900, Ralph and Terry Kovel, Random House Reference, 2004.

Kovel's American Collectibles 1900-2000, Ralph and Terry Kovel, Random House Reference, 2007.

Magazines

American Antiquities Journal
126 E. High Street
Springfield, OH 45502
(937) 322-6281
www.americanantiquities.com/journal.html

Antique Trader Weekly
700 East State Street
Iola, WI 54990-0001
www.antiquetrader.com

AntiqueWeek
27 North Jefferson Street
Knightstown, IN 46148
(765) 345-5133
www.antiqueweek.com

Maine Antique Digest
911 Main Street
Waldoboro, ME 04572
www.maineantiquedigest.com

Southeastern Antiquing & Collecting Magazine
P.O. Box 510
Acworth, GA 30101
(888) 388-7827
www.go-star.com/antiquing

Resources and References

The following books, booklets, and online publications will give you a ready reference to the many questions you're likely to have as you start and maintain your home-based antiques business. You may find some of the books at your local library or as used editions on websites such as Amazon.com, while you'll find the business and government publications ready to download as Adobe PDF files on the websites listed with them.

Government Publications

Small Business Administration

The following titles are available for download from the SBA website (www.sba.gov) in PDF format for Adobe Acrobat Reader (available as a free download from Adobe at www.adobe.com.).

ABCs of Borrowing— #FM1

Advertising— #MT11

Business Plan for Home-Based Business— #MP15

Checklist for Going Into Business— #MP12

Computerizing Your Business— #MP14

Creative Selling: The Competitive Edge— #MT1

Marketing for Small Business, An Overview— #MT2

Marketing Strategies for Growing Businesses— #EB2

Planning and Goal Setting for Small Business— #MP6

Pricing Your Products and Services Profitably— #FM13

Problems in Managing a Family-Owned Business— #MP3

Recordkeeping in Small Business— #FM10

Researching Your Market— #MT8

Signs: Showcasing Your Business on the Street— #MT12

Understanding Cash Flow— #FM4

Internal Revenue Service

The following instruction forms are available for download from the Internal Revenue Service website (www.irs.gov) in PDF format for Adobe Acrobat Reader.

Business Use of Your Home— #587

Miscellaneous Deductions— #529

Recordkeeping for Individuals— #552

Starting a Business & Keeping Records— #583

Tax Guide for Small Business— #334

Travel, Entertainment, Gift and Car Expenses— #463

Antiques Price Guides and Reference Books

Price Guides

(The publishers listed issue these guides annually with updated information.)

Antique Trader's Antiques and Collectibles Price Guide, Krause Publications, WI

Flea Market Trader, Collector Books, Paducah, KY

Garage Sale & Flea Market Annual, Collector Books, Paducah, KY

Kovels' Antiques & Collectibles Price Guide, Crown Books, NY

The Official Price Guide to Antiques and Collectibles, House of Collectibles, NY

Pictorial Price Guide to American Antiques, Penguin Putnam, NY

Schroeder's, Collector Books, Paducah, KY

Wallace-Homestead Price Guide to American Country Antiques,
    Wallace-Homestead Book Company, Radnor, PA

Warman's Antiques and Collectibles Price Guide,
    Wallace-Homestead Book Company, Radnor, PA

Reference Books

The following are just a few of the dozens of titles available, and many are updated regularly. Check your local library for other books on specific antiques.

The Bulfinch Anatomy of Antique Furniture, Bulfinch Press, MA

From Collector Books, Paducah, KY:

Antique Tins: Identification and Values, Fred Dodge

Elegant Glassware of the Depression Era, Gene Florence

The Encyclopedia of Carnival Glass, Mike Carwille

Fostoria Stemware, Milbra Long and Emily Seate

Made in Japan Ceramics Identification & Values, Carole White

Milk Glass, Betty Newbound

From Hobby House Press, Grantsville, MD:

Blue Book of Dolls and Values, Jan Foulke

From Wallace-Homestead Book Company, Radnor, PA:

Warman's English & Continental Pottery & Porcelain, Susan D. Bagdade and Allen D. Bagdade

Useful Websites

Accounting Software and Materials

Dome Publishing Company - www.domeproducts.com

Iambic.com - www.iambic.com

Intuit - www.intuit.com

Antiques Information
The Antiques Almanac.com - www.theantiquesalmanac.com

Book Publishers
Amazon.com - www.amazon.com
Shire Publications, Ltd. - www.shirebooks.co.uk

Banking Services
Merchant Services - www.merchantservices.com
PayPal - www.paypal.com

Business Information
American Bar Association Legal Topics - www.abalawinfo.org
American Bar Association's online referral service - www.findlegalhelp.org
American Institute of Public Accounts - www.aicpa.org
Business Licenses - www.businesslicenses.com
Small Business Administration - www.sba.gov

Computer Equipment
Computer-Show.com - www.computer-show.com
SquareTrade.com - www.squaretrade.com
TigerDirect.com - www.tigerdirect.com
UsedLaptopComputers.com - www.usedlaptopcomputers.com

Internet Promotion
Blogger.com - www.blogger.com
GetListed.org – http://getlisted.org
Google - www.google.com

Miscellaneous
Anywhocom - www.anywho.com
AutoTrader.com - www.autotrader.com
EverydayPlastics.com - www.everydayplastics.com
Van Dyck's Restorers - www.vandykes.com
Welcome Wagon - www.welcomewagon.com

Online Auctions

Ebay.com - www.ebay.com

Ruby Lane - www.rubylane.com

TIAS - www.tias.com

Phone and Internet Services

AT&T - www.att.net

Clear Wireless Internet - www.clearwirelessinternet.com

Tracfone.com - www.tracfone.com

Verizon - www.verizon.net

Printing

Checks Unlimited - www.checksunlimited.com

VistaPrint.com - www.vistaprint.com

Shipping

Federal Express - www.fedex.com

United Parcel Service - www.ups.com

United States Postal Service - www.usps.com

Website Services

FreeWebSites.com - www.freewebsites.com

GoDaddy.com - www.godaddy.com

Tripod - www.tripod.lycos.com

Worksheets

Detail of Monthly Expenditures

MDSE AND MATERIALS PAID BY CASH AND CHECKS					OTHER EXPENDITURES BY CHECKS AND CASH				
Date	Payee	Check No.	Amount		Date	Payee	Check No.	Acct. No.	Amount
1					1				
2					2				
3					3				
4					4				
5					5				
6					5				
7					5				
8					6				
9					6				
10					7				
11					7				
12					7				
13					15				
14					15				
15					17				
16					21				
17					21				
18					28				
19					30				
20					30				
21					30				
22									
23									
24									
25									
26									
27									
28									
29									
30									
	Carried Forward					**Carried Forward**			

Shop	Furniture	Glassware	China	Other	Prices	Remarks

Code	Item Description	Cost	Price	Sold At	Date	% Markup

Code #	Item Description	Purchase Price	Original Price	Sale Price

Date: _____

Goals for this year:

1. _____
2. _____
3. _____
4. _____

Goals for second year:

1. _____
2. _____

Goals for fifth year:

1. _____
2. _____

Month	Campaign	Budget
January		
February		
March		

Month	Campaign	Budget
April		
May		
June		
July		
August		
September		
October		
November		
December		

Index

About the Author

As an avid collector of a variety of antiques and collectibles for the last twenty years, Bob Brooke knows what he's writing about. Besides writing about antiques, Brooke conducts seminars on antiques for various organizations, including the Smithsonian Institution in Washington, D.C. In addition, he has also sold in flea markets and shops. His antiques articles have appeared in many antiques and consumer publications, including *British Heritage, AntiqueWeek, American Antiquities, Southeastern Antiquing and Collecting Magazine, History Magazine,* and many others. To read more of his articles, visit his main website, Writing at Its Best (www.bobbrooke.com) or his specialty antiques site, the Antiques Almanac (www.theantiquesalmanac.com).